The Green Challenge

Despite considerable media and popular interest in environmentalism, environmental movements and Green parties, there has been relatively little systematic academic assessment of the factors involved in the formation, development and electoral performance of Green parties in Europe.

The Green Challenge is an up-to-date comparative analysis of the rise, development and varying electoral successes of Green parties in western, southern and central Europe. It provides a common comparative perspective and contextual setting through which the very different fortunes of individual Green parties operating in different national circumstances can be analysed. By using a comparative thematic perspective rather than a pre-ordained theory, *The Green Challenge* not only points out the deficiencies of existing theoretical studies but illuminates the primary factors which have helped to make the rise of political ecology such an important development in contemporary Europe.

Its conceptual unity and coherent approach make it essential reading not only for students of Green politics but for Green activists and anyone interested in the rise of political ecology.

Dick Richardson is a Senior Lecturer in International Relations and Green Politics, University of Teesside. **Chris Rootes** is a Senior Lecturer in Sociology and Director of the Centre for the Study of Social and Political Movements, University of Kent at Canterbury.

The Green Challenge

The development of Green parties in Europe

Edited by
Dick Richardson and Chris Rootes

London and New York

First published 1995
by Routledge
11 New Fetter Lane, London EC4P 4EE

Simultaneously published in the USA and Canada
by Routledge
29 West 35th Street, New York, NY 10001

Typeset in Baskerville by
Ponting–Green Publishing Services, Chesham, Bucks
Printed and bound in Great Britain by
T.J. Press (Padstow) Ltd, Cornwall

British Library Cataloguing in Publication Data
A catalogue record for this book is available from the
British Library.

Library of Congress Cataloging in Publication Data
A catalogue record for this book has been requested.

ISBN 0–415–10649–4 (hbk)
ISBN 0–415–10650–8 (pbk)

Contents

Illustrations

Contributors

Martin Bennulf is a researcher in the Department of Political Science at the University of Gothenburg.

Clive H. Church is a Professor of European Studies at the University of Kent at Canterbury.

Alistair Cole is a Lecturer in Politics at the University of Keele.

Nicolas Demertzis is an Assistant Professor in the Department of Communications and Mass Media at the University of Athens.

Brian Doherty is a Lecturer in Politics at the University of Keele.

E. Gene Frankland is a Professor of Political Science at Ball State University, Indiana.

Petr Jehlicka is a research student in the Global Security Programme at the University of Cambridge and was formerly a researcher at the Academy of Sciences, Prague.

Tomas Kostelecky is a researcher at the Institute of Sociology, Academy of Sciences, Prague.

Martin Rhodes is a Lecturer in Government at the University of Manchester.

Dick Richardson is a Senior Lecturer in International Relations and Green Politics at the University of Teesside.

Benoît Rihoux is an Assistant in the Department of Political and Social Sciences at the Catholic University of Louvain.

Chris Rootes is a Senior Lecturer in Sociology and Director of the Centre for the Study of Social and Political Movements at the University of Kent at Canterbury.

Gerrit Voerman is Director of the Documentation Centre for Dutch Political Parties at the University of Groningen.

Foreword

The Green Challenge is an extremely important book. It is the first academic study to set Europe's Green parties within an explicitly political context as participants, challengers and potential successors to the current accepted political orthodoxies.

Green Party activists in the UK are often asked, 'but why don't you do as well as *Die Grünen?*' This book provides useful answers. It examines the political circumstances in a number of European countries, assessing how the development of Green parties has been assisted or held back by the availability of political space and looking at how individual parties have exploited that space.

The writers make clear that there is no perfect model for the development of a Green party; each has arisen from particular circumstances but all share the conviction that current political practices and beliefs must change fundamentally if the world is to have the chance of peaceful, equitable and lasting survival.

The dual challenge facing Green parties is clear from this study. The first challenge is that posed to existing political power and we see how it has responded: through dirty tricks, co-option of the easier policies or attempts to co-opt the parties into compromising alliances, and through outright opposition, which has brought together management and workers against the Greens. The second challenge is that posed to the Greens themselves: how have they adapted to the shift from parties of opposition to ones of proposition as they have gained political representation? How have they coped within the political arena without losing their political identity and integrity? How do they maintain and enlarge their political space?

These are important questions for the developing Green political movement. Serious studies such as this will help us see ourselves more clearly and enable us to learn and draw strength from each other so that we can maximize our political effect and bring about the ecologically sustainable future for which we are all working.

I look forward to the next volume with great anticipation!

Jean Lambert
*Chair, Green Party Executive and former UK representative
to the Green group in the European Parliament*

Introduction

Dick Richardson and Chris Rootes

One does not need to be a committed supporter of a Green party to recognize that Greens have become a more or less permanent feature on the European political scene and one that is growing in visibility. The highly publicized failure of the German Greens to retain their parliamentary representation at national level after the 1990 unification election, the similar loss of parliamentary status by the Swedish Greens in 1991 and the very public internal wranglings of British and French Greens should not be allowed to obscure the more or less steady progress the Greens have made in other countries and, fairly generally, at regional and local levels. Almost everywhere in western Europe, the Greens are more established political parties now than they were even five years ago. Clearly, the widespread dismissal of the Greens as a merely transient and irretrievably marginal phenomenon has been proved wrong.

1989 was a very significant year for the Greens. First, they did extraordinarily well – often in very unlikely places – in the elections for the European Parliament. Second, they were at the forefront of the opposition to the state-socialist regimes of central and eastern Europe. In recognition of the high profile of the Greens and their breakthrough in public acceptance across the whole continent of Europe, the European Consortium for Political Research sponsored a workshop on the Green challenge to political orthodoxy at its Joint Sessions at the University of Essex in March 1991. The idea for this book originated at those sessions.

The book is not, however, a collection of conference papers. The chapters assembled here have been specially commissioned to address the central theme which emerged in the course of our discussions at Essex: that the principal factor in the rise and development of Green parties, and their electoral successes, has been the varying impact of political competition upon them, within the overall context of heightened environmental consciousness. The fortunes of national Green parties clearly have been influenced by competition between them and other parties, but also – perhaps especially – by competition among already established parties and actors. In organizing this book around the theme of political competition, our aim is not merely to add to the volume of literature which *describes* Green parties, but to explain *why* Green parties have developed so differently in different European countries.

We have not tried to cover all European countries or all European Green parties. An exhaustively comparative book would either have been much longer and correspondingly more expensive, or the individual chapters would have been too short to give an adequate analysis of any individual case. We have instead opted to cover a broad sample of European cases in greater depth. Some countries selected themselves because of their sheer size and their prominence within European political arrangements: Germany, Britain, France and Italy. Other countries have been included because of the distinctiveness and intrinsic interest of their experience of Green party development; in this category we include Belgium, Sweden, The Netherlands and Switzerland. Inevitably, constraints of space and time have dictated the omission of several cases – especially those of Austria, Finland and Portugal – which, on grounds of intrinsic interest, we should have liked to include. Nor could we cover all countries in which Green parties have been less prominent; instead we have attempted to achieve a balance by including chapters on two such cases: one on Greece, which in some respects can be taken as illustrative of the travails of Green parties in the Mediterranean periphery generally; and one on Czechoslovakia which, though it is in many ways not typical of post-Communist states, does at least raise most of the problems which confront Green parties elsewhere in central and eastern Europe.

In editing the book, we have given our contributors a fair degree of latitude in the interpretation of the central theme and, although we have endeavoured to standardize the general style, the methodology and conclusions of each chapter are the responsibility of its author.

Editing this volume has been an interesting – indeed salutary – experience. The patience of those contributors who met our original deadline has been sorely tried, but so was our own when two authors who had promised chapters withdrew at the last minute. We should therefore like to record our special thanks to Martin Rhodes and Gene Frankland for providing the chapters on Italy and Germany at very short notice. We should like, too, to thank the Royal Mail for unfailingly managing the overnight delivery of mail between villages at the northern and southern extremities of England.

February 1994

Chapter 1

The Green challenge
Philosophical, programmatic and electoral considerations

Dick Richardson

Green political ideas are hardly new. Xenophon, among other ancient Greeks, is alleged to have set out the main principles of the Gaia hypothesis, on which much Green thinking is based, over 2,000 years before James Lovelock developed the modern, scientific version. Green political parties, on the other hand, are a distinctly modern phenomenon. It was only in 1972 that the first Green party was established (the New Zealand Values Party) and in 1979 that the first Green member was elected to a national parliament (Daniel Brelaz in Switzerland). Now, Greens sit in democratic assemblies at local government level throughout Europe and in a great number of national assemblies, including the former Soviet satellite states in eastern and central Europe. They represent a challenge to political orthodoxies of both left and right in three main respects: philosophical, programmatic and electoral.

THE NATURE AND CONTEXT OF THE GREEN CHALLENGE

Given that Green ideas coexisted with the major religions of the world through to late medieval times and never entirely disappeared, it is perhaps surprising that Green political parties did not develop with the emergence of the political state. The fact that they did not develop until the late twentieth century can be attributed to a number of factors. Primarily, however, the rise of industrial society in the late eighteenth and nineteenth centuries stimulated the emergence of anthropocentric rather than bio-centric ways of thinking. By the twentieth century, the industrial world-view, based on the conquest of nature ('domination theory' – the philosophical aspect), materialism (the spiritual aspect) and consumption (the economic aspect), predominated over the Gaian view to such an extent that, to all intents and purposes, it became non-existent as far as practical politics was concerned.

There have always been critics of industrial society and the industrial world-view, but before the 1960s the apparent success of industrialism in raising living standards, at least in the so-called developed world, made many critics appear irrational and nostalgic for a pre-industrial Eden that never existed. In the 1960s, however, there was a surge of interest in the natural environment from a scientific and economic point of view, and this was to have a profound impact on the way the environment was viewed in intellectual, if not yet political, circles. In 1962, for example, Rachel Carson published *Silent Spring*, a damning indictment of the overuse of pesticides and their deleterious effects on natural systems. Although calling for greater scientific enquiry, Carson's work represented an indirect attack on prevailing scientific reductionist theories. Damned by much of the scientific establishment of the time as 'emotional', the conclusions of *Silent Spring* are now generally accepted. Indeed, many of the pesticides attacked by Carson are now banned.

In 1967 E.J. Mishan attacked the prevailing economic orthodoxy of industrialism in *The Costs of Economic Growth*. This was followed in 1968 by the establishment of the Club of Rome, an informal international association of scientists and industrialists concerned about the impact of industrialism and the industrial ethic not only on human society but on the planet itself. The Club's major publication, *The Limits to Growth* (1972), was extremely influential in questioning the ability of the planet to sustain the lifestyles emerging in the developed world. The Earth's resources were seen to be finite; it was not a question of *if* the planet's resources would run out at contemporary rates of consumption, but *when*.

1972 marked a watershed in the development of Green ideas. The publication of *The Ecologist*'s *A Blueprint for Survival* alongside *The Limits to Growth* inaugurated not only an intellectual debate on what were to become known as green issues, but also the first inklings of a political debate, sometimes known as The Great Doom Debate. Four considerations prompted the publication of *Blueprint*. First, there was the perception that, if current patterns of material consumption and resource depletion were allowed to persist, the life-support systems of the planet would be irreversibly disrupted and society would inevitably break down. Second, there was an awareness that governments throughout the developed world were either refusing to face the relevant facts or were briefing their scientists in such a way that their seriousness was played down. Third, there was seen to be a need for national and international movements which would complement the work of concerned scientists and industrialists such as those in the Club of Rome, if necessary assuming political status and contesting national elections. Finally, there was a realization that the movements envisaged would not succeed unless they had previously formulated a new philosophy of life, whose goals could be achieved without destroying the environment, together with a precise and comprehensive action programme for bringing about the kind of society in which it could be implemented (*The Ecologist* 1972: 1).

In Britain, the authors of *Blueprint* anticipated the establishment of a Movement for Survival (MS), a coalition of autonomous environmental groups whose aim would be to influence government. There was no suggestion of setting up a new political party; indeed this possibility was specifically discounted (Parkin 1989: 214). However, the environmental groups which the authors of *Blueprint* anticipated would join the new movement proved unenthusiastic about even a modicum of participation in the political process. As a result, the editor of *The Ecologist*, Edward Goldsmith, who was committed to initiating political action, decided to join an infant grouping set up in an estate agent's office in Coventry in February 1973. Originally called 'People', it changed its name to the Ecology Party in 1975 and then to the Green Party in 1985.

The circumstances in which the UK Green Party was formed in 1973 were, in one sense, particular. But they also illustrate the conjuncture of forces in which emergent Green groups in each European state had to take decisions for future action. The kernel of the problem as far as each group was concerned lay in the four considerations behind *Blueprint*, more especially the third and fourth: the need for political action and the need for a new philosophy of life and a comprehensive programme towards a new style of society. While many people could understand and accept the critique of industrial society put forward in *Blueprint*, fewer saw the need for a new philosophy of life and/or a separate programme of political action, let alone a new political party. In other words, even at this early stage in the development of the Green movement in Europe, there was a distinction between individuals who wanted to participate in the political process and those who did not.

There was also a distinction, which was later to become even more important, between ecologists and environmentalists: between those who cared for the environment because of the intrinsic value that they associated with the Earth (ecologists) and those who cared for the environment simply for the betterment of human society (environmentalists). Such distinctions revolved around two key questions. Could environmental action be secured within existing political parties? Should political action stop at environmental action, or should it go further into social, cultural and ecological action? The answers to these questions would depend not only on the nature of the personal responses to the questions themselves, but on the political systems and traditions in each individual state. What appeared to be appropriate in one state might not be appropriate in another. Thus, in practice, Green parties in some countries were to develop along ecological lines, imbued with a Gaian philosophy of life; in others they developed along environmentalist lines; some were to develop connections with other political traditions; others sought to develop a practical coalition of ecologists and environmentalists.

During the early 1970s, few political observers, and even fewer political scientists, appreciated that a new political philosophy was emerging, one that was biocentric rather than anthropocentric. As far as politicians were concerned, the ideas raised by *Blueprint* and similar publications were regarded simply as issues which, given time, would go away of their own accord, new issues taking their place. On the surface, this appeared to be a realistic assessment of the situation. The UK Ecology Party remained the only national Green party in Europe throughout the 1970s and its political significance was negligible. Certainly, the Greens were no threat to the established parties.

Beneath the surface, however, a number of developments had occurred which were to have a profound significance in the 1980s and beyond. On the one hand, serious scientific studies began to validate the majority of the conclusions of *Blueprint* regarding the impact of industrial society on the natural environment. In Europe and North America, forests and lakes began to die under the impact of acid rain. The problems of ozone layer depletion, global warming, the destruction of the tropical and coniferous forests, desertification, the impact of population growth and the pollution of the seas and rivers – to mention only a few – became the concern of all (even politicians) whereas previously they had been dismissed as the meanderings of cranks.

Modern biocentric philosophy began to emerge. Central to it was planet Earth and the limits to growth hypothesis of the Club of Rome and *The Ecologist*. Theories of holism, of humankind being part of a greater natural system, began to be espoused. Many were based on ancient folklore. One of the most quoted references was from a speech by an unknown native American chief in answer to a demand by the US President that Indian lands be sold:

> All things are bound together.
> All things connect.
> What happens to the Earth
> happens to the children of the Earth.
> Man has not woven the web of life.
> He is but one thread.
> Whatever he does to the web,
> he does to himself.
>   (Anon. 1984)[1]

Such suggestions could be – and were – dismissed as the further ramblings of cranks. However, in 1979 a new dimension was added to the argument with the publication of James Lovelock's *Gaia: A New Look at Life on Earth*. Lovelock's thesis was that the Earth is controlled by its living organisms and that these organisms behave as a single entity. All life-forms are interconnected in a self-sustaining biosphere. As Lovelock himself put it, 'we share the chemistry of all the non-humans among which we live; everything that lives on earth is made of the same stuff' (quoted, Porritt 1984: 207). Perhaps unconsciously, Lovelock, an acclaimed scientist who had worked for the American space agency NASA, gave scientific and intellectual backing to the emerging theories of holism.

Lovelock's thesis was greeted by the scientific establishment as a heresy, much as the religious establishment in medieval times greeted Galileo's ideas: two leading scientific journals, *Nature* and *Science*, refused to publish his ideas. Lovelock was challenging conventional wisdom which held that life on the planet evolved separately from the planet itself. Indirectly, he seemed to be challenging not only the orthodoxies of reductionism, Baconian science, Cartesian reason and religious dogmatism, but the political philosophies which rested on those orthodoxies. It is little wonder, therefore, that Greens have taken up Lovelock's theories and adapted them to their political programmes. From a Gaian viewpoint, all attempts to rationalize a subjugated biosphere with humankind in charge are doomed, because humankind is a part of nature, not above it. This is the basis of the Green challenge at the philosophical level.

Given the different philosophical basis of the Greens, it has always been difficult for politicians and political scientists to place them on the conventional left–right spectrum. Richard Gott, for example, has described the Nazis as 'enthusiastic Greens' on the grounds that Hitler was a vegetarian and Hess an ardent homeo-path and student of Rudolf Steiner, founder of the anthropo-sophical movement and early Green thinker (Gott 1989). Peter Brooke, on the other hand, has suggested that the UK Green Party is an 'extreme socialist party' on the grounds that it would abolish the House of Lords and cancel Third World debts (Brooke 1989). What both fail to appreciate is that Greens cannot be seen in conventional left–right terms since it is impossible to place a biocentric philosophy or party on an anthropocentric spectrum. As Jonathon Porritt puts it:

> The politics of the Industrial Age, left, right and centre, is like a three-lane motorway, with different vehicles in different lanes, but all heading in the same direction. Greens feel that it is the very direction that is wrong, rather than the choice of any one lane in preference to the others. It is our perception that the motorway of industrialism inevitably leads to the abyss – hence our decision to get off it, and seek an entirely different direction.
>
> (Porritt 1984: 43)

If the philosophical basis of the Green programme is different from that of the established political parties, so too is the nature of the society which Greens seek to attain. Whereas established parties, whether left, right or centre, espouse the concept of a consumer (or at least materialist) society based on economic growth, Greens accept that the finite nature of the Earth's resources makes continued economic growth impossible. In contrast, they espouse the concept of a conserver society, a society which it is within the capacity of the planet to sustain. The exact nature of such a society was still being debated during the early 1980s, when the majority of west European Green parties were formed and when no such parties existed in the Soviet satellite states. Not surprisingly, therefore, there are differences of approach among the various national parties. However, by 1989 most of the west European parties came together to adopt the following line in their policy document for the European elections:

> The key to a conserver economy is to take and to use only what we really need: green politics is about 'enough', not about 'more and more'. In many areas of human activity it may well mean using less – less energy and fewer resources. This in turn would create less pollution. More things would be repaired, restored and recycled. We wouldn't always insist on 'new and better'.
>
> In a green conserver economy, wellbeing would be measured not merely by the amount we spend. . . . It would be measured in terms of good health, clean air, pure water, unpoisoned food, stimulating education, cultural diversity, safe and friendly neighbourhoods, the variety of plants and animals sharing our environment.
>
> In a conserver economy, values change too. A 'developed country' would no longer be one that can dominate world markets, but one which has the ability to house and feed its population properly . . . . It would measure its success in terms of a healthy environment, its ability to care for its people and share its wealth, and its capacity to guarantee the wellbeing of as yet unborn generations.
>
> (Green Party 1989)

The European election manifesto has been quoted at length because it demonstrates that the Green vision of the future incorporates aspects of environmentalism as well as ecologism. All things being equal, few would disagree with the need for a healthy environment, adequate housing, clean air and so on. What ecologists question is the ability of a materialist economy based on the 'god of growth' to achieve such ends. As far as Greens are concerned, an ever-expanding economy merely eats up the dwindling resources of the planet, spewing out waste as pollution to the detriment of future generations.

> That's why we have a world in which the rich minority is able to dictate the living standards of the poor majority. That's why the atmosphere is so polluted that we are now faced with potentially disastrous climatic change. That's why trees are dying from acid rain, and why our streams and rivers are so dirty . . . . Any government which remains a slave to the endless expansion of

consumption, driven remorselessly by the futile goal of economic growth at any cost, can never call itself green. It can only ever be grey.

(Green Party 1989)

Doubtless few voters in the 1989 European elections, certainly in the UK, appreciated the very different vision of society being offered by the Greens: the concept of a no-growth or even negative growth economy with reduced standards of living as currently measured. Nevertheless, that is arguably the most important element of the Green challenge at the programmatic level.

At the same time, the Green vision of society is not simply concerned with ecology and the environment and their relationship with the economy. Neither is it confined to the relationship of humankind with nature. It concerns the whole gamut of socioeconomic and political activity. In this respect, the biocentric philosophy of the Greens equates the needs of the planet with the needs of the person, the rights of the person with the rights of the planet (Ecology Party 1983: 3). Anthropocentric politics, whether right, left or centre, are seen as exploitative politics, the politics of alienation and destruction, of both people and planet. In contrast, the Green vision of society is one of co-operation and consensus, with policies geared towards the long-term sustainability not only of planetary ecosystems but of human society itself. Central to this vision are the concepts of social justice, non-violence, decentralization, gender and racial equality, participatory democracy and individual human rights. Such concepts are not the exclusive preserve of the Greens; indeed, the Green political programme encompasses many individual aspects of other political traditions and programmes – socialist, liberal, conservative, Marxist, anarchist. But the underpinning philosophy is different, as is the goal.

THE ELECTORAL CHALLENGE

Many Green activists, even today, are averse to participation in what they term 'grey' political society. This is particularly true in states such as Britain, whose first-past-the-post electoral system makes it difficult for any new party to secure parliamentary representation. In such circumstances, many individuals prefer to participate in extra-parliamentary movements such as the Hunt Saboteurs organization or go into practical self-sufficiency, for example, in communes or through the purchase and running of organic farms. Others prefer to develop their own individual green spirituality. Many decide to participate in environmental action groups, for example, Greenpeace and Friends of the Earth, where environmentalists and ecologists coexist in reasonable harmony. In so doing, they may get ecological as well as environmental ideas on to the political agenda. However, as the 1970s progressed into the 1980s, more and more individuals, both in Britain and elsewhere in Europe, came to believe that pressure group activity and personal spirituality were no substitute for political action. Green parties were formed on a national basis, and began to develop an electoral challenge to the traditional political parties. It is this third element of the Green challenge – the electoral challenge – with which this book is primarily concerned.

In analysing the development of national Green parties, there is no such thing as a putative norm. As indicated previously, different decisions were made by individual Green groups operating in diverse and distinctive national and political circumstances. In some countries, as in Britain, the Green Party chose the path of ideological purity, of ecologism. In others, notably West Germany, Greens chose to develop in association with other political traditions, especially, but not exclusively, the anarchist and socialist traditions. In yet others, including France, there are separate ecological and environmental parties, each regarding themselves as Green. In most countries, however, ecologists and environmentalists coexist, not always happily, within the same party.

At this point, readers should consult the flow chart (Figure 1.1), which represents diagrammatically the historical evolution of Green politics and Green parties in a theoretically pure form. It is not suggested that it represents a stereotype of Green development, nor that it accords with political reality in any one state. Rather it illustrates the context in which emergent Green groups in the 1970s and 1980s took decisions as to what kind of party, if any, they wished to establish. Especially important in this respect are the links between Green politics and grey politics represented by the arrows across the Green–grey divide. Greens were not working in a political vacuum, but within political systems established by non-Green parties. Choices had to be made as to how to come to terms with political exigencies within each individual state. A Green world-view and a Green programme did not necessarily result in a Green political party, except in the formal sense that 'Green' was included

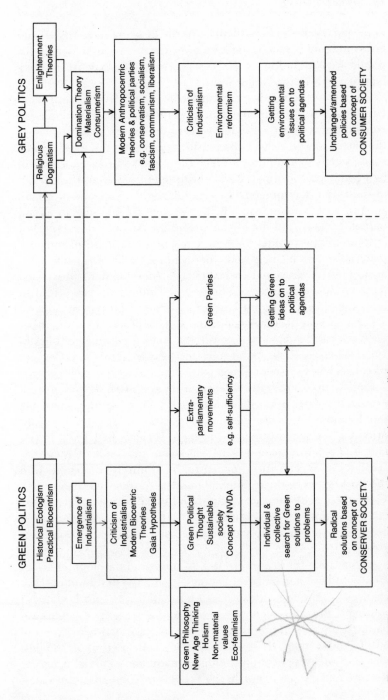

Figure 1.1 The historical evolution of Green and grey politics

in the party's name. In particular, the divide between ecologists and environmentalists was often seen to be narrow enough to allow for political co-operation in the short term at the expense of ideological purity in the longer term.

Given that the major common factor in the development of all Green parties is the existence of an ecological and environmental consciousness, together with a perceived need for political action, the extent to which that consciousness permeates within individual states becomes all-important. Here, there appears to be a correlation between levels of ecological and environmental awareness and levels of industrial development. In general, the less developed a state, economically and industrially, the weaker the impulse to Green party formation and the less successful the party. In this respect, it is important to consider the concepts of post-industrialism and post-materialism. It is suggested, for example, that it is only when economies have reached a certain stage of development, when basic material needs have been satisfied, that individuals can afford to look ahead to a different kind of society and engage in political action to that end. However, not only has the post-materialism thesis been criticized as inconsistent with the empirical evidence (Bürklin 1984; Eckersley 1989), but it relies too heavily on the West German case, which is atypical of Green party development.

Equally, there are many different visions of post-industrial society, even in the states of northern Europe. The predominant view, one put forward by environmentalists, is that of a technologically-oriented, service-inspired and affluent society (Bell 1973; Frankland and Schoonmaker 1992: 42–54). But this is not a Green view at all; rather it is an anthropocentric view entirely compatible with the world-views of the traditional political parties of left and right. The Green, ecological view of post-industrial society is very different: it is that of the conserver society, with its decentralized economy in which manufacturing industry is no longer dominant (Marien 1977: 416).

At the same time, a severe lack of industrial development does appear to have a negative effect on Green party development. For example, in the less industrialized but rapidly urbanizing states of southern Europe, such as Greece and Portugal, the political battleground is still dominated by the struggle between right and left. In these states, the political agenda is focused upon the best means of securing economic enhancement and material progress. Relative to the states of northern Europe, environmental consciousness is low and environmental action even lower. It is not that environmental problems do not exist, or are not recognized – the massive air pollution around Athens, for example, is both recognized and a national scandal in Greece. Rather the governments of southern European states, supported by their populations, feel there are greater priorities. Thus Green party development on the southern periphery has been retarded.

Similarly, while environmental groups may have been at the forefront of the opposition to Communist rule in eastern Europe, it is only too apparent that it is not the environmental degradation which took place under the former regimes but problems of national identity and the move towards market-oriented economies which have dominated the political agenda of post-Communist states. Green groups played an important part in the 'velvet revolution' in Czechoslovakia, but the subsequent democratic elections focused on economic development and the dismantling of the Communist political structure (1990) and the split between Slovakia and the Czech Republic (1992).

The relevance but overall inadequacy of the concepts of post-materialism and post-industrialism in explaining Green party development has led a number of political scientists, notably Herbert Kitschelt, to seek an alternative explanation in terms of political opportunity structures. Kitschelt's approach takes into account both structural and institutional factors and emphasizes the impact of new social movements and the importance of precipitating conditions such as the nuclear issue in the late 1970s and early 1980s. He stresses the role played by political parties within the opportunity structure, and in particular points to the political space which opened on the left with the rightward shift of existing socialist and social democratic parties in the 1960s and 1970s (Kitschelt 1986, 1988, 1989; Kitschelt and Hellemans 1990). Nevertheless, there are a number of deficiencies in Kitschelt's approach, apart from the fact that he places too much emphasis on the West German and Belgian cases and barely considers southern Europe. More especially, he attaches low importance to electoral systems as a factor making for Green electoral success, and fails to appreciate the distinctiveness of ecological identity and its ideological divergence from New Left politics.

In practice, it can be seen that there are four general constraints on the development of Green parties. The first is the underlying divergence between ecologism and environmentalism, not always apparent even to individual members of the green movement; there are inherent difficulties in biocentrists endeavouring to work within anthropocentric political structures. The second is the divergence between individuals and groups who wish to participate directly in the party political process and those who prefer to work through pressure groups and/or the traditional political parties. The third is the state of economic and industrial development, which helps to condition environmental and ecological awareness. The fourth factor, allied to the third and particularly concerned with eastern and southern Europe, is the circumstances in which democratic political systems themselves emerged. This latter factor is seen most clearly in the first post-Communist elections in eastern Europe, but can also be seen operating in certain countries, for example, Spain and Greece, which emerged from authoritarian rule at a somewhat earlier date.

On top of these general constraints on Green party development and success, there are a number of peculiarly national constraints. Especially important are institutional structures, for example, the openness (or otherwise) of civil bureaucracies to ecological and environmental ideas: the more closed the bureaucracy, the more likely that green ideas are expressed through party political activity; the more open the bureaucracy, the more likely that Green parties, if established, are marginalized, as in Britain. Political tradition can also act as a constraint. The prime consideration, however, is the nature of the electoral system, which provides constraints and opportunities for the political expression of both ecologism and environmentalism, and sets the ground rules for party-political competition.

In Great Britain, the marginalization of the UK Green Party as an electoral force at national level has led to a greater concentration on the development of a 'pure' political programme. First published in 1974, but continually updated, *Manifesto for a Sustainable Society* is a highly developed, explicitly ecological programme of political action. The possibility of incorporating a socialist element into the programme was rejected at an early stage. However, the lack of political success at national level, with the significant exception of the Euro-elections in 1989, has led to a number of activists propounding more environmentalist views and flirting with other political parties, primarily the Liberal Democrats, in order to advance green ideas more quickly. But in general, despite numerous internal ructions, the party has held together well on the ideological front. At the same time, the lack of electoral success, at local as well as national level, has meant that many would-be activists have preferred to concentrate on pressure group politics rather than join the Green Party.

A similar situation has occurred in France, which (except for a brief flirtation with proportional representation in 1986) has its own double-ballot version of the first-past-the-post system for National Assembly elections. However, conditions in France are complicated by three further factors. First, because historically France has suffered less from the impact of industrialization than many other countries, the environment has been less of an issue in national elections. Second, after the Second World War, in the light of continuing fossil fuel deficiencies, French administrations chose to invest heavily in nuclear power, achieving a nationwide pro-nuclear consensus which cut across the development of both ecological and environmental politics. Third, individual person-alities, especially those with a sound local or regional base, have traditionally assumed rather greater importance in French national politics than in most other developed states. This has especially been the case under the Fifth Republic. Therefore, it is perhaps not surprising that from an early date green politics in France tended to factionalize around personalities and regional and local associations, which hindered the development of a single unified party with a coherent ecological programme. Even after Les Verts was founded in February 1984, problems arose, especially in the form of the personal ambition of the charismatic Brice Lalonde, the leading environmental campaigner who became Minister of the Environment in Michel Rocard's 1988 government. Lalonde, the *eminence grise* of Green politics in France, in 1990 founded Génér-ation écologie, a rival party to Les Verts, with the support and blessing of President Mitterrand, who wanted to draw Lalonde and his supporters into his presidential grouping of parties. Environ-mentalist in nature and supportive of both nuclear power and nuclear defence, Génération écologie can hardly be considered a Green party, even if Lalonde's supporters regard it as one.

The founding of Génération écologie is an excellent illustration that the mere existence of 'Green' or 'Ecology' in the name of a party does not by itself substantiate the party's Green credentials. Certainly as far as the traditional democracies in western Europe are concerned, the rise of environmental consciousness in the 1970s and 1980s, coupled with the Green electoral successes initiated by Die Grünen in the Bundestag elections of 1983, has alerted traditional political parties to the electoral advantages of giving their policies an environmental tinge. That political colours can be usurped is demonstrated by the Dutch case: the ideologically pure De Groenen has consistently failed to gain representation in a national assembly where less than 1 per cent of the national vote can secure a seat. Instead, a combination of four older 'small left' parties took the title Groen Links (Green Left) in an effort to reverse their declining electoral fortunes. Mainly because of their strong organization and the collaboration in 1979 of one of them (the PPR) in the Co-ordination of Green and Radical Parties, they were able to gain acceptance among Green parties elsewhere in Europe. This, together with the Dutch political culture of consultation and collectivism, and the increased importance attached to the environment by the traditional political parties, culminating in the National Environmental Policy Plan of 1989, has helped to limit the development of a purely ecological party in the Netherlands (Van der Straaten 1992: 68).

In general, the more proportional the electoral system, the easier it is for Green parties to gain representation in national assemblies. This can be seen, for example, in Belgium, where Ecolo (in Wallonia) and Agalev (in Flanders) have been continually represented in both houses of the national parliament since the early 1980s. The Belgian case also provides an instance where ecologists and environmentalists coexist in reasonable harmony. Moreover, uniquely in Belgian politics, Ecolo and Agalev have bridged the linguistic divide by forming a single group in both the Chamber of Representatives and the Senate, despite the fact that Senate rules do not formally provide for 'interlinguistic' groups.

States with a threshold system of proportional representation, for example, Sweden and West Germany, have a built-in yardstick for the measurement of electoral success. In such systems, in theory, the ease with which Green parties achieve parliamentary representation should be proportionate to the threshold. Again, however, the situation is materially affected by differing political traditions and structures. Thus, in Sweden, where the threshold is 4 per cent, the Green Party (Miljöpartiet de gröna) was unable to gain representation in the Riksdag until the election of September 1988. In contrast, in West Germany, with its 5 per cent threshold, Die Grünen entered the Bundestag at its second attempt, in March 1983.

In all cases, the development and electoral success of Green parties has been conditioned to a significant extent by party political competition within the overall context of ecological and environmental awareness. In Britain, for example, the factor of political competition at a time of rising environmental consciousness predominated in the one major success of the UK Green Party, the 15 per cent of the national vote which it achieved in the 1989 elections for the European Parliament. Similarly, in West Germany, the configuration of the leading parties in the late 1970s and early 1980s left a niche for the development of an ecological–environmental party with radical socialist leanings. The success of Die Grünen in securing parliamentary representation in 1983 undoubtedly stimulated the development of Green parties in other states.

West Germany has often been taken as the paradigmatic case of Green party development and success. In fact, it is entirely singular. Historically, with their semi-socialist and semi-Marxist origins, Die Grünen have developed along very different lines to the majority of Green parties in Europe, especially in terms of ideology and organization. In many respects, their ideological configuration is more akin to Groen Links in the Netherlands than to any of the other European Green parties which have achieved parliamentary representation. At the January 1984 meeting of the European Greens, which sought to establish a common Green programme for the Euro-elections of June 1984, Die Grünen championed the cause of the Green Progressive Accord (the forerunner of Groen Links) at the expense of De Groenen. Thus began a long and frequently thorny relationship between the German and the other major European Green parties. In the aftermath of the 1984 Euro-elections, Die Grünen refused to consider the establishment of a Green Group within the European Parliament, and instead forged ahead with a group called the Green Alternative European Link (GRAEL) based on themselves, the Dutch GPA and two Italian Marxists.[2] It was not until 1987 that Die Grünen began to change tack and move closer to the central Green position at both the philosophical and programmatic levels. In this respect, the European elections of 1989 marked a watershed in that Die Grünen came to accept a common programme with the other major European Green parties, with a specifically ecological basis. Given the major successes of Green parties throughout Europe in those elections, Die Grünen and their MEPs had no real alternative but to join the new Green Group in the European Parliament.

The philosophical conjuncture of European Green parties was

consummated at a meeting of the Co-ordination of the European Greens in Helsinki on 19–20 June 1993. This meeting, at which 23 out of the 24 member parties were represented, along with eight out of 10 parties (mostly from the former Soviet Union) in the process of applying for membership, endorsed a common statement, 'The Guiding Principles of the European Greens'.[3] The foreword to the statement identified the ecological basis of Green thinking and the planetary crisis and affirmed that, while technological development might delay the deterioration of the environment for a time, the ecological and social collapse of civilization could not be prevented without a fundamental change in the ideology of unquestioned material growth (European Greens 1993: 2). The statement delineated a political programme aimed at implementing these principles in the very different circumstances of western, northern, southern and eastern Europe. These principles related specifically to policy positions at international fora, member parties retaining autonomy in policy-making at national level. More particularly, it was intended that the principles be incorporated in the campaign material for the elections to the European Parliament in June 1994 (Green Party 1993: 1).

CONCLUSION

In analysing the nature and context of the Green challenge to political orthodoxy, it is evident that no single factor can account for the differential development and varying electoral success of individual Green parties. Political ecologism has established itself in different ways, in different states, at different times, at different levels: theoretical, programmatic, electoral. The fundamental factor is the development of an ecological consciousness; but the way in which this consciousness has expressed itself in political terms is by no means uniform. Facilitative and defacilitative factors vary from state to state, and may change from year to year, even month to month. Given the diverse nature of Green parties, no one general theory can adequately explain either their development or success – or, indeed, their failures. What *can* be said is that the *electoral* challenge of the Greens itself has implications for the theoretical and programmatic challenges, and that the implications will be different according to the different national parties. The common ground discovered at Helsinki may or may not last. The one certainty is that the Green challenge exists and is here to stay.

NOTES

1 The statement is usually attributed to Chief Seattle.
2 GRAEL comprised one part of a broader organization, the Rainbow Group, formed by a number of smaller parties in the European Parliament to gain access to the Parliament's special facilities for political groupings. However, as a political formation, GRAEL lacked both ideological and organizational coherence and was of marginal relevance to the Parliament's proceedings. It was initially boycotted by the Belgian Greens, though they joined later in an unsuccessful attempt to influence its political direction.
3 The one member state not represented was the MDP from Portugal; the two applicants not represented were the Green parties of Albania and Lithuania.

REFERENCES

Anon. (1984) *How Can One Sell the Air?*, Dorchester: Prism.
Bell, D. (1973) *The Coming of Post-Industrial Society*, New York: Basic Books.
Brooke, P. (1989) *The Green Party and the Environment*, London: Conservative Research Department.
Bürklin, W. (1984) *Gruene Politik: Ideologische Zyklen, Waehler und Parteien System*, Opladen: West Deutscher Verlag.
Carson, R. (1962) *Silent Spring*, Harmondsworth: Penguin.
Eckersley, R. (1989) 'Green Politics and the New Class: Selfishness or Virtue?', *Political Studies* 37: 218.
The Ecologist (1972) *A Blueprint for Survival*.
Ecology Party (1983) *Politics for Life*, London: Ecology Party.
European Greens (1993) *The Guiding Principles of the European Greens*, Brussels: European Greens Information Office.
Frankland, G. and Schoonmaker, D. (1992) *Between Protest and Power: The Green Party in Germany*, Boulder, Colo. and Oxford: Westview.
Gott, R. (1989) 'The Green March', *Guardian*, 17 March.
Green Party (1989) *Don't Let Your World Turn Grey*, London: Green Party.
—— (1993) *Green Link* 7.
—— (annual) *Manifesto for a Sustainable Society*, London: Green Party.
Kitschelt, H. (1986) 'Political Opportunity Structures and Political Protest: Anti-Nuclear Movements in Four Democracies', *British Journal of Political Science* 16: 57–83.
—— (1988) 'Left Libertarian Parties: Explaining Innovation in Competitive Party Systems', *World Politics* 40(2): 194–234.
—— (1989) *The Logics of Party Formation: Ecological Politics in Belgium and West Germany*, Ithaca, NY: Cornell University Press.
Kitschelt, H. and Hellemans, S. (1990) *Beyond the European Left: Ideology and Political Action in the Belgian Ecology Parties*, Durham, NC: Duke University Press.
Lovelock, J. (1979) *Gaia: A New Look at Life on Earth*, Oxford: Oxford University Press.

Marien, M. (1977) 'The Two Visions of Post-Industrial Society', *Futures*, October.

Meadows, D.H. *et al.* (1972) *The Limits to Growth*, London: Earth Island.

Mishan, E.J. (1967) *The Costs of Economic Growth*, Harmondsworth: Pelican.

Parkin, S. (1989) *Green Parties: An International Guide*, London: Heretic.

Porritt, J. (1984) *Seeing Green*, Oxford: Blackwell.

Van der Straaten, J. (1992) 'The Dutch National Environmental Policy Plan: To Choose or to Lose', *Environmental Politics* 1: 45–71.

Chapter 2

Germany

The rise, fall and recovery of Die Grünen[1]

E. Gene Frankland

The electoral successes of the West German Greens (Die Grünen) during the early 1980s made them the paradigmatic case of Green politics. In contrast to other Green parties, Die Grünen soon became a power in national party politics. Their unexpected defeat in the all-German elections on 2 December 1990 shook the party from top to bottom and sent a chill through the European family of Green parties. However, media reports of the Greens' demise turned out to be greatly exaggerated; 1991–1993 has seen their successes in a series of *Land* (state) elections, in reforming party structures, and in merging with the East German Bündnis 90 (Alliance 90).[2]

Although the German Greens have been the most prominent of European Green parties, their origins and early development are not typical. In retrospect, they appear to have been relatively advantaged by both 'problem push' and 'opportunity pull' (Rüdig 1989) during their mobilization. However, after the mid-1980s, the Greens as an organized party began to encounter less favourable internal and external circumstances. Then in 1990, German unification transformed the political agenda and challenged the relevance of the 'almost established' (Veen and Hoffmann 1992) Greens. This chapter examines these phases in the development of the Green Party, particularly in view of the changing nature of party-political competition.

THE RISE OF THE GREENS

The formative period for the Greens was between 1977 and 1980. The major issue that energized the local and regional alliances that created the Green and Alternative Lists was nuclear power. The

nuclear issue brought together radical leftists, conservative ecologists and apolitical local residents. Beginning in 1977, Green
candidates scored breakthroughs in local elections, which stimulated the launching of *Land* parties. A national alliance of Green
activists won 3.2 per cent of German votes in the 1979 European
Parliament elections. Before the end of the year, the Bremen Green
List had won the first Green seats in a Landtag (state parliament).

On 13 January 1980, an alliance of activists, more diverse than
that which had contested the Euro-elections, officially launched the
Greens as a new national party. The founders shared a deep
discontent with the 'party cartel' in Bonn. They agreed that the
pillars of the new party would be grass-roots democracy, social
concern, ecology and non-violence, but they began to splinter over
the specifics of the federal programme. The Green Party survived
its disappointing results (1.5 per cent) in the October 1980 federal
election and the departure of most of its conservative wing by 1981.

During their early years, the Greens were discounted by the
hostile press as a one issue (environment) party and as a hodge-
podge of protest groups; in either case, they were seen as a transient
phenomenon. However, the Greens'[3] entry into four more Landtage during 1981–1982 suggested otherwise. The Greens' national
profile was emerging as a radical democratic movement–party of
socialist and liberal ideals coming together behind an ecological
banner. They challenged the postwar consensus of West German
élites that the established order of representative institutions and
passive citizenship should be preserved, that economic growth and
consumerist lifestyles should be encouraged, and that engagement
in the Western Alliance, with its policy of nuclear deterrence,
should be maintained. Furthermore, the Greens took up the
neglected causes of women, foreign workers and assorted disad-
vantaged groups.

Social scientists have explained the Greens' emergence in terms
of changing social structures and shifting values. From Inglehart's
perspective (1990), there has emerged throughout western Europe
a new educated middle class who have grown up under conditions
of relative peace and prosperity. Accordingly, post-1945 generations are more likely to be 'post-materialists', showing greater
sensitivity to quality of life issues and seeking to maximize opportunities for self-expression and participation. Post-materialist values
have been clearly reflected in the demands of the new social
movements that began springing up during the 1970s, especially in

West Germany (Markovits and Gorski 1993: 10–14). Cross-national surveys have indicated that the West German Greens have higher proportions of post-materialists[4] among their supporters than not only other German parties, but also other Green parties (Kaelberer 1992).

Another perspective, which depends less on pre-adult social-ization, holds that there would have been no Green party in West Germany without severe environmental problems (Rüdig 1989). The 'economic miracle' brought unprecedented prosperity but also unprecedented pollution, which after decades of intensive industrialization in a densely populated country was hard to ignore. According to Eckersley's synthesis (1989: 221), the new educated middle class is most likely to be aware of environmental degrada-tion and to be 'least constrained from pursuing remedial action' because of 'its relative structural autonomy from the production process' and 'its adherence to the culture of critical discourse'. During the late 1970s, with the major parties demonstrating a lack of responsiveness to environmental concerns, national polls indi-cated a potential electorate of 15–20 per cent for a hypothetical national environmentalist party.

The other major root of the Green phenomenon goes back to the New Left student movement of the late 1960s. There were student protests in almost all industrialized democracies, but what was unique about the German protest action was its durability, variability and influence. The Green Party was to become the institutional embodiment of many ideals and practices developed during the days of the Extra-parliamentary Opposition (APO). Generational conflict was more acute in West Germany than in other industrialized democracies. New Left students, in coming to terms with the heavy burdens of Germany's history, were con-fronting the silence and complacency of their elders. In contrast to other student radicals, young West Germans felt a crisis of identity as well as a crisis of authority. In effect, the New Left was engaged in a dual protest against the present Bonn Republic and the past Third Reich (Markovits and Gorski 1993: 21–22). Seen from the most 'front-line' country in an East–West nuclear confrontation, the future did not seem reassuring either. Thus the intensity of the generational conflict in West Germany is missed if one over-emphasizes the period effects of postwar affluence and security.

During the 1970s, some '68ers took up the challenge of 'march-ing through the institutions' to democratize politics and society, while others became members of fragmented Marxist and Maoist groupings. Many became engaged in local non-partisan citizen groups pushing for action on concrete problems neglected by the established parties. Rapid industrialization, unplanned urbanization and, above all, the nuclear issue, helped to connect a New Left student generational cohort and a larger number of citizens who felt that policy reforms were needed. Compared to other Green parties, the German Greens during their mobilization could draw upon the energy and experience of a relatively large pool of unattached young educated activists.

POLITICAL OPPORTUNITY STRUCTURE

Societal changes, value shifts and controversial issues can go only so far in explaining the rise of the Greens; one must also consider the 'political opportunity structure'. Surging movements do not necessarily translate into new parties if parliamentary, administrative and/or judicial élites respond to new demands and have the institutional capacity to innovate. A comparative study of antinuclear movements (Kitschelt 1986) concludes that the relatively closed political input structures and relatively weak output structures of the West German political system encouraged its antinuclear movement to pursue a confrontational strategy that set the stage for the emergence of the Green Party.

The electoral system is a legal manifestation of the political opportunity structure. Since 1953, only the Christian Democrats (CDU/CSU), the Social Democrats (SPD) and the Free Democrats (FDP) had independently cleared the 5 per cent threshold to win seats in the Bundestag. The electoral experiences of environmentalists during the late 1970s taught them that to gain national representation they would have to have allies. Subsequently, the 5 per cent threshold became a vital ingredient of the 'glue' holding the Greens' heterogeneous activists together. Furthermore, under German electoral law there are no required constituency deposits for candidates, and parties winning 0.5 per cent or more of the votes qualify for campaign reimbursements from public funds. The fact that a national alliance of Greens (SPV) qualified for DM 4.5 million as a result of their showing in the 1979 Euro-elections and the prospects of generous public funding as a consequence of participating in Bundestag elections clearly encouraged the formation of a national Green party in early 1980.

Nor should one overlook the opportunity provided by the German federal system for a new party to win seats in the Landtage, which are more significant policy arenas than the local and regional councils of unitary systems. By clearing electoral hurdles in a number of *Länder* during the early 1980s, the Greens gained national media attention and built up financial resources, parliamentary skills and political credibility.

The political opportunity structure encompasses the pattern of party competition as well as legal/institutional characteristics. Comparative studies (Rüdig 1991: 30; Müller-Rommel 1990: 22) indicate that the more successful Green parties have emerged where social democratic parties have held or shared national power. According to Kitschelt and Hellemans (1990: 4), this is because 'Governmental participation rendered conventional leftist parties inaccessible to the demands of the new social movements.' In corporatist welfare states, social democratic parties worked closely not just with their traditional allies, labour unions, but also with corporate élites. These cosy relationships encouraged preservation of the status quo – not reformism – and thus opened up a political space for a 'left–libertarian' opposition.

In its postwar quest for national power, the SPD after the late 1950s leaned increasingly towards the centre. The Grand Coalition with the CDU/CSU (1966–1969) confirmed the fears of many leftist students: the SPD had become part of the establishment. Nevertheless, some held out hopes for progressive changes under Brandt's SPD–FDP government. But after Schmidt replaced Brandt as Chancellor in 1974, the SPD retreated from its reform agenda, alienating its young left-wingers. Despite evidence of changing public opinion in the early 1980s, the SPD leadership maintained its support for nuclear power plants and for NATO's deployment of new nuclear missiles in West Germany. In 1983, the Greens were able to campaign as the aspiring parliamentary arm of both the anti-nuclear movement and the peace movement, and of the new social movements in general.

The numerical pattern of party competition also may facilitate new party success. The West German party system had developed with a restricted number of relevant actors. Because the SPD and the CDU/CSU rarely had a realistic chance of winning absolute majorities, the FDP, by receiving over 5 per cent of the votes, had disproportionate policy influence in West Germany's 'two-and-a-half' party system. The Greens' entry into *Land* elections coincided with the failure of the FDP to clear the 5 per cent hurdle in a number of *Länder* during 1978–1983. The Greens were better positioned for political relevance than other Green parties that competed in more fragmented party systems, where major parties had alternatives in coalition-building.

THE GREENS AS 'ANTI-PARTY' PARTY

The Bonn Basic Law (1949) 'constitutionalized' political parties. Subsequent federal laws and court decisions helped the consolidation of a party state (*Parteienstaat*) in West Germany. Through the years, the SPD, the CDU/CSU and the FDP voted themselves increasing levels of public funding for campaign expenses, parliamentary salaries and 'educational' foundations. They monopolized political recruitment and influenced top appointments in other societal institutions. All three parties attracted increasing numbers of civil servants as members. The CDU/CSU and the SPD claimed to be *Volksparteien* (people's parties), yet in many senses they had become *Staatsparteien* (parties vitally connected to the state).

Political scientists found declining levels of public satisfaction with the Bonn parties during the 1970s. Raschke (1983) attributes this trend to four tendencies of the major parties: overaccommodation of vested interests, overgeneralization of appeal, overinstitutionalization and 'overloading' (inability to meet rising expectations). Opinion polls indicated more West Germans were active in citizen action groups than were members of the major parties (Helm 1980). Differences of opinion emerged within the new social movements in the late 1970s over the desirability of a national Green party. Some activists rejected the idea because they equated any party organization with hierarchy, careerism and corruption. Those, arguing that a national Green party would increase the visibility of 'new politics' issues and augment the resources of movement groups, prevailed.

The Greens' federal programme (1980: 5) declares, 'We have decided to create a new type of party structure founded upon grassroots democracy and . . . decentralization.' The founders of the Greens, several of whom had as party members (typically of the SPD) experienced the frustrations of intraparty 'democracy' West German style, envisaged their party as the countermodel of the major parties: a semi-institutionalized, non-professionally led, bottom-up organization. Although the Greens' organizational chart resembled those of the major parties, their anti-élitist rules contrasted sharply. They not only took a collective approach to leadership but also limited the tenure and resources of leaders, and forbade the simultaneous holding of party office(s) and a parliamentary seat. In 1983, the Greens mandated mid-term rotation of Bundestag seats of Green deputies, who were also required to donate most of their salaries to fund ecological projects. The federal party charter emphasizes the autonomy of state and local parties.

Although party membership grew from 18,000 to 40,000 during the 1980s, the Greens' leaders never sought aggressively to maximize membership (even the FDP had a membership roughly double that of the Greens during the decade). Some were sensitive to the trade-off between size and internal democracy; most viewed movement activists as de facto members in most circumstances.[5] Qualitatively, the Greens' membership has been distinctive because of its deep distrust of 'media-genic' leaders and its indirect loyalty (via faction or issue-constituency) to the party.

In short, the Greens entered national politics as a 'new type of party' that, activists hoped, would combine the best features of movement and party. However attractive the Greens' alternative party organization was to the surging ecological, peace and feminist movements of the early 1980s, its overly amateurish characteristics would complicate long-term electoral competition with the major parties.

THE ELECTORAL PERFORMANCE OF THE GREENS, 1983–1989

The Greens broke the Bonn parties' decades long monopoly of Bundestag seats in October 1983. Mainly at the expense of the SPD, they polled 5.6 per cent of the national vote, and as a result formed a parliamentary group of 27 Green deputies. Four years later, the Greens won 8.3 per cent of the national vote, again at the expense of the SPD, and expanded their representation to 42 deputies. The party also performed well in the European Parliament elections, winning 8.2 per cent of German votes in 1984 and 8.4 per cent in 1989. By winning between 5.9 and 11.8 per cent of the votes, they held seats in eight of 11 Landtage at the end of the decade. Their *Land* electoral successes had noteworthy consequences: displacing the FDP as the third party, reducing the political power of the SPD, creating the possibility (in two cases the actuality) of SPD–Green coalitions and/or forcing new elections. Furthermore, some 7,000 Green local councillors had been elected, and in a number of major cities local Greens had become an important variable in power equations.

While the peace issue waxed and waned, the environmental issue hovered near the top of the West German political agenda during the mid- and late 1980s. The mass media's coverage of ecological issues increased, the Greens' dire predictions about acid rain were supported by scientific studies, eco-disasters, such as at Bhopal, Chernobyl and Basel, and repeated local stories about toxic chemicals reinforced the Greens' critique of modern industrial society. National surveys indicated that the public viewed the Greens as the party best suited to solve environmental problems.[6]

Numerous studies have revealed the Greens' electorate as disproportionately young, secular, educated, new middle-class citizens in large cities and university towns who have (or are studying towards) public service or high-tech employment. To this post-materialist constituency, the Greens have added voters in areas adversely affected by massive developmental projects, for example, power plants, airports, superhighways. They also have served as a vehicle for protest voters sending a message to the major parties, often entangled in scandals, to clean up their acts. The Greens' national programmes steadily devoted more attention to women's issues. In the early 1980s, polls indicated that the Greens tended to draw relatively more support from men; by the end of the decade, they tended to draw more from women. In the early years, the Greens could appeal as the youthful party of dynamism, freshness and convictions, adding a streak of colour to the grey West German partisan landscape. By the end of the decade, survey evidence indicated the 'greying' of the Greens' electorate.

The Greens' electoral onslaught suffered its first major setback in May 1985 elections in North Rhine Westphalia, the most populated of the German *Länder*. The results demonstrated the volatility of the Greens' new middle-class voters, who helped the local Greens in autumn 1984 gain almost 9 per cent of the vote and in spring 1985 only mustered 4.6 per cent for the state Greens. The Greens' campaign was marred by internal party conflicts and amateurish gaffes, especially a proposal to decriminalize sex be-

tween adults and children which almost ended up in the party's
Land programme and received national media coverage. The SPD
ran an aggressive campaign that focused on the leadership qualities
of Minister-President Johannes Rau and capitalized on the 'ir-
responsibility' of the Greens. Winning 52.1 per cent of the vote, the
SPD retained its absolute majority.

Since 1983, the SPD's challenge has been to co-opt the post-
materialist issues of the Greens without alienating its traditional
materialist working-class supporters. In Saarland and Schleswig-
Holstein, young dynamic SPD leaders appealed for votes on the
issues of environmental protection, women's equality and regulated
growth, and portrayed a vote for the Greens as a vote for the CDU.
The Greens failed to score a breakthrough in either *Land* during
the 1980s. At least in these states, where there was relatively low
urbanization and few university students, the SPD was able to
achieve a balance between the New Left and the old.

The decline in party identification, the rise of a more educated
electorate, the increase in ticket splitting and issue voting are
transnational trends within the 'First World' of industrialized
democracies. German electoral law provides the opportunity to cast
two votes[7] – the first for a constituency representative, the second
for a party list – and the ideological proximity of the Greens and
the SPD on many issues provides the rationale for tactical voting by
politically informed, weak party identifiers. Therefore, SPD-leaning
post-materialist voters will tend not to give their second votes to the
Greens if the SPD stands a real chance of winning a majority. On
the other hand, they will be tempted to vote for the Greens if the
SPD has little chance of winning a majority, as was the case in the
1987 Bundestag elections. In other words, the Greens' electoral
performance of the 1983–1989 period may be understandable
more as 'dealignment' than 'realignment'.

By the end of the decade, the Greens had carved out their niche
as the fourth national party (in some *Länder* the third party). In
January 1989, the Alternative List won 11.8 per cent of West Berlin
votes, the best Green showing ever in a *Land* election, and became
the SPD's partner in a short-lived coalition. Yet late 1980s electoral
successes barely disguised the changing context of political competition: the new social movements were subsiding, Green party in-
fighting was turning off supporters, and the major parties were
showing resilience.

THE CRISIS OF PARTY DEVELOPMENT

A decade after their birth, one critical observer portrayed the Greens as 'legally a party, structurally an alliance, and at least according to their understanding, a movement' (van Hüllen 1990: 6). During the early 1980s, the Greens pronounced themselves a movement-party, with the party as the manoeuvring 'leg' in electoral and parliamentary activities for the more important, supporting 'leg', the grass-roots movements. Critics of the formation of a national Green party had feared that it might sap the vital energy of the extra-parliamentary movements. However, it is difficult to blame the mid-1980s decline of movement activism on the Green Party (Zeuner 1985). Contrary to the 'two leg' model, movement groups soon were turning to the parliamentary groups for 'support'. The party was having difficulties relating to changing societal circumstances. The majority of Green activists had a lot of ideological capital invested in the concept of *Basisdemokratie* (grass-roots democracy), which meant that the party should focus on more than electoral competition.

At the outset most Green activists favoured a strategy of 'fundamental opposition' (refusing to compromise basic principles in order to share governmental power) but electoral successes brought immediate opportunities to affect the balance of power in a couple of *Länder* and suggested future prospects for doing so in Bonn. Even where Green deputies were limited to an opposition role, they became fully engaged in parliamentary activities and had access to resources (budgets, staffs and media) which overshadowed those of the party leadership.

By the mid-1980s, the party's red–green (left) versus green–green (right) cleavage had been supplanted by the *Realo* (realist) versus *Fundi* (fundamentalist) cleavage.[8] In general, *Realos* emphasized parliamentary politics and reform proposals, and favoured sharing power with the SPD, while *Fundis* emphasized extra-parliamentary politics and radical declarations, and opposed sharing power with the SPD. The factional balance of power varied regionally, with Hamburg one of the fundamentalist strongholds and Hesse one of the realist strongholds. As a general rule, in the more mixed *Länder* and in Bonn, realists were overrepresented in parliamentary groups while fundamentalists were overrepresented in party executives. Throughout the decade, polls indicated that most Green voters, even in Hamburg, favoured sharing power with the SPD. Bitter factional conflicts between *Realo* and *Fundi* celebrities began to alienate a number of Green supporters. These well-publicized feuds provided support for the major parties' view that the Greens were too irresponsible, unreliable and immature to bring about positive changes.

The Greens' wide diversity of ideological perspectives[9] coupled with high decentralization of power to produce a 'stratarchical, disjointed framework party' in which careerist 'political entrepreneurs', not grass-roots activists, prevailed (Kitschelt 1989: 295). Practical experiences raised questions about the functionality of anti-élitist rules. Only unrepresentative kinds of members were motivated to hold non-salaried, burdensome party offices. Mid-term rotation of seats disrupted the work of already hard-pressed parliamentary groups.[10] Collective leadership tended to produce a divided leadership fighting for factional interests rather than integrating the party around common interests. Because of the lack of ideological consensus and the diffusion of power, factions and special issue groups could contest the public meaning of the Greens' programme. One critical observer concluded, 'The Green party . . . seems little more than a convenient label for a disjointed and divided assortment of policies' (Kolinsky 1989: 8). The political credibility the Greens needed in order to carry through their policy alternatives was in short supply.

While the SPD was renewing itself by borrowing green themes and promoting a new generational cohort into leadership, the Greens were not only squabbling at the national level but shrivelling at the grass roots. As measured by attendance at party meetings, Green activism sank to new lows in the late 1980s. In some *Länder*, the Greens' local councillors *were* the local party activists, while the Greens' parliamentary groups had siphoned off activists essential for the vitality of the state party organization.

A moderate group of Greens (Aufbruch 88) sought to reawaken the grass roots by calling for a membership ballot on rival manifestos. *Fundis* favoured the status quo, which had allowed them disproportionate influence on programmatic and strategic development. Aufbruch and *Realo* leaders were unable to push aside the non-dogmatic and fundamentalist lefts so that the party could be adapted to changing competitive conditions. The majority of federal party delegates favoured a 'pluralistic' leadership, in which leftists counterbalanced realists and moderates. Questions of party reform were sidetracked.

In retrospect, the Greens underestimated the adaptability of the major parties, all of which 'greened', at least in terms of rhetoric, discovered the talents of female party members for office and talked about balancing ecology and economics. Furthermore, with the winding down of the Cold War, all were becoming peace parties. The Greens' core voters would not easily be persuaded by these 'conversion experiences', but a cautious estimate would place such voters at 4 per cent of the late 1980s national electorate. It was becoming apparent that a generational shift of societal values was not going to sweep the Greens onward no matter how chaotic their public image. In short, as the major parties were getting their acts together, the Greens were losing the advantages of a grass-roots democratic organization without gaining the advantages of a professional electoral organization (Maier 1990).

GERMAN UNIFICATION AND THE 1990 CAMPAIGN

The national unity question abruptly transformed the political environment of the Greens, leaving them confused, ambivalent, and discordant, while Kohl's CDU/CSU–FDP government boldly seized the political initiative. The Greens have been many things to many people, but they have *not* been nationalists! Their 1980 federal programme made one passing reference to German unification, premised on the dissolution of both military blocs. Later the Greens pushed to remove the clause about German unification from the preamble of the Basic Law. In 1990, after public debate had already shifted to how and when unification should occur, Green activists were still arguing over how the 'two German state' concept would work, how a 'third way' between corporate capitalism and state socialism could be followed by East Germany (Fücks 1991: 33).

Although many East German environmentalists favoured evolving as a decentralized movement, proponents of a Green party, citing the rush of events, prevailed in November 1989. From the outset, the East Greens were more environmentally focused, more homogeneous and more pragmatic than the West Greens (Veen and Hoffmann 1992: 144–146). They were also smaller in membership (claiming 3,000 plus in 1990) and in electoral support (receiving only 1.97 per cent in the March 1990 East German parliamentary elections).[11]

The West German Greens had maintained contacts with East

German dissidents, who favoured a bloc-free democratic socialist GDR, since the early 1980s. These dissidents, who also were to misjudge the power of nationalism, became the core around which citizen movements formed in 1989 (Markovits and Gorski 1993: 248–252). To contest the March 1990 elections, New Forum, Democracy Now and the Initiative for Peace and Human Rights formed an electoral alliance, Bündnis 90, which proclaimed its independence from all West German parties. While the West German Greens provided limited assistance to Bündnis 90 and the East Greens, the major parties utilized their resources to dominate their emerging sister parties and to take control of the campaign. Eastern amateurs turned out to be no match for western professionals; Bündnis 90 received only 2.9 per cent of the votes.

Although the unification issue was on the fast track with Kohl's government in the driver's seat after March 1990, it was not until September 1990 that the West Greens finalized an electoral arrangement with their eastern allies. Sensitive to the citizen movements' concern with autonomy, the West Greens agreed to campaign only in the West while East Greens ran as part of Bündnis 90 in the East; after election day East and West Greens would merge.[12] Their common electoral platform was preoccupied with likely negative effects of German reunification. Its authors saw the democratic revolution of 1989–1990 as having been betrayed by party élites determined to carry out the 'annexation' of the GDR, whatever the costs. On the unification issue, one national survey indicated that the West Greens were out of touch with 66 per cent of their supporters (Mannheim 1990: 72).

The Greens' attempts to refocus the campaign on global warming and ozone holes – 'Everybody talks about Germany, we speak about the weather' – smacked of too-clever amateurishness. Overall, the West Greens made ineffective use of the media, did not showcase their leading personalities and continued to feud in public. On the eastern side, Bündnis 90 was outspent and out-organized by the major parties. SPD Chancellor candidate, Lafontaine, also had qualms about rapid unification and had a positive track record on many issues that appealed to the Greens' post-materialist constituency. The Greens did not expect to do well in such competitive circumstances. Yet some encouragement could be drawn from the October state election results in Bavaria where the Greens were returned to the Landtag, and in the five new eastern *Länder* where Bündnis 90/Grüne candidates won 6.9 per cent of the overall votes.

Virtually all national polls indicated that the Greens would clear the 5 per cent threshold.

The West German Greens ended up with only 4.8 per cent of the votes in western Germany and lost all their Bundestag seats, while their allies managed 6.1 per cent of the votes in eastern Germany and won eight seats. Why were the pollsters wrong? Almost 250,000 former Green voters did not turn out, and these non-voters had not shown up in many polls. Second, although the SPD lost badly in the election, some 600,000 former Green voters switched to the SPD late in the campaign. Third, the Greens lost votes to new parties: the ex-communists (PDS/LL) and the Greys (formed by the Grey Panthers, a senior citizens' lobby, that was allied with the Greens in 1987). Nevertheless, if the West Greens had fused with their eastern counterparts before the election, together they would have won 26 seats. Thus, short-term unfavourable competitive conditions and poor strategic choices interacted with long-term organizational shortcomings to produce the West Greens' 'débâcle' on 2 December 1990 (Poguntke 1993: 382–386).

REFORM AND RECOVERY, 1991–1993

The unexpected defeat of the West German Greens shook the party from top to bottom and raised second thoughts within Bündnis 90 about the wisdom of fusion with losers.[13] *Realos* and Aufbruch leaders immediately seized the initiative by proposing major structural reforms to remedy the lack of forceful national leadership in the party. Spokespersons of the undogmatic left (Linken-Forum) also urged rationalizing the party organization, but favoured retaining the separation of party office and parliamentary mandate. The fading minority of *Fundis*[14] spoke out for reviving grass-roots democracy through extra-parliamentary opposition, *not* reforming the party organization to be more like the major parties.

The Hesse Greens portrayed the *Land* election in Hesse on 20 January 1991 as a test of the national destiny of the Green Party. Their *Realo* approach involved a disciplined and structured campaign that made special efforts to mobilize young voters, showcase party leader Joschka Fischer and present the Greens as thoughtful reformers. The Hesse Greens were aided by the interjection of the Gulf War issue into the campaign, which allowed them to demonstrate against possible German involvement. The campaign strategy succeeded as the Greens won 8.8 per cent of the Hessen vote and entered a coalition with the SPD. The reformist impetus was reinforced by the results of the Rhineland–Palatinate election of 21 April 1991, when its moderate Green Party won 6.4 per cent of the vote, better than in the 1987 *Land* election and in the 1990 all-German election. Survey evidence indicates that the Greens benefited from pro-SPD tactical voters who favoured a Red–Green coalition (Mannheim 1991b). However, the victorious SPD leadership opted for a coalition with the FDP.

At the Neumünster federal party conference (26–28 April 1991) two-thirds majorities voted to eliminate term limits of party leaders, streamline the federal executive committee, increase the role of state party leaders and parliamentary deputies by replacing the federal steering committee with a new *Länderrat* and set up dual chairs with a Green from the East and a Green from the West. However, the proposal to abandon the rule forbidding the simultaneous holding of a party office and a parliamentary mandate failed narrowly.[15] Another outcome was the tumultuous exit from the party of the last of the leading *Fundis*, Jutta Ditfurth, and her entourage. A rival Alternative List, supporters of fundamentalist views, won a mere 0.5 per cent of the votes in the Hamburg election of 2 June 1991. The Hamburg Greens (GAL), who had fallen apart due to factional in-fighting and had to be pieced back together – minus far leftists – after December 1990, polled 7.2 per cent. The departure of the fundamentalist left in Hamburg and elsewhere has clarified the political profile of the Greens as a reformist party.

Electoral successes have continued at the *Land* level. In September 1991, Bremen Greens increased their share of the vote to 11.4 per cent and joined a coalition with the SPD and the FDP (corresponding to the coalition in which Bündnis 90 has participated in Brandenburg following the October 1990 elections in that state). Survey evidence indicates that many voters saw the Bremen Greens as having a track record of realistic and diligent political work (Mannheim 1991a). In April 1992, although overshadowed by media coverage of the gains by the right-wing Republikaner, Baden-Württemberg Greens achieved their best ever vote – 9.5 per cent. As a result the CDU conducted coalition talks with the moderate south-western Greens before settling on a grand coalition with the SPD. In the April Schleswig-Holstein election, the Greens won 4.97 per cent (but no seats), more than double their 1988 result. Lastly, in September 1993 the Hamburg Greens (GAL), stressing the credibility and competence of their list headed by the popular Krista Sager, polled 13.5 per cent, the highest percentage ever won by Greens anywhere in a Landtag election. By attracting former SPD voters, the GAL more than doubled its votes since 1991. Despite the preference of a majority of SPD voters for a red–green coalition (Mannheim 1993b: 48), the SPD leadership chose to share power with a breakaway faction (Statt Partei) of the CDU.

During 1991–1993, Green politics on the state and national levels moved in a less polemic, more pragmatic direction. Professionalization, greater attention to the media and more time spent on organizational tasks seemed to have paid off. Yet the context of party competition was also changing as public anxieties about unification's social and economic costs steadily grew. It is possible to see in the state election results the Greens, like the extreme right-wing parties, reaping a bonus from the increasing discontent with the major parties' policy performance at both state and national level.

It had long been apparent to most observers that some sort of 'marriage of convenience' (Schoonmaker 1992) would be necessary between the Greens and Bündnis 90 if they were to have a credible chance of winning 5 per cent of all-German votes, especially in times of resurgent 'old politics' concerns with economic security and national identity. Bündnis 90 had been as heterogeneous as the Greens were during their mobilization phase. A vocal minority of its New Forum activists was 'unwilling to trade their movement credentials for what they perceive as an organizational straitjacket of a party' (Schoonmaker 1992: 9). On the other hand, most easterners tended to be pragmatic; yet they did not want to be simply swallowed up by the larger, wealthier and more aggressive Greens.

After some public misunderstandings, the parties formed a commission, equally representing 37,000 Green Party members and 3,000 Bündnis 90 members, which in mid-1992 began work on an association contract. The major issue turned out to be the unified party's name. The easterners prevailed as Bündnis 90/Die Grünen became the official name of the party, with 'Greens' the shortened version. The commission voted to add several provisions to the Green Party charter to protect the special interests of the easterners. For example, they may form an intraparty association, *Bürgerbewegung* (citizen movement), and they are overrepresented on the federal executive committee. The association contract was put to a membership ballot in April 1993; the Greens' membership voted 91.8 per cent in favour of fusion as did 85.7 per cent of Bündnis 90 members (Raschke 1993: 927). Doubtless party unification will not go so smoothly, but easterners and westerners are now committed to common campaigns on social justice, peace and ecology. In December 1993 the Mannheim research group (1993a) projected an all-German vote for the unified Green Party of 10 per cent.

CONCLUSIONS

Despite the Greens' defeat in the uniquely unfavourable conditions of the first all-German elections, they remain the most successful of European Green parties. Postwar socio-economic transformations and an acute generational gap provided the social base for the rise of the Greens. Converging policy frustrations and precipitating events (especially involving the nuclear issue) provided the impetus towards Green Party formation. West Germany's political opportunity structure provided footholds for the Greens' quick ascent to national political relevance. During its first decade, the major obstacle to the Green Party's success often seemed to be its own internal contradictions.

As of early 1994, the (unified) Greens hold seats in the European Parliament, the Bundestag,[16] 13 of 16 Landtage and hundreds of local councils. Their electoral performance has altered the pattern of coalition politics in several *Länder* and many localities: there are Green ministers, state secretaries, departmental heads and mayors. Even where confined to the opposition, the Greens have had an undeniable impact on the environmental programmes of the major parties, especially of the SPD. As a feminist party, they have contributed to the changed public discourse on the role of women in German society (Markovits and Gorski 1993: 273). From the outset, the Greens have opposed the revival of militarism, nationalism and racism in the Federal Republic. Critical observers have credited the Greens with integrating youthful protest into the party system and strengthening the control ('oversight') functions of parliamentary bodies (Veen and Hoffmann 1992: 158–159).

Nevertheless, Green prospects for the mid- and late 1990s must be viewed cautiously. Although national polls during 1992–1993 have shown the Greens well above the 5 per cent threshold, they still lack the safety net of loyal partisans on which established parties may depend. And, although the Greens' recovery in recent *Land* elections has been remarkable, one should note that, as 'second order' elections, these tend to be characterized by lower turnouts and fewer inhibitions about protest voting. Beyond these caveats are the historic uncertainties of politics in the united Germany.

At least in the near future, the German policy agenda will be heavily weighted with materialist or 'old politics' issues. In December 1993 (Mannheim 1993a), only 6 per cent of western Germans cited environmental protection as one of the most important problems facing the country; it does not even register among eastern Germans. In the longer run, the backlog of ecological disasters will have to be addressed in eastern Germany, but for now, unemployment is at the top of the problem list for eastern Germans (78 per cent) and for western Germans (63 per cent); in both cases, these percentages are significantly higher than in 1992 (Mannheim 1992). Economic policy has never been the strong card of the Greens, who have long attributed – without reservations – higher priority to environmental protection than economic growth. Furthermore, this survey indicates that the number two and three problems are law and order and foreigners in the East, and foreigners and inflation in the West. Since early confrontations, the Greens have retained a deep suspicion of the police. Of all the parties, they have adopted the most permissive approach to asylum-seekers, and they are out front in advocating full citizenship for foreign residents. Such policy orientations would seem unlikely to have wide appeal under current socio-economic circumstances.

There is little evidence of a sizeable post-materialist constituency, such as the West German Greens had during the 1980s, to build upon in the East. Yet, the major parties also lack stable foundations in the East: support in eastern Germany for the CDU, for example, has fallen from 45 per cent to less than 25 per cent. Although the odds are against the PDS's return to the Bundestag in 1994,[17] its 21.5 per cent share of the votes in the December 1993 Brandenburg local elections suggests that it may have a future as the eastern party of resentment. Thus, the Greens will have to define a space between a lingering PDS and a recovering SPD in the East.

The SPD leadership has chosen a centrist strategy of electoral competition for the mid-1990s. Despite their voters' preferences, the Rhineland–Palatinate SPD and the Hamburg SPD declined the opportunity to share power with reformist Greens. In the midst of a decade of economic anxieties, SPD national party leader, Rudolf Scharping, reasons that there are more ready gains to be won at the CDU's expense than the Greens'; therefore, his party should distance itself from the Greens. Such a strategy opens up the grand coalition option, but also allows for combinations with the FDP and/or the Greens. With the post-Genscher FDP falling behind the Greens in the polls, the numbers are not adding up to an SPD–FDP majority. The Greens have not ruled out a coalition with the SPD, but they have been critical of its rightward drift. With the Lafontaine 'left–libertarian' strategy shelved, a space to the left of the SPD is opening for the Greens in western Germany, where the PDS is not a factor. According to Kitschelt's analysis (1993: 106–107), such spatial conditions have worked in favour of the Greens in the past.

The pattern of party competition is further complicated by the extreme right-wing parties, which in the West have shown ability to take votes from not only the CDU but also the SPD in 'second order' elections. If the Republikaner and the German People's Union (DVU) were to co-operate (still a big 'if') and enter the Bundestag, coalition politics would become even more interesting with five or six parties represented. A grand coalition might then leave the Greens as the major opposition party. At state level, *Ampelkoalitionen* of the SPD, FDP and Greens have worked, but would there be sufficient commonalities regarding defence and foreign policies? At a special November 1993 conference, 90 per cent of Green delegates voted to continue their party's opposition to the use of military force as a tool of foreign policy. While the major parties have favoured European economic and political union, the Greens have envisaged Europe evolving as a large, loose confederation of nations and regions that does not threaten anyone (or any species) at home or abroad.

In sum, the Greens have risen, fallen and recovered in little more than a decade. Their electoral shock therapy in December 1990 facilitated an overdue clarification of party identity and consolidation of party organization. The Green Party still has a distinctive profile, more regionally diverse, decentralized, participatory and élite-challenging than the major parties. As Poguntke (1993: 401) reminds us, the Greens 'have retained most essentials of *Basisdemokratie*'. Furthermore, they have remained committed to their other pillars: non-violence, social concern and ecology. The Greens seem likely to return in force to the Bundestag in October 1994. Their long-term future will be shaped by outside forces, but it will also depend to a significant extent upon their own performance. Nationally, the Greens must expand their core electorate, recruit a politically astute (and accountable) leadership and cultivate more 'civility' within their active membership.

NOTES

1   In addition to the sources cited in the text, this chapter relies upon the author's collaborative works with the late Don Schoonmaker, especially *Between Protest and Power: The Green Party in Germany* (Boulder, Colo. and Oxford: Westview Press 1992).

2   The official name of the party is now Bündnis 90/Die Grünen. This chapter prefers the common name, the Greens, in most circumstances. In the text any general reference to German Greens means West Greens prior to 3 December 1990, when East and West Greens officially merged; after that and until May 1993 (when the union with Bündnis 90 became official) it means East and West Greens.

3   The leftist Alternative List first won seats in the West Berlin parliament in 1981. From the outset it has been an ally of the West German Greens and after 1985 it became the officially designated state association of the federal Green Party in West Berlin.

4   A large number of Green supporters, nevertheless, have mixed post-materialist/materialist values as operationalized by the Inglehart scheme (1990).

5   Movement groups have had the right to speak at party conferences. Their activists have been nominated and elected as Green parliamentary candidates though they have not been party members. They have also served on specialized working groups at all levels that focus on the Greens' programmatic development.

6   See, for example, the EMNID survey reported in *Der Spiegel*, 6 May 1986: 46.

7   The German electoral system allocates parliamentary seats proportionally according to the 'second' votes for party lists. Winning a plurality of 'first' votes determines district winners, whose seats are subtracted from the total list seats won by the party. If a party should win more seats via 'first' votes than those qualified for by 'second' votes, these are kept as bonus seats and the size of the Bundestag is temporarily expanded. To be proportionally represented, a party must win 5 per cent of 'second' votes or three district seats. (There was no threshold clause in the March 1990 East German parliamentary election.)

8   Distinctive groups have existed within both wings. For example, the *Fundis* included eco-socialists of the Hamburg ex-communist variety and radical ecologists of the Frankfurt variety. Furthermore, there were noteworthy non-aligned groups, such as autonomous feminists, and eco-libertarians, as well as numerous one-issue specialists.

9   Raschke (1991: 22) identifies four divergent ideological perspectives – feminism, fundamentalism, eco-socialism and eco-reformism – behind the Greens' factional conflicts during the 1980s.

10   By the late 1980s, the federal party and nearly all *Land* parties had

abandoned mid-term rotation for deputies. Several, however, restricted the deputies' tenure to two legislative periods.

11 The East German Greens ran in alliance with an independent women's association (UFV). After the campaign they feuded over who would get the seats in the Volkskammer and parted company.

12 The West German Greens successfully challenged in the Federal Constitutional Court the use of the 5 per cent clause in the first all-German Bundestag elections on the grounds that it would discriminate against the new parties of East Germany. As a result the electoral law was temporarily changed so that a party earning 5 per cent in the East or West would qualify for representation.

13 On 3 December 1990, the West German and East German Greens had officially merged.

14 The Trampert–Ebermann eco-socialist group had withdrawn from the Greens to form a new radical leftist association in early 1990. Some remaining far leftist Greens defected later to the reform communists (PDS/LL), whose campaign won 0.3 per cent of western German votes on 2 December 1990.

15 Several state parties, for example, Hesse, voted to abandon the incompatibility rule at the *Land* level. The *Länderrat* represents a partial phase-out of the federal rule since state parliamentary deputies are now part of the federal party leadership.

16 Two of the eight Bündnis 90/Grüne candidates elected in 1990 were members of the East German Greens. Others of the eight have subsequently taken active roles in the B'90/Green Party.

17 Because the PDS lacks a base of support in the more populated West, its only possible route back into the Bundestag would be by winning district seats in the East. Three direct wins would be necessary to qualify for their proportion of all-German seats.

REFERENCES

Die Grünen (1980) *The Program of the Green Party* (English Translation), Bonn: Die Grünen.

Eckersley, R. (1989) 'Green Politics and the New Class: Selfishness or Virtue?', *Political Studies* 37(2): 205–223.

Fücks, R. (1991) 'Ökologie und Bürgerrechte: Plädoyer für eine neue Allianz', in R. Fücks (ed.), *Sind die Grünen noch zu retten?*, Reinbek: Rowolt, pp. 33–43.

Helm, J. (1980) 'Citizen Lobbies in West Germany', in P.M. Merkl (ed.), *Western European Party Systems*, New York: Free Press, pp. 576–596.

Inglehart, R. (1990) *Culture Shift in Advanced Industrial Society*, Princeton, NJ: Princeton University Press.

Kaelberer, M. (1992) 'The Emergence of Green Parties in France and Germany', paper presented at the German Studies Association conference, Minneapolis, 1–4 October.

Kitschelt, H. (1986) 'Political Opportunity Structure and Political Protest: Anti-Nuclear Movements in Four Democracies', *British Journal of Political Science* 16(1): 57–83.

—— (1989) *The Logics of Party Formation: Ecological Politics in Belgium and West Germany*, Ithaca, NY: Cornell University Press.

—— (1993) 'The Green Phenomenon in Western Party Systems', in S. Kamieniecki (ed.), *Environmental Politics in the International Arena*, Albany, NY: State University of New York Press, pp. 93–112.

Kitschelt, H. and Hellemans, S. (1990) *Beyond the European Left: Ideology and Political Action in the Belgian Ecology Parties*, Durham, NC: Duke University Press.

Kolinsky, E. (1989) 'Introduction', in E. Kolinsky (ed.), *The Greens in West Germany: Organization and Policy Making*, Oxford: Berg, pp. 1–8.

Maier, J. (1990) 'Die Grüne Parteien in Westeuropa', *Die Grünen: Monatszeitung*, Bonn: Die Grünen.

Mannheim, Forschungsgruppe Wahlen e. V. (1990) 'Bundestagswahl 1990: Eine Analyse der ersten Gesamtdeutschen Bundestagswahl am 2. Dezember 1990', *Berichte* No. 61 (Mannheim).

—— (1991a) 'Wahl in Bremen: Eine Analyse der Bürgerschaftswahl vom 29. September 1991', *Berichte* No. 66 (Mannheim).

—— (1991b) 'Wahl in Rheinland-Pfalz: Eine Analyse der Landtagswahl vom 21. April 1991', *Berichte* No. 64 (Mannheim).

—— (1992) *Politbarometer* No. 12 (Mannheim).

—— (1993a) *Politbarometer* No. 12 (Mannheim).

—— (1993b) 'Wahl in Hamburg: Eine Analyse der Bürgerschaftswahl vom 19. September 1993', *Berichte* No. 69 (Mannheim).

Markovits, A.S. and Gorski, P.S. (1993) *The German Left: Red, Green and Beyond*, New York: Oxford University Press.

Müller-Rommel, F. (1990) 'Political Success of Green Parties in Western Europe', paper presented at American Political Science Association conference, San Francisco, 30 August–2 September.

Poguntke, T. (1993) 'Goodbye to Movement Politics? Adaptation of the German Green Party', *Environmental Politics* 2(3): 379–404.

Raschke, J. (1983) 'Jenseits der Volkspartei', *Das Argument* 25(1): 54–65.

—— (1991) *Krise der Grünen: Bilanz und Neubeginn*, Marburg: Schüren.

—— (1993) *Die Grünen: wie sie wurden was sie sind*, Cologne: Bund-Verlag.

Rüdig, W. (1989) 'Explaining Green Party Development: Reflections on a Theoretical Framework', paper presented at the UK Political Studies Association conference, University of Warwick, Coventry, 4–6 April.

—— (1991) 'Green Party Politics Around the World', *Environment* 33(8): 7–9, 25–31.

Schoonmaker, D. (1992) 'The Green Alliance: A Marriage of Convenience', paper presented at the German Studies Association conference, Minneapolis, 1–4 October.

van Hüllen, R. (1990) *Ideologie und Machtkampf bei den Grünen*, Bonn: Bouvier.

Veen, H.-J. and Hoffmann, J. (1992) *Die Grünen zu Beginn der neunziger Jahre*, Bonn: Bouvier.

Zeuner, B. (1985) 'Parlamentarisierung der Grünen', *Prokla* 61: 13–18.

Chapter 3

France

Pas comme les autres – the French Greens at the crossroads

Alistair Cole and Brian Doherty

Before 1989 the new wave of Green party politics which had influenced most of the rest of western Europe seemed to have bypassed France. In that year, however, the French Green Party (Les Verts) followed a modest success in the March local elections (8 per cent in towns with over 9,000 inhabitants) with an impressive 10.59 per cent in the European elections. This gave the movement nine MEPs, the largest number of any of the European Green parties. This was not quite the rise from nowhere that it might have seemed: Les Verts first emerged in the mid-1970s and can look back on a history of intermittent minor successes, including the 3.8 per cent vote for Antoine Waechter in the 1988 presidential election.

Between 1989 and 1992, Les Verts maintained a relatively high level of public support in the polls and electoral contests (around 14 per cent). However, French Green politics was complicated by the emergence in 1990 of a rival party, Génération écologie, led by Brice Lalonde, an ecologist presidential candidate in 1981 and, as an independent, Minister of the Environment in the Socialist government from 1989 to 1992. In the 1992 regional elections the two parties were in competition, Génération écologie narrowly outdistancing Les Verts (7.1 per cent to 6.8 per cent). A long history of animosity between Lalonde and the leaders of Les Verts, as well as deeply opposed political styles, have meant that the obstacles to the unity of the two camps are substantial. Yet, despite their rivalries, they concluded an electoral agreement in November 1992 in order to run a single Green candidate in each constituency from the first ballot in the legislative elections of March 1993. The performance of the Entente écologiste in the National Assembly elections of March 1993 will be considered below.

THE GREENS IN THE FRENCH PARTY SYSTEM

In the past, good reasons have been given for believing that the French party system was a particularly uncongenial environment for green politics (Kitschelt 1990). According to Wilson (1988: 526), French parties resisted the challenge of alternative political organizations for five main reasons. First, the major parties were themselves reforming or emerging. Second, the central political battleground of the 1970s was that between left and right, an arena in which alternative organizations had no part. Third, class confrontation remained important in France and encouraged citizens to identify with established vehicles for class conflict rather than turn to alternative political organizations unrelated to class; even the new Socialist Party, though it articulated many of the demands of new social movements, retained a political discourse centred on class conflict. Fourth, the centralized and aloof pattern of policy-making in the Fifth Republic insulated the political system from alternative groups and their issues. Finally, the tradition of political protest in France made the new groups of the 1970s seem little different from a long succession of others which had advocated mass action.

The contours of the French party system in the 1970s also discriminated against the breakthrough of new political forces in more subtle ways. The party system of 1978 has been described as a bipolar quadrille: four parties of roughly equal weight distributed the preferences of the electorate evenly between left and right coalitions (Cole 1990: 3–24). This pattern was in part encouraged by the second-ballot electoral system, which discriminated against all forms of minority parties (see below, pp. 60–61); this was evident in 1978 when ecologist candidates obtained some 2 per cent of the vote in the Assembly elections to no obvious political effect (Bridgeford 1978). It was also in part a consequence of the fact that the Fifth Republic had not yet managed to achieve an alternation in power: aspirations for social change (including ecological change) rested firmly upon the mainstream left-wing parties, especially the Socialist Party (PS). The ecological constituency was thus imperfectly represented by existing political parties, such as the PS, or the Parti Socialiste Unifié (PSU), or else by effective pressure groups such as Les Amis de la Terre.

The penetration of the Front National (FN) from 1982 onwards, combined with the historic decline of the Communist Party (PCF), followed by the breakthrough of the Greens in 1989, fundamentally altered the structure of the French party system. If the break-through of the FN had indirectly benefited the PS (by causing divisions among the conservative RPR and UDF), the emergence of the Greens after 1989 threatened the Socialists, in part because the Greens provided a rallying point for disillusioned ex-Socialists, but also because any weakening of the PS almost mechanically strengthened the RPR–UDF bloc. With significant votes for both the Front National and the Greens in the 1989 European and 1992 regional elections, and the poor performance of the governing Socialists (23.4 per cent in 1989, 18.9 per cent in 1992), the French party system appeared considerably less stable in the early 1990s than it did in the early 1980s. Yet, although the points made by Wilson now seem less powerful, each of the five principal features of the French party system that he emphasized can still be seen as influencing the character of green politics in France.

- The attempt by the Socialist Party to remain open to new ideas and new movements in the 1970s meant that, in elections, the Greens were always competing with the Socialists for the support of a new social movement-oriented left (Ladrech 1989). During the 1980s, the evolution of the PS into a more traditional social democratic party of government increasingly left the Greens rather than the Socialists as the beneficiaries of endorsements from key social movement actors such as Harlem Désir (former leader of SOS-Racisme), and led to the recruitment of New Left intellectuals such as the economist Alain Lipietz and the psycho-analyst Félix Guaterri.
- Surveys of French voters show an increase in the numbers of those who see the left–right spectrum as politically irrelevant. Issues such as the future of Europe, immigration, racial conflict and the environment have become more important in French politics and have proved difficult for the existing parties to assimilate. The French Greens have always refused to align themselves formally with either left or right, and this may now seem a more appropriate strategy than it did in the 1970s. Yet, despite their claims to be new, most Green activists and voters do regard themselves as lying on the left, although not necessarily the left as represented by the PS or PCF.
- The failure of the Greens to articulate more of the non-environmental dimension of their politics has meant that they

have tended to be seen as a single-issue party whose role is essentially to pressure government on environmental issues. Conscious of this, the leaders of the Entente écologiste constructed their 1993 electoral campaign so as to emphasize issues other than the environment.

- The rapid success of the Greens since 1989 has been founded on good performances in elections based on proportional representation (although the rule is not an absolute one, as the Greens' strong showing in the 1989 municipal elections confirms). Their consequent representation in regional assemblies and the European Parliament has given Les Verts new powers, resources and credibility. Until the approach to the 1993 National Assembly election, the second-ballot electoral system was always perceived to be an insuperable barrier to significant Green representation in National Assembly elections, but the continuing opinion poll strength of the Greens suggested that a unified Green alliance might obtain representation even under that system.

- The concentration on the development of a party since 1984 is a strategic move away from protest and towards cultural change and the use of power within existing political institutions.

LES VERTS

The evolution of the French Greens away from a political culture based on protest to a more electorally oriented politics was achieved only gradually, imperfectly and with difficulty. When the Greens first emerged in 1974 as a loose coalition to promote ecological ideas through the presidential campaign of Réné Dumont, they were still clearly marked by the legacies of the student movement of May 1968. In the early to mid-1970s, it was difficult to distinguish the influence of political ecology from a more general *gauchisme* (Pronier and le Seigneur 1992).

The nuclear question was of primary importance in shaping the character of the French ecology movement during the 1970s. Other ecological conflicts were secondary. The absence of sufficient legal avenues of protest meant that in France, by contrast with Britain, anti-nuclear conflicts became more broadly political (Rüdig 1990). There was no single-issue environmental movement which was able to separate the technical questions of ecology from the issues of democracy, the role of the state and control of information.

The death of a demonstrator after serious violence at Malville in 1977 fractured the anti-nuclear movement and proved to be an important turning-point. Many activists sought a less confrontational form of politics, while others regarded the police action as a declaration of war by the state and pursued a campaign of direct action. Despite some success, such as the abandonment by the Socialist government of the proposed nuclear site at Plogoff, after the Malville demonstration the anti-nuclear movement could no longer mobilize the same degree of public support. Thus, when President Mitterrand failed to fulfil his promise of a moratorium on nuclear plants in 1981, the movement was unable to react effectively.

For many Greens, an important legacy of this period was an acceptance of the difficulty of sustaining over a long period a broad social movement based on protest. Greens increasingly sought to influence the mainstream parties, especially the Socialists, within whose ranks ecologist currents were present. Disillusion with the Socialists was all the more bitter after May 1981, when it became clear that the new government would pay little more than lip-service to key ecological themes. Indeed, after 1981, the movement entered a period of retrenchment in which the various Green organizations explored different strategies. Unity between the two main wings of the ecologist movement was achieved at Clichy in January 1984 and resulted in the formation of Les Verts (Hainsworth 1990).The key groups which came together to form Les Verts were Les Verts: parti écologiste, created in 1981 out of the Mouvement d'écologie politique (MEP) which had been born in the 1970s, and Les Amis de la Terre (AT). AT has been described as an 'organization of experienced activists, combining ideological debates with "alternative" actions on the ground' (Biffaud and Jarreau 1989). Their chief spokesperson was initially Brice Lalonde, originally a member of the PSU, the ecologist candidate in the 1981 presidential election. In 1981, AT joined with former MEP activists to create the Confédération écologiste. Lalonde refused to associate himself with the creation of the unified Green Party.

It is possible to identify various formative influences underpinning the creation of Les Verts. The years of polarized confrontation over the nuclear question were the first such influence. The second major influence was their long experience of poor electoral performances. Between 1974 and 1989, they did not manage to achieve 5 per cent in a national election, and had only occasional success in local elections. Throughout the 1970s, the Green vote proved volatile, increasing from 1.7 per cent for Dumont in the 1974 presidential election to scores as high as 10 per cent in Paris in municipal elections in 1977, only to fall back again to 2.14 per cent in the 1978 National Assembly elections. The best performances were for Green candidates in presidential elections and for Green lists in European elections fought under proportional representation. Brice Lalonde's 3.37 per cent in 1981 represented a marked improvement on the 1978 total and propelled Lalonde to the forefront of ecologist personalities; Waechter's 3.8 per cent in 1988 was better still. In the European elections, the Greens obtained 4.4 per cent in 1979, but a rather disappointing 3.4 per cent in 1984 when they were faced with competition from an alternative list (Entente radicale et écologiste – ERE) led by Lalonde, in alliance with the left-Radicals and the renegade centrist Olivier Stirn.[1]

The use of proportional representation for European elections undoubtedly assisted the Greens, although the fact that there was no automatic relationship between the type of electoral system used and the Greens' electoral fortunes was demonstrated by the poor ecologist performance in 1986 (1.2 per cent overall, 2.4 per cent where lists were presented), despite the adoption of proportional representation for that election. In neither 1979 nor 1984 were the Greens able to break the 5 per cent threshold for representation in the European Parliament. The Greens maintained a consistent 3–4 per cent of the vote throughout the 1980s, although they remained largely restricted to their regional bastions in Alsace and Normandy (Bennahmias and Roche 1992: 74–75). The best Green performances occurred where the left parties were divided, or when they had disillusioned their own supporters. The Greens also performed well in certain municipal contests fought under the second-ballot system; the success of Green candidates in 1989, for instance, depended mainly on local environmental factors or the weight of specific personalities.

The role of presidential elections deserves closer analysis. The first round of a French presidential election offers voters an opportunity to cast an expressive vote before choosing between the two leading candidates, almost invariably one from the right and one from the left, in the second round. The first round has proved fruitful territory for ecologist candidates. The national prominence given to candidates at presidential elections in France tends, inevitably, to personalize political competition. While Green candidates were far less susceptible than those of the mainstream parties, the presidential factor was not completely without effect: following relatively successful presidential campaigns in 1981 and 1988, Lalonde and Waechter enjoyed a national prominence which escaped other Green personalities. While this occasionally led to difficult relations with grass-roots supporters, it is indicative of the pressures operating within the French political system that Waechter and Lalonde remain by far the two best-known French Greens.

The third major formative influence lies in the effect of divisions over strategy among Greens. In fact, strategic arguments have been endemic throughout the history of the French Green movement. In the 1970s, the main disagreement was over whether the Greens should participate in electoral politics or remain principally a social movement. At this stage, the movement was only loosely organized, with Les Amis de la Terre providing the most cohesive link between the diverse local organizations. There was no permanent national Green Party organization, merely electoral campaigns organized on an *ad hoc* basis. For some, elections were a diversion from the more important activity of direct action against the nuclear industry. There were regional differences in the character of the movement as well, with a regionalist flavour in Brittany, a strictly ecological agenda in Alsace and a more utopian left current in Paris.

Many of those who accepted elections as a necessary part of the movement's activity were none the less critical of the style of Lalonde's 1981 presidential election campaign. In contrast to the strongly thematic campaign mounted by Dumont in 1974, Lalonde pushed his own personality to the fore and played down some of the more radical themes that had characterized earlier campaigns. Lalonde's 1981 campaign represented the first attempt to adapt the Greens to the realities of the French political system, and to portray the Greens as most effective when acting as a pressure group in relation to other parties. Even at this stage, Lalonde was moving towards his later expressed argument that, rather than seeking to politicize ecology, the Greens should seek to ecologize politics.

By the time of the formation of Les Verts in 1984, Lalonde had already moved too far away from the new social movement culture of the new organization to find it attractive. The bitterness underlying the split between Lalonde and Les Verts dates from this period, but rather than simple opportunism by Lalonde, it reflected serious divergence about the appropriate scope and direction of green politics. Les Verts traditionally represented the more radical, new politics agenda, while Lalonde favoured a more pragmatic environmentalism, tied loosely to the left, but led by politicians free from strict party ties or close control by social movements.

Thus, from their inception, Les Verts were confronted by ecological and environmentalist forces from outside the party, as well as riven by divisions from within. It is possible to identify within the party various currents articulated by recognizable clusters of personalities, both in terms of broad philosophical tendencies and varying strategic positions. In the first category, Dupin (1989) identified strict environmentalists, anti-nuclear activists, Third World enthusiasts and those representing the traditions of the alternative left. At the level of political strategy, the party was divided between strict autonomists and those conceiving of Les Verts as a party of the alternative left tradition. The personalities associated with these strategies varied over time, but from 1986 to 1993 Waechter was usually associated with the principle of Green autonomy. The most recognizable internal constellations were: those supporting Waechter; the 'alternative left' culture represented initially by Yves Cochet and Didier Anger; and the Verts et pluriels group, animated by Dominique Voynet, which sought to bridge diverse opinion within the party. Latterly, individuals such as M.-C. Blandin have come to form recognizable groups on their own, tied to the exercise of a specific political function and regional identity (in Blandin's case as president of the Nord-Pas de Calais region).

ORGANIZATION AND STRATEGY IN LES VERTS

The strategy of Green parties is more dependent than that of traditional parties on the consciously ideological form of the party organization. The power of party activists in Les Verts reflects, with minor Gallic differences, the forms of Green parties in most other western European states. The central organization is extremely weak, with only minimal control over local organizations. The internal decision-making processes are based mainly on direct democracy, with the party's sovereign annual assembly remaining open to all members (around 600 to 700 members usually attend out of a total membership of some 5,000) (*Libération*, 9 November 1991). As well as providing the major forum for strategic debates, the annual assembly is also the occasion when support for the party's various tendencies can most accurately be judged. Between its annual assemblies, the party is governed by an Executive College, composed of 11 members drawn from the *Conseil national inter-regional* (CNIR). Rather than nominating an official leader, Les Verts designate four national spokespersons: after the 1991 AGM, these were Waechter, A. Buchmann, Didier Anger and Dominique Voynet; in 1992, Waechter's historic rival, Yves Cochet, replaced Anger to form a finely balanced collective leadership (*Libération*, 2 December 1991; *Le Monde*, 1 December 1992). The leadership exercised by Waechter has been informal, and has always been strongly contested from within the movement. The Executive College is supervised by the CNIR. This, the second forum for grass-roots control of the leadership, is made up of 120 members, three-quarters of whom are elected as representatives of the regions, with the remainder elected by proportional list at the national AGM.

As with other Green parties, Les Verts' statutes are designed to limit the power of any leadership group. A complicated points system allows individuals to hold more than one office, but prevents excessive concentrations of power in the hands of any one individual. By comparison with other Green parties, Les Verts seem to have persisted longer with features of the grass-roots democratic organization which have elsewhere been regarded as counter-productive. Thus it was that eight Green MEPs rotated their positions as Euro-deputies half way through their terms of office. There has, as yet, been no move similar to those taken by Greens in Germany and Britain to change the AGM from an open assembly to one based on delegates. In fact, even quite small changes of party statutes, supported by both Waechter and Cochet, failed at the 1990 Assembly (*Le Monde*, 6 November 1990). After his difficulties at the 1992 AGM, Waechter vowed once again to place statute reform on the agenda.

As in other Green parties, there is no unified leadership in Les Verts; instead, fluid factions representing different sides in internal conflicts have risen and fallen according to the level of support received from activists. Despite the existence of divisions over the party organization and its ideology, strategic divisions have prevailed over all others. In particular, Les Verts have repeatedly been split over how to maintain a distinctive presence within the French party system without becoming absorbed into bipolar conflicts between left and right.

In 1986, the veterans of the 1970s, Anger, Cochet and Jean Brière (until then the principal national spokespersons for Les Verts), effectively found themselves sidelined by a new faction within the party led by the hitherto little-known Waechter from Alsace. Waechter reflected the predominantly ecological concerns of the movement in Alsace, as distinct from the New Left positions associated with the then leadership. His opposition to any agreement with the New Left, in the form of the PSU and others, had the support of a diverse coalition of grass-roots activists, pure Greens and anti-leftists. Waechter refused to define Les Verts as an additional marginal formation of the extreme left. His political message was therefore one of Green autonomy. This perspective was not shared by all leading personalities within Les Verts. The long years of electoral failure had convinced Cochet, from Brittany, that the best hope for the Greens lay in seeking some concessions and possibly ministerial posts from the Socialists. For the majority of Green activists, this was anathema in view of the Socialist government's record on ecological issues. Events such as the Rainbow Warrior affair of 1985 served only to exacerbate ill-feeling towards the Socialists.

At the AGM of Les Verts in 1986, Waechter was able to secure a two-thirds majority for his motion that ecology was not available for marriage. From 1986 onwards, Green autonomy became the defining creed of the majority current within Les Verts. Although portrayed by the media as decidedly uncharismatic and unpresidential, Waechter's stress on autonomy, combined with a recentring of the movement on ecological themes, unified Les Verts and left him in the position of de facto leader of the party. In the period after 1986, Les Verts insisted that they sought radical changes, based on attracting support from a cultural majority, before they could consider exercising power. Waechter's strategy appeared vindicated by Green successes after 1986. Ironically, though, these successes exposed the limitations of this purist position. Les Verts were, to some extent, victims of their own success, since success intensified pressures to engage in alliance-building of the type associated with other French parties. The fact is that the French party system places a high value on parties able to construct alliances, but penalizes those that, through choice or necessity, remain without allies.

Les Verts' relations with other parties were not limited to the PS and Génération écologie. The strict autonomy line embodied by

Waechter encountered its severest challenge when Les Verts were forced to determine their strategy towards the Front National. At the AGM in Strasbourg in November 1990, Cochet and others proposed a motion to the effect that the Greens should not always insist on retaining a candidate in the second round if to do so meant facilitating the election of a Front National candidate. Those close to Waechter suspected this as a means of forcing the Greens to respect a 'Republican Front' strategy of the type espoused by the Socialists. Such a strategy, they reasoned, would weaken the Greens' identity and would probably benefit the Socialists alone. Cochet's position was rejected by two-thirds of the AGM, which decreed instead that the Greens should reject all other parties of the Fifth Republic. This hard-line position alienated a fraction of potential Green voters worried by the rise of Le Pen; to many, the Greens appeared guilty of wilfully ignoring the distinctions between Le Pen's extreme right and the democratic parties (Pronier and le Seigneur 1992: 198ff.).

The anti-leftism which propelled Waechter to prominence became more difficult to justify with the disappearence of the alternative left after the failure of Pierre Juquin's 1988 presidential candidacy and the influx of activists from these movements into the Greens. Waechter seemed to have accepted this in 1991 when he welcomed a subdued Juquin into the Green fold. This ecumenical gesture was opposed by more fundamentalist ecologists who contended that a small pure party was preferable to a larger one whose Green ideology was under threat. Yet Waechter remained too isolationist for many within the party; in 1991, a new group, Verts et pluriels, which originally aimed to bridge the division of the party into two rival wings, emerged around Voynet. The support for both Waechter and Cochet was diminished at the 1991 Assembly in Saint Brieuc: the motion sponsored by Waechter obtained 45.6 per cent, with the main opposition to Waechter crystallized around the motion signed by Cochet (23.4 per cent); a total of six other lists together obtained 30.6 per cent (*Libération*, 9–10 November 1991). By the Chambéry assembly of November 1992, Voynet's motion obtained 37 per cent support from the AGM, as opposed to only 30 per cent for Waechter. Waechter managed to secure a bare 51 per cent majority within the executive only by allying with the anti-Maastricht elements he had fought so tenaciously during the campaign for the 1992 referendum (*Libération*, 16 November 1992), and he was forced to accept his two main rivals – Voynet and

Cochet – as national spokespersons, along with the faithful Buch-mann (*Le Monde*, 1 December 1992). The CNIR, which met to elect the new leadership on 28–29 November 1992, could not agree on who should occupy the key post of National Secretary: Waechter's candidate failed to obtain the necessary 60 per cent.

Waechter's influence within Les Verts has clearly diminished since 1986–1990. Yet the personalization encouraged by the French political system has, to the chagrin of the Greens, tended to maintain Waechter in the forefront of ecologist personalities, along with his ubiquitous rival Lalonde. Unlike any other party within contemporary French politics, Les Verts' internal organ-ization means that Waechter's leadership status is informal, con-ditional upon his ability to maintain the support of fragile and changeable alliances. This was illustrated when, prior to the referendum on the Maastricht Treaty in September 1992, Waechter proved incapable of bringing Les Verts around to support the Treaty, with the result that the party refused to take an official line either for or against. While Waechter personally undertook a low-profile campaign in favour of Maastricht, other leading Greens, such as Voynet and Blandin, opposed the treaty.[2]

Faced with the challenge posed by Lalonde, Waechter engaged in a series of U-turns: first he entered discussions with the Socialist government of Pierre Bérégovoy, where the prospect of Vert ministers was openly envisaged, and then, following the breakdown of negotiations with the Socialists in September 1992, Waechter swallowed his pride and concluded a comprehensive electoral pact for the 1993 legislative elections with Génération écologie. This illustrated that Les Verts had become infected with a new sense of political realism and had become a little more *un parti comme les autres*. The price paid for this new electoral realism was opposition from some grass-roots activists disillusioned by the politics of pragmatism; such disillusion was apparent at the 1992 Chambéry AGM, which grudgingly approved the agreement with Génération écologie but delivered a personal rebuff to Waechter.[3]

GÉNÉRATION ÉCOLOGIE

The contrast between Génération écologie and Les Verts is striking, in terms of organization, strategy and personality. Lalonde founded Génération écologie in May 1990, when he was Minister of the Environment in the centre-left government of Michel Rocard. He was actively encouraged in this by President Mitterrand, who aspired not only to halt the progress of Les Verts but also to promote alternative sources of party support to that provided by the unpopular Socialist Party. Such presidential connivance initially prevented Les Verts from taking Lalonde's movement too seriously; the party was forced to change tack when Génération écologie surprisingly emerged ahead of Les Verts in the regional elections of March 1992. The movement was also initially welcomed by the Socialists, since it appeared as if it had been created to undermine Les Verts by regrouping environmentalists and ecologists who suppported Mitterrand under an alternative banner. As Lalonde's movement developed, however, the PS came to view it with less equanimity.

The available evidence suggests that Génération écologie recruited many of its members and candidates from disaffected members of the PS: either those who felt slighted by their own party organization, or those who wanted to protest against the abandonment of socialist principles by that party. Lalonde himself grew more critical of the government, and resigned as Minister of the Environment in advance of the regional elections, provoking the familiar charge of opportunism. Distance from the Socialists, however, did not mean proximity to Les Verts.

Although Lalonde made several offers of electoral alliance to Les Verts during 1991, he also denounced them as ecological fundamentalists. Lalonde's support for the Gulf War, strongly opposed by Les Verts, also differentiated the two parties. Lalonde sought to present his own rather technocratic environmentalism as more moderate and practical than the radicalism of Les Verts. The success of Génération écologie in the 1992 regional elections depended in part upon the already significant popularity of Lalonde himself (Pronier and le Seigneur 1992: 139). Polls suggested that in comparisons of the capabilities of the two leaders, Lalonde was judged more competent and sincere than Waechter. Génération écologie also benefited from the support of that fraction of the left-wing electorate which was dissatisfied with the Socialists, but which sought a party which identified with the left and was less fundamentalist than Les Verts.[4] There was some understandable confusion between the two rival Green lists in the 1992 regional election. Their programmes were superficially similar and, in these circumstances, voters may have chosen between movements on the basis of the qualities of their most prominent public personalities. But the fact that Génération écologie was able to present lists in 85 departments revealed the existence of a genuine political formation, albeit one that often took over networks shaped by ex-PS politicians anxious to avoid defeat. The great novelty of Génération écologie was that it allowed double membership and thereby managed to attract to its banner personalities who had no intention of quitting their original parties (Barbier 1992).

Despite its success in the 1992 regional election, Génération écologie faced several problems. The organization was very much the creation of Lalonde and a small network based in Paris and, in many areas, its newly elected councillors faced problems in working without a local political organization. These problems were reflected in the organizational structure of Génération écologie: Lalonde remained strongly opposed to a culture based on party militants, and this was reflected in his minimal concessions to internal democracy in the early stages of the movement. All candidates for the 1992 regional election were approved by the national office in Paris. There was no congress in the first 18 months of the party's existence, and its programme was drawn up by its National Executive. Lalonde hinted at, and then postponed, plans to enhance internal democracy within Génération écologie in May 1992, but, in the event, the entire process of reaching an electoral agreement with Les Verts for the 1993 election was co-ordinated from the summit, with little grass-roots participation (Feltin 1992). Faced with such centralization, a number of early enthusiasts (including Haroun Tazieff, leader of an immigrant organization) left the movement. At its second congress in November 1992, Génération écologie experienced a new level of division when two 'historical chiefs' of the movement, Bernard Frau and François Donzel, announced their decision to quit (*Libération*, 16 November 1992).[5] Lalonde was openly accused of right-wing deviation for adopting a tough anti-socialist political stance, the logic of which was debatable in a movement which contained so many ex-cadres, elected officials and activists from the PS. Yet Lalonde continued to be acclaimed in presidential style by the mass of activists, in contrast with the reception reserved for Waechter among Les Verts.

Notwithstanding Lalonde's centralist pretensions, the decentralized reality which prevailed among Les Verts was to some extent repeated within Génération écologie. The central organization lacked the means to control the activities of its representatives in the provinces. Indeed, regional diversity prevailed in both organizations. This may be illustrated by assessing the coalitions formed after the regional elections of March 1992. In the Nord-Pas de Calais, for example, Génération écologie firmly opposed the Regional Council presided over by Les Verts Blandin in alliance with the PS and PCF. In Languedoc-Roussillon, by contrast, Génération écologie councillors generally voted with the PS, against the regional alliance formed by the UDF, the RPR and Les Verts. In Lorraine, Les Verts rallied to provide unofficial support for the regional administration of G. Longuet, president of the conservative Parti républicain; Génération écologie councillors were more reserved. Finally, in Bourgogne Les Verts formed part of a coalition centred around the PS, which Génération écologie refrained from supporting. Apart from local rivalries between the two formations, purely ecological concerns were uppermost in the constellation of these alliances: in Lorraine, for example, Les Verts obtained a 100 per cent increase in the regional environment budget, the creation of a regional agency for the environment and support for environmentally friendlylocal companies (*Libération*, 14–15 November 1992).

Les Verts might plausibly claim to be a movement of civil society, but Génération écologie, if it was not conceived as little more than a temporary label to provide an organizational framework for Lalonde's presidential ambitions, appears more as an aspiring classical party organization. Even if Génération écologie is able to establish effective local organizations outside Paris, it may face problems if there are demands for more internal party democracy.

THE 1993 ELECTION

Various interpretations have been advanced for the breakthrough of Les Verts during the 1980s and the emergence of Génération écologie in 1992.

First, the rise of the French Greens forms part of a broader Europe-wide movement based on the saliency of environmental concerns among the electorate. Sympathy for the Green movement rose as concern with environmental problems grew. In one poll prior to the 1992 regional election, 84 per cent of those questioned admitted to some degree of support for the Greens. In 1989, over 90 per cent of French people were said to be concerned about pollution; for 41 per cent of those surveyed, the state of the environment was a priority, and for 53 per cent it was important but not a priority (Bennahmias and Roche 1992: 183). Understood as the defence of the environment, green issues have, at least at the level of political discourse, become consensual in France as in the rest of western Europe.

Second, the breakthrough of the Greens is testimony to the breakdown of the Socialist electoral coalition. The evidence suggests that Les Verts provided a rallying point not only for groups of the alternative left, such as the PSU or Juquin's critical Communists, but more generally for idealistic left-wing voters disillusioned with the pragmatism and technocratic solutions proposed by the Socialist government. Its early abandonment of environmental pledges was undoubtedly important in this respect, as were the politics of austerity adopted after 1983 and the general shelving of any ambition beyond short-term economic management and economic growth. Opinion poll evidence also pointed to Génération écologie attracting considerable sympathy from former Socialist voters: a majority of the Green electorate of 1993 had voted for the PS in 1988.

Third, the French Greens are a manifestation of discontent with the political system. The rise in the Green vote coincided with a period of crisis for the established parties. With the FN and the Green parties able to claim 20–30 per cent of the vote between them, there are clear signs of disenchantment with the political system as articulated through the established political parties. But it is clear that there is no unified protest vote in France; voters for the FN and the Greens are clearly opposed on the nature of and solution to the problems facing the nation. The oscillation in the fortunes of Les Verts, the emergence of Génération écologie and the disappointing electoral performance of the Entente écologiste in 1993 prove that the Green vote is fragile. Both Les Verts and Génération écologie have benefited from their status as virgin parties: until recently, neither has been associated with the exercise of significant political power and neither has had the opportunity to become embroiled in debilitating political scandals of the type that have afflicted the PS and the RPR. Evidence of minor political corruption even among Les Verts reveals not only the ubiquity of the problem in a country in which continuous election campaigns force parties to pursue unorthodox methods of raising finance, but also that Les Verts do not have a monopoly of political virtue (Gattegno 1991).[6]

The conclusion of an electoral pact with Génération écologie before the 1993 National Assembly election was a rare instance of political realism on the part of Waechter. The existence of rival

Green candidates in the first round of an election fought under a majority electoral system would have proved devastating, since they would rarely, if ever, have surpassed the 12.5 per cent necessary to proceed to the second round.[7] The electoral agreement of November 1992 made the achievement of such a target feasible. Under the terms of that agreement, the two organizations agreed to present single candidates for the first ballot in all constituencies, to contest second ballots wherever Green candidates obtained the support of 12.5 per cent of registered voters in the first ballot and to refuse to back any candidate in the second round where Green candidates failed to overcome the 12.5 per cent threshold. In theory, moderate Socialist candidates would receive the same treatment as those of the Front National.

After the agreement, Waechter cautiously suggested that the Green parties might win between 30 and 40 seats; Lalonde, characteristically, predicted 60 to 70. A more sober assessment concluded that Green candidates stood a realistic chance of election in 13 seats where Green lists had outpolled Socialists in the 1992 elections and where the PS–PCF–Green total surpassed 50 per cent (*Libération*, 14–15 November 1992). In the event, only two Greens broke through the 12.5 per cent barrier to contest the second round: Voynet in Jura and C. Barthet in Haut-Rhin. Neither was elected, although both managed substantially to improve upon the combined first round vote for the left and the ecologists. The failure of either Waechter or Lalonde to achieve the 12.5 per cent threshold must be regarded as a stark defeat for both men and testament to their deficiencies of political leadership.

CONCLUSION

If the Greens have so far made only a modest electoral breakthrough in France, they have nevertheless succeeded in broadening their appeal. Initially concentrated among middle-class professionals (Bennahmias and Roche 1992: 169), the Green vote has, in terms of occupational class, come gradually, and especially after 1989, to approximate a cross-section of the electorate.[8] This progress may, however, create problems for the Greens in the form of conflicts between activists, who remain concentrated among the younger, highly educated members of the new middle class,[9] and voters. A more serious worry is the stability of the Green vote. Green voters are relatively young (those of Génération écologie especially so) and young voters are notoriously volatile. Moreover, in recent years and even in the modest circumstances of 1993, the Greens have increasingly attracted those who previously voted for the PS; despite Waechter's argument for a new society, Green supporters and activists alike have become increasingly likely to classify their position as 'on the left' rather than 'beyond left and right'. This carries the twin risks that the Greens will be popularly regarded as simply a specialized fragment of the left, and that a resurgent PS might win back the allegiance of those who deserted it for the Greens.

The state of political competition, the structure of the party system and the weakness of the Socialist government obviously aided the Green parties throughout the 1980s and early 1990s. The disappointing result of March 1993, however, confirmed doubts that the electorate mobilizable by the Green parties in non-decisive elections would remain committed to them in more important elections. Far from demonstrating the Greens' autonomy from the Socialists, exit polls suggested that the Entente écologiste had suffered from the public's failure adequately to distinguish between the Socialists and the Greens (*Libération*, 23 March 1993). The decision to downplay environmental themes during the election had made the Greens appear as *un parti comme les autres*. Nevertheless, the 7.63 per cent of the vote captured by the Greens in 1993 was by far their best result in any decisive election (parliamentary or presidential).

Taking the period as a whole, the success of Les Verts since 1989, and latterly that of Génération écologie, is symptomatic both of the erosion of the bipolar bases of the French party system as developed in the 1960s and 1970s and of the emergence of political ecology as a powerful European movement with an impact upon mainstream political activity. Support for the Greens represents something more than single-issue environmentalism and something less than the ecological conversion spoken of by Waechter. It was always unlikely that Green voters would remain patient enough to support Waechter's original strategy of awaiting the creation of a Green cultural majority before attempting to begin a programme of social change. The Green parties are seen by supporters and others alike as a source of pressure on the political system and, without some results, that pressure will seem ineffectual.

The strategic divergences prevailing within the Green parties during and after the 1993 election recalled those of the mid-1980s.

The response to Rocard's call in February 1993 for a political 'Big Bang' revealed the division and confusion reigning among Green personalities. Lalonde, initially sceptical about Rocard's initiative, was forced to rally once it became clear that the former premier enjoyed widespread support. Yet any endorsement of the idea of a recomposition of the party system inevitably weakens the appeal of the Greens as a specific, original movement. However vigorously Lalonde denounced the incumbent government, this was one further instance of the Greens' inability to differentiate themselves from the Socialists. The PS leadership's offer to withdraw in favour of Green candidates on the second ballot, unilaterally if necessary, helped further to confuse the identity of the Greens as separate from the PS.

The traditional strategy of Green autonomy – *ni gauche, ni droite* – was inherent in the November 1992 electoral agreement which committed both Les Verts and Génération écologie to an autonomous stance in relation to other parties. In practice, certain leading Green figures lent their support to Socialist candidates desperately fighting for survival in the second ballot; in return, prominent Socialists queued to register their support for Voynet's second-ballot campaign in the Jura. It seemed likely that the poor performance of the Greens would strengthen those within both formations, Voynet among them, in favour of a party realignment or closer co-operation with other progressive political groupings, especially since Rocard's take-over of the Socialist Party in April 1993. For the moment, the political ambiguity and eclecticism of the French Greens remains their most distinctive trademark.

The systemic pressures of the Fifth Republic have not totally bypassed the Green parties. The fact that the parties were forced into an electoral agreement is one sign of their impact. The personal rivalries encouraged by the direct election of the President are another.[10] Yet, as the ebullient democracy and anti-élitism of Les Verts testifies, such pressures remain less compelling for the Greens than for other French parties. To this extent, the French Greens remain *pas comme les autres*.

NOTES

1 Lalonde, Stirn and François Doubin (left-Radical) all later served in Michel Rocard's government.
2 Local Green activists whom Alistair Cole met in Lille in September 1992

were furious that, as they saw it, Blandin had sided with Le Pen for the pleasure of upsetting the local Socialists.

3 The electoral agreement was approved by 70 per cent of conference delegates; Waechter's motion trailed that of Voynet.

4 See the *Libération* (1992) collection for survey evidence.

5 Frau had come to Génération écologie from the PS in 1990; Donzel had been a close adviser of Lalonde at Environment.

6 Allegations of improper methods of rising campaign finance were also levelled against Lalonde's movement by Barbier (1992).

7 In fact, this threshold represents 12.5 per cent of the registered electorate, i.e. around 20 per cent of those actually voting.

8 In this respect Les Verts and Génération écologie are very similar (*Libération*, 23 March 1992).

9 Surveys in 1989–1990 showed the membership of Les Verts as comprising schoolteachers (35 per cent) and health and social work professionals (12 per cent), a profile similar to that of the PS in the 1970s; most clearly underrepresented were manual workers (3 per cent). Most Green activists were relatively young (20 per cent under 30 in 1989–1990, and 50 per cent aged between 31 and 45) and had some form of higher education (only 20 per cent had qualifications inferior to the *baccalauréat* (Bennahmias and Roche 1992: 115; Prendiville and Chafer 1990:185).

10 The parties appear divided over who should represent Green political opinion in the 1995 presidential election: Waechter and Lalonde have each laid down a marker; Voynet must not be discounted.

REFERENCES

Barbier, C. (1992) 'Génération écologie: la galaxie Lalonde', *Le Point*, 29 February.

Bennahmias, J.L. and Roche, A. (1992) *Des Verts de toutes les couleurs: histoire et sociologie du mouvement écolo*, Paris: Albin Michel.

Biffaud, O. and Jarreau, P. (1989) 'Des babas cool de 1968 jusqu'au parlement européen', *Le Monde*, 19–20 November.

Bridgeford, J. (1978) 'The Ecologist Movement in the French General Election of March 1978', *Parliamentary Affairs* 31(3).

Cole, A. (ed.) (1990) *French Political Parties in Transition*, Aldershot: Dartmouth.

Dupin, E. (1989) 'Une carte unique pour plusieurs identités', *Libération*, 31 May.

Feltin, M. (1992) 'Lalonde à la hussarde', *La Croix*, 19 May.

Gattegno, H. (1991) 'L'argent noir des verts', *Le Nouvel Observateur*, 19 December.

Hainsworth, P. (1990) 'Breaking the Mould: the Greens in the French Party System', in A. Cole (ed.), *French Political Parties in Transition*, Aldershot: Dartmouth.

Kitschelt, H. (1990) 'La gauche libertaire et les écologistes', *Revue Française de Science Politique* 40(3): 339–365.

Ladrech, R. (1989) 'Social Movements and Party Systems: The French Socialist Party and New Social Movements', *West European Politics* 12(2): 262–279.

Libération (1992) *Tout sur les écologistes*, Collection no. 9.

Prendiville, B. and Chafer, T. (1990) 'Activists and Ideas in the Green Movement in France', in W. Rüdig (ed.), *Green Politics One*, Edinburgh: Edinburgh University Press.

Pronier, R. and le Seigneur, V.J. (1992) *Génération Verte: les écologistes en politique*, Paris: Presses de la Renaissance.

Rüdig, W. (1990) *Anti-Nuclear Movements*, London: Longman.

Wilson, F.L. (1988) 'When Parties Refuse to Fail: The Case of France', in K. Lawson and P. Merkl (eds), *When Parties Fail*, Princeton, NJ: Princeton University Press.

Chapter 4

Britain

Greens in a cold climate

Chris Rootes

If the existence of a large environmental movement and high levels of popular concern about the environment are taken as indicators of the extent of likely support for a Green party, the British case must, to the casual observer, appear paradoxical. On the one hand, the environmental movement in Britain comprises a rich variety of groups, campaigns and networks sustained by a high level of public concern with environmental matters, and it is plausibly claimed that 'Britain has the oldest, strongest, best-organized and most widely supported environmental lobby in the world' (McCormick 1991: 34). On the other hand, the British Green Party, although it was the first such party in Europe, now appears weak by the standards of most of the larger and more economically developed societies of western Europe.

The party's early progress was painfully slow.[1] Formed in 1973 and calling itself 'People' to emphasize its differences from conventional parties, the party first contested a national election in February 1974 when its five candidates polled an average of 1.8 per cent. The four candidates who contested the October 1974 election did less well, averaging just 0.7 per cent (Rüdig and Lowe 1986: 267). It changed its name to the Ecology Party in 1975, but by 1978 still had only about 550 members. In order to enhance its visibility during the 1979 general election campaign, it decided to field the 50 candidates necessary to secure a 5-minute radio and television election broadcast. The party's 53 candidates managed an average of only 1.5 per cent of the vote, but the publicity excited a surge in membership to over 5,000. The three Ecology candidates in the June 1979 Euro-elections polled 4.1, 3.9 and 3 per cent respectively (Parkin 1989: 221–222).

During the 1980s, while Green candidates were securing election to national parliaments across western Europe, the British party had to be content with a handful of seats on parish, district and county councils (Parkin 1989: 223–228). If the party's showing in local elections was modest, its performance in elections for the national parliament was dismal. At the 1983 general election, Ecology Party candidates attracted an average of barely 1 per cent of the votes cast in the 106 constituencies where they stood. In 1987, the Green Party, as it was by then known, fared little better, its 133 candidates polling on average 1.4 per cent. In an electorate of some 42 million, the Greens had attracted just 90,000 votes (Byrne 1989: 104). Ecology Party candidates fared a little better in the 1984 elections to the European Parliament, winning an average of 2.6 per cent in the 16 divisions[2] they contested, and a best ever individual result of 4.7 per cent.

In short, until 1989, in elections at every level, Green candidates secured a proportion of the popular vote that, with only a few very localized exceptions, was little better than derisory, their only consolation being that they quite consistently fared better than the candidates of the extreme left and extreme right (Taylor 1985: 162).

The poor electoral performance of the Greens was not, however, simply a reflection of massive indifference towards environmental or even ecological issues on the part of the British public. Neither the size of the environmental movement nor the opinion poll evidence suggest that the British were consistent laggards in the development of environmental consciousness. If, during the early 1980s, they appeared relatively less concerned about the environment than some of their fellow Europeans, Eurobarometer data suggest that, during the 1970s, the British had, if anything, been not less but more concerned about the protection of the countryside and the fight against pollution than were other Europeans (Watts 1987: 56). Moreover, since 1974, successive national surveys have found majorities approaching 90 per cent in favour of further action to protect the countryside (Heath et al. 1990; Young 1987 and 1989).

There is even survey evidence showing that there has for some time been considerable potential support for a Green party in Britain. In 1983 a poll suggested that 12 per cent of the electorate might be prepared to vote for a Green candidate if she or he were believed to have a chance of winning (Parkin 1989: 223). In the event, in the 1983 general election only 1 per cent of those who had the opportunity to vote for a Green candidate actually did so. In 1984 31 per cent told interviewers for the Eurobarometer that it was possible they might vote for 'an ecologist party' (Inglehart and Rabier 1986: 466), yet, in the 1984 European elections, fewer than 3 per cent of voters who had the opportunity actually voted for a Green candidate.

The simplest explanation for the failure of potential support to be translated into votes, and what most distinguishes Britain from those countries where Green parties have flourished, is the operation of an electoral system based upon simple plurality voting ('first-past-the-post') in single-member constituencies. Such a system tends to make elections contests between the two or three candidates or parties who appear most likely to have some chance of winning and is responsible both for sustaining the two-party system that dominates parliament and for presenting nearly insuperable obstacles to the entry of new parties into parliamentary politics. The perception that the candidates of new or minor parties have little chance of being elected creates the impression that a vote for them is a 'wasted' vote, and the consequent lack of credibility depresses the vote that such parties attract. The problem for the Greens, like the Liberals before them, is to surmount the threshold of credibility beyond which diffuse support is translated into votes.

This system presents particular obstacles to the progress of the Green Party even among those who are sympathetic to what they perceive to be its aims (Rüdig and Lowe 1986). Because the party lacks credibility as an electoral force, even members of environmental organizations do not usually vote for Green candidates in national elections.

THE GREEN PARTY IN THE 1989 EUROPEAN ELECTIONS

Given their lack of previous success and the tendency of the electoral system to turn elections into straight fights between the major political parties, it is less difficult to understand why the Greens should have failed to elect a single Member of Parliament than it is to explain why they should suddenly have done so well in the 1989 elections to the European Parliament, especially since the electoral system employed for the European elections was the same as that used in national parliamentary elections. Yet, in the European elections, the Green Party not only won almost 15 per cent of the national vote, but polled over 20 per cent in 17 divisions in England, came second ahead of Labour in six and ran third in all but two other divisions in England and Wales.

This success was remarkable for two reasons: first, it was the highest percentage of the national vote ever won by a Green party in any European state, and, second, it was attained by a party which had never before contested as many as a quarter of the seats at any election in Britain and none of whose candidates in previous national and European elections had attracted so much as 5 per cent of the vote.

How, in the light of their previous failures, is the spectacular rise of the British Greens in 1989 to be explained? One possibility is that it was a reflection of an equally sudden and spectacular increase in the British public's interest in and concern about environmental matters. Another is that it was made possible by a change in the balance of political competition among British political parties, a change which provided a Green Party audacious enough for the first time to contest every seat in Britain with an unprecedented window of opportunity.

There can be no doubt that the British public's concern about the environment did increase towards the end of the 1980s. The reasons are complex, but they include the belated discovery of global environmental issues by both public and government, a series of well-publicized alarms about food and water safety and the impact of the development boom of the last few years of the decade.

During the first half of the 1980s, the Eurobarometer surveys showed the British to be less concerned about global environmental problems than the Germans, Danes or Italians (Watts 1987: 61). One probable reason is that transnational environmental problems are less salient to the inhabitants of an island on the margin of Europe than to people whose countries are obliged by geography to import much of the pollution generated by their neighbours. They are less salient, too, in a country whose problems are not those of economic growth and success but of relative economic decline. Deindustrialization – the dismantling of traditional heavy industry and the general decline of manufacturing – meant that the objective seriousness of environmental pollution actually declined in Britain during the first half of the 1980s (Watts 1987: 19–20, 24). It meant, too, that unemployment and economic concerns were firmly entrenched at the top of the public's political agenda, and economic development was more desired than feared. If the British have not been conspicuously less concerned with the environment than other Europeans, it is nevertheless true that, for much of the 1970s and 1980s, they were relatively distracted by economic problems from environmental anxieties, just as most continental European countries had been during the period of postwar reconstruction. Moreover, because of the generally depressed level of economic activity in Britain during the 1980s, relatively little development perceived as threatening to the environment was proposed: the nuclear energy programme was virtually stalled, the extension of the national motorway network all but ceased and economic development could plausibly be conjoined with the rehabilitation of urban environments blighted by the Industrial Revolution.

The revival of the economy towards the end of the 1980s brought with it a significant increase in the number of motor vehicles on the roads and, especially in already highly populated southern England, a development boom which markedly increased the pressure upon the environment. Major development projects like the high-speed rail link from London to the Channel Tunnel provoked well-publicized protests, and in towns and villages throughout the south there were conflicts between residents concerned to protect the quality of their environment and the proponents of housing, office and road developments.

The most spectacular evidence of heightened concern with the environment was the apparent conversion of Margaret Thatcher. In September 1988, at the end of a speech to the annual dinner of the Royal Society, Mrs Thatcher surprised her audience with a declaration of commitment to preserving the balance of nature. Conservative leaders were surprised at the response to Mrs Thatcher's speech and taken aback by the number of environmentalist motions presented to the party conference a month later (Flynn and Lowe 1992: 25–28). The Prime Minister rose to the occasion, telling the conference that 'no generation has a freehold' upon the planet but merely 'a life tenancy with a full repairing lease'. Whether Mrs Thatcher's speeches were a cynical and opportunistic attempt to leap aboard the already rolling bandwagon of increasing anxiety about the environment detected by opinion pollsters, or whether they represented a genuine if belated acceptance by the Prime Minister and her advisers that the balance of scientific evidence about the state of the global environment had tipped in favour of the alarmists, their effect was dramatically to heighten the prominence of environmental issues and to give unprecedented respectability to their articulation.

Although there had for some time been increasing media

attention to environmental matters, the real explosion of coverage
came after the Prime Minister's speeches and reached a crescendo
by the spring of 1989. In February 1989 the cover of the *Sunday
Times Magazine* proclaimed that 'The world is dying' and the
paper's main news pages began a long-running campaign against
the polluters of Britain's rivers. The new awareness of global
environmental problems such as the depletion of the atmospheric
ozone layer and the 'greenhouse effect' of carbon dioxide emissions
was conjoined with more parochial concerns. Looming large
among them, and given massively heightened salience by the
government's announced intention to privatize the water-supply
companies, was anxiety about the quality of drinking-water. A series
of near-panics about the safety of such basic foods as eggs, and even
the government's belated campaign to encourage motorists to
switch to unleaded petrol, served to enhance the credibility of
environmentalists. The British, having been compelled by the
issues on their doorsteps to act locally, began to think globally. The
more radical environmentalist organizations were immediate beneficiaries: in 1988–1989 Friends of the Earth grew from 31,000 to
125,000 paid-up members, and Greenpeace from 150,000 to
281,000 (Frankland 1990: 13).

Yet, important though the 1988–1989 surge of public concern
was, it needs to be kept in perspective. It is estimated that the
combined membership of all environmentalist organizations in
Britain increased from 3 million in 1983 to nearer 5 million by early
1989 (Burke 1989). While it is clear that some organizations did,
as Burke suggests, experience unprecedented growth at the end of
the decade, for most of them growth in the latter part of the 1980s
might more accurately be described as a rather modest acceleration
of a long-term trend (cf. *Social Trends* 19 and 21).[3]

The increased environmental concern of the late 1980s was
paralleled by a change in the balance of political competition which
also benefited the Green Party. One of the liabilities under which
the Greens had long laboured was lack of visibility. A party which
contests only a fraction of the seats at an election, has meagre
campaign funds and negligible access to party political broadcasts
is ill-placed to compete at national level with established political
parties. At local level, where personalities and local issues have
more impact, the Greens had begun to have some modest impact,
particularly in parish council elections. The May 1989 County
Council elections raised the ratchet another notch: the Greens

fielded 600 candidates, retained the seat on the Isle of Wight that they had gained by the defection of a Liberal councillor, averaged over 8 per cent where they stood and secured individual results of over 20 per cent in widely dispersed parts of England.

The publicity attracted by their performance in the County Council elections, coming on top of the general increase in environmental concern, meant that the population had been softened up as never before for the Green assault. The decision to contest all 78 British seats at the 1989 European elections was a matter of some controversy within the Green Party, but it, and the skilfully exploited broadcasting time it earned them, had the effect of making the Greens more visible throughout Britain than they had ever previously been. Even so, their performance might have been a deal more modest had not the major political parties been in some disarray.

The Conservatives, as the party in government, were almost bound to lose support in a 'second order' election at mid-term in the national parliamentary calendar, but their position was particularly weakened by the unpopularity of the recently introduced poll tax[4] and by the fact that their campaign for the European elections was widely criticized as 'negative' even by party members. The Labour Party was, after a comprehensive policy review, in a better competitive position than for some time, but its changed stance on nuclear issues had alienated some of its more radical supporters and left the Green Party as the only party in England committed to unilateral nuclear disarmament. The Liberal Democrats were still suffering from the adverse publicity attracted by the wrangling between Liberals and Social Democrats in the course of the incomplete merger between the former Alliance parties; the heavy losses they sustained in the County Council elections exacerbated their decline in the opinion polls just as campaigning in the local elections had exhausted the energies of their activists. In the European elections, defending no seats and reckoning that the only one they had any chance of winning was Cornwall and Plymouth, the Liberal Democrats concentrated their resources in that one division and made little attempt to campaign elsewhere.

Thus the competition the Greens encountered in June 1989 was less formidable than at any previous election. They were especially well placed to gain from the weakness of the Liberal Democrats since the Liberals had not only become the traditional party of protest but had had a relatively good record on environmental policy (Breach 1990; Porritt and Winner 1988: 72). For much of the 1980s, when on the basis of European comparisons the Greens might have been expected to make some progress in Britain, the Liberal–SDP Alliance had appeared the best hope of political innovation and the Greens had made negligible impact. Given the encouragement the British electoral system gives to tactical voting, it is reasonable to assume that many potential Green voters had voted for Alliance candidates because they appeared to stand a better chance of overturning Conservative or Labour majorities. In view of the vulnerability of the Conservatives, and to a lesser extent Labour, to protest voting in 1989, the weakness of the Liberal Democrats left the Greens unusually well placed.

Both the poll data on the previous allegiances of Green voters and the local and regional variations in the distribution of the Green vote demonstrate the effects of political competition. According to an NOP poll in July 1989, 29 per cent of those who voted Green in the European elections said they had voted Conservative in 1987, 18 per cent Labour, 27 per cent Alliance, 6 per cent Green and 15 per cent had not voted at all. Thus although the Greens did benefit from the collapse of the Alliance, it is no less clear that they benefited from defections from the Conservatives and, to a lesser extent, from Labour.[5]

When results are compared division by division, the same pattern is evident. There is a strong positive correlation ($r = 0.61$) between the 1989 Green vote and the Alliance vote in 1984, but an even stronger one ($r = 0.79$) between the 1989 Green and 1984 Conservative votes (Adonis 1989: 267). Thus the best predictor of the Green vote in a division was not the level of previous support for the Alliance, but that for the Conservatives. In all six divisions in which the Greens came second in 1989 the Conservatives had in 1984 polled over 50 per cent and Labour had trailed the Alliance by more than 5 per cent. It appears that in these Conservative strongholds, with Labour not a credible contender and the Liberal Democrats unable to mount a strong challenge, many voters turned to the Greens, whether as a vehicle for diffuse anti-government protest or as the clearest expression of environmental concern. There is evidence that a vote for the Greens was not merely a protest vote: three-quarters of Green voters told NOP in July 1989 that they regarded voting Green as 'mainly a vote in favour of them' rather than 'mainly a vote against the other parties'.

If the local balance of political competition explains the Greens' greatest successes, it also explains their failures. The Greens' most anomalous results were in Scotland, Wales North and Cornwall and Plymouth, the only areas in which other minor parties campaigned strongly: the Scottish National Party throughout Scotland, the Liberal Democrats in Cornwall and Plymouth and Plaid Cymru in Wales North. Only in Cornwall and Plymouth did the Greens fail to outpoll the Liberal Democrats. Elsewhere in England the Green vote declined quite consistently with distance from the relatively affluent, Conservative-dominated south: in the south it averaged 20.3 per cent, in London 16 per cent, in the Midlands 14.7 per cent, in the north 12 per cent. In only three English divisions, all Labour strongholds in the north-east, did the Greens poll less than 10 per cent. In Scotland the Greens averaged 7.2 per cent and came fourth in all eight divisions.

The Greens' success in 1989 should not be overestimated. Even by the standards of 'secondary' elections, the turnout was low (36 per cent) and it was for a parliament few voters knew much about, let alone regarded as a significant locus of power (Niedermayer 1990). It is unlikely that they were much more knowledgeable about the policies of the Green Party; because of their limited campaign resources and because the Green surge came late in the campaign, their policies received relatively little exposure and were not subjected to close scrutiny by the other parties; thus few voters can have realized how radical they were. Nor was the Green vote sufficiently concentrated geographically to establish areas of local strength upon which future victories might be built; even by comparison with that of the Liberal Democrats, it was relatively evenly spread. Moreover, survey evidence suggests that far from tapping a larger reservoir of latent support for the Greens, the 1989 result may have represented a maximal realization of their appeal; in the immediate aftermath of the election, over half of those who voted Green declared the intention of voting for a traditional party in a general election, and none of those surveyed who voted for any other party in 1989 intended in future to vote for the Greens (Rüdig and Franklin 1992: 43, 46).

The main impact of the Green surge of 1989 was upon the policies of the mainstream political parties. Each revised its pro-gramme to give greater prominence to the environment, and the Liberal Democrats pledged themselves to making it a central plank of their platform. It is no doubt partly in response to this that the Greens' standing in the opinion polls, which peaked at 10 per cent in June 1989, sank to 2 per cent by the end of 1990, while support for the Liberal Democrats rose. Whereas the Liberal Democrats proved quite effective at organizing the vote in local contests and at by-elections for the national parliament, the Green Party, lacking an effective election machine, failed completely at parliamentary by-elections. Only in the less intensely contested arena of local elections, and even then only in those relatively scattered places where it had active local organizations, did the Greens manage respectable results.

Nothing more clearly demonstrates the extent to which the Greens' success in 1989 depended upon an extraordinary state of political competition than the contrasting result in 1992.

THE GREEN PARTY IN THE 1992 GENERAL ELECTION

The 1992 general election was little short of a disaster for the Green Party. It fielded more candidates than ever before (256 compared with 133 in 1987, and 106 in 1983), but the average share of the vote gained by these candidates was, at a little over 1.3 per cent, fractionally lower than in 1987. The Greens did a little better in England (1.33 per cent) and in Wales (1.25 per cent) than in Scotland (1.08 per cent), but although they polled consistently better than the handful of candidates of far left parties, even the Green Party's best result (3.8 per cent in Islington North) was only fractionally better than the best result for the extreme right British National Party (3.6 per cent in Bethnal Green).

The cost to Green Party funds of £128,000 in lost deposits might have been worthwhile had the intervention of Green candidates served to make the environment a major electoral issue, but in the event it was scarcely mentioned by the major parties at any point during the campaign. The televised 5-minute election broadcast the Green Party earned by reason of the number of its candidates was amateurish and unpersuasive by comparison with that of 1989 and, because party election broadcasts were rescheduled away from their traditional slots preceding the main mid-evening television news, it is probable that the Green Party broadcast was seen by many fewer voters than was the 1989 broadcast.

Given the character of the British electoral system, national general elections are always unpromising contests for the Greens. The 1992 election was especially so. In the most closely fought election in almost two decades, the intensity of the efforts of the major parties to mobilize their supporters and the unprecedented pressure upon voters to vote tactically when opinion polls suggested that a handful of votes really might determine the outcome combined to make the task of minor parties like the Greens even more than usually difficult.

The weaknesses of each of the major parties from which the Greens had profited in 1989 had, by 1992, largely been repaired. The Labour Party, after the completion of its policy review and in the wake of the expulsion of many of the better-known supporters of the Trotskyist *Militant*, mounted a vigorous campaign and for the first time in many years appeared capable of winning. In 1989, the Liberal Democrats had been at the nadir of their fortunes, but three years later the wrangles surrounding the party's formation were largely forgotten: it had a new and forceful leader, its recovery in the opinion polls had been spectacular and it had won some notable by-election victories. Even the Conservative Party was in better shape: it was well advanced in the process of disencumbering itself of the hated poll tax and had a new and more emollient leader. The closeness of the contest and the uncertainty of the outcome served to encourage wavering supporters of the Conservatives to return to the fold and, late in the campaign, to persuade others nervous at the prospect of a Labour or coalition government to vote for the known quantity of a Conservative government. The result was that the Liberal Democrats, who had been riding so high in the polls that they seemed likely to hold the balance of power, were subjected to a classic third-party squeeze. The sole bright light in this dismal landscape shone in the Welsh constituency of Caredigion Goggled Penfro where Cynog Dafis, jointly endorsed by Plaid Cymru (Welsh nationalists) and the Green Party, was elected (Carter 1992b).[6]

An added complication for the Greens was the reappearance of the Liberal Party. Formed by the minority of members who chose not to sink their differences with former Social Democrats in the formation of the Liberal Democrats, the Liberal Party is, in terms of policy, much the closest party to the Greens. The intervention of a Liberal candidate in a seat for which a Green candidate was standing might, therefore, have been expected to split the left–libertarian vote and to depress the percentage of the vote attracted by the Green candidate. This indeed seems to have happened, but the effects appear more modest than might have been expected. In the 34 constituencies contested by both parties, the Greens outpolled the Liberals in 15. On average, Green candidates competing with Liberals attracted 1.16 per cent of the vote compared with 1.36 per cent in those seats where there was no Liberal candidate. In fact, it appears that it was the Liberal vote that suffered more in these contests: whereas the 38 Liberal candidates who did not have to contend with Green competition averaged 1.88 per cent, those competing with Greens averaged 1.44 per cent (or 1.23 per cent if we exclude the outlying case of Leeds West in which Michael Meadowcroft, contesting the seat he held between 1983 and 1987, secured 8.3 per cent). The Liberal vote was, then, more depressed by the intervention of a Green candidate than was the Green vote by the presence of a Liberal. In so far as the Green vote appears the more resistant to the intervention of another non-established party, it is less fairly characterized as a diffuse protest vote than is that of the Liberals.

Nevertheless, the Greens were clearly victims of tactical voting. Their worst result by comparison with 1987, and one of only two seats in which the Green vote fell by more than half compared with the 1987 result (0.6 per cent compared with 1.5 per cent), was Eastbourne, where the Liberal Democrat MP elected at the 1990 by-election faced an uphill struggle to prevent the Conservatives regaining the seat. The Green vote also appears to have been squeezed in a number of other seats where the Liberal Democrats were in close competition with the Conservatives.

But if the Greens suffered from the effects of political competition, they also benefited in a number of constituencies where the result was never in doubt. Their best individual result and 15 of the 21 cases in which the Greens attracted at least 2 per cent of the vote were in seats where the re-election of a Labour MP was a foregone conclusion. The most likely explanation is the prominence the Green Party gave, in its 1992 campaign, to unilateral nuclear disarmament and, in particular, its emphatic rejection of the Trident programme. In safe Labour seats, erstwhile Labour voters disillusioned by the Labour Party's abandonment of unilateral nuclear disarmament could vote Green without any fear that by doing so they would contribute to the election of a Conservative MP.

The modest concentration of support for the Greens in urban, Labour strongholds contrasts sharply with the pattern of their support in the 1989 European election when their best results were in relatively rural, safe Conservative seats in the south of England.

The shift of support to urban, Labour-held seats, coming on top of the very low correlation between the Green vote in those European parliamentary divisions which the Greens contested in 1984 and their vote in the same divisions in 1989, confirms the lack of any stable constituency or regional base to the Green vote.

The example of Cynog Dafis' success might encourage other local Green parties to collaborate with other minor parties, but the general weakness and lack of significant geographical concentrations of support for the Greens severely limits their attractiveness as partners in the eyes of other parties. The election of Dafis apart, the 1992 election marked a step forward for the Green Party only in the number of candidates it presented. There appears now to be, in England, a hard core of about 1 per cent of the electorate who are prepared to vote Green in a national election and to resist all exhortations to vote tactically. The small proportion of the vote it has been able to attract, the low correlation between the results obtained in particular constituencies at successive elections and the shift from rural to urban locations in its decidedly modest concentrations of electoral support, all suggest that the Green Party remains as far away as ever from any substantial electoral advance in national politics.

LOCAL ELECTIONS

At the local level, the Greens remain at least a modest electoral force in some areas. In 1989 Green candidates averaged 8.64 per cent in local election contests with two or more other candidates, but their share of the vote in such contests fell away thereafter, to 6.5 per cent in 1990, 5.17 per cent in 1991 and 3.82 per cent in 1992 (Rose 1993). Yet this overall ebbing of the Green tide conceals an increasing number of individual successes. Thus, despite the decline in the overall Green vote in 1991, the Greens gained 12 new seats, held five and lost three, to give them a total of 26 district councillors on 14 authorities, as well as two county councillors and a Scottish regional councillor. The 1992 general election may have given the Greens a drubbing but, within weeks, and despite the continued slide in their share of the vote, they polled well enough in local elections to retain most of their council seats. More remarkably, in the midst of massively unfavourable publicity during the 1992 annual conference, a Green candidate came within 100 votes of winning a local by-election in Oxford.

The 1993 County Council elections were more encouraging for the Greens. Their 566 candidates (compared with 645 in 1989) averaged 5.7 per cent of the vote and, for the first time since 1981, a Green candidate who had not previously held the seat as a representative of another party gained a County Council seat. This gain and another near miss, both in Oxford, demonstrate the relevance to the Greens of the lore of conventional politics: each was built upon persistent campaigning and perennial candidature by high profile candidates backed by a tightly knit and energetic local party organization. The exceptional level of organization and activity of the Oxford City party gave Oxfordshire Greens the best average results in England (21 candidates averaged 9.56 per cent). Above average results were also obtained in the neighbouring counties of Gloucestershire and Hereford and Worcester. If these results suggest that the Greens may, as the Liberals did before them, build local success upon sustained local campaigning, the fact remains that whatever electoral success the Greens have enjoyed has come in 'secondary' elections in which the conditions of political competition are much less severe than in elections to the national parliament.

ENVIRONMENTAL AND ECOLOGICAL MOBILIZATION

In other European countries, where Green parties are represented in parliament, the ecological and environmentalist cause benefits from enhanced visibility and access and, sometimes, from financial support as well. There, ecologists may use Green parliamentary representatives as a conduit for influence through the formal political process or, as in Germany, they may employ a dual strategy of party and movement, in which the party serves to channel into the formal political process issues which have been raised by the extra-parliamentary movement. In Britain, neither strategy is available; the poor prospects for a Green party under present electoral arrangements compel ecologists and environmentalists to adopt other tactics.

The relative closure of the British electoral process has been balanced by an administrative structure relatively open to the representations of environmental lobby groups. As a result, the institutional environment in Britain has generally favoured the 'bureaucratic accommodation' of environmental interests. Because the doors of the civil service in Whitehall have been partly open even as those of the Parliament at Westminster were closed, environmentalist organizations have tended to adopt a posture of negotiation and consultation with officialdom rather than protest and confrontation. This is true even of organizations such as Friends of the Earth and Greenpeace. When they have taken spectacular protest action it has been as a tactical device to attract media attention and so to raise the visibility of an issue which might then be placed upon the political agenda and discussed with government, rather than as a strategic alternative to such negotiation (Rüdig and Lowe 1986: 270; McCormick 1991: 157–158). The consequence is that even such activist environmentalist organizations now enjoy the status of expert witnesses, consulted by government departments and agencies on environmental matters (McCormick 1991; Lambert 1992).

It might be thought that the predominance of moderate, reformist environmentalism over radical ecologism is a product of the peculiar civility of British political culture, but the survey evidence suggests that the British differ little from the West Germans in their dispositions towards protest or towards political participation in general (Rootes 1992). What is different is the way national political institutions shape the translation of such dispositions into action. The virtual absence of a radical ecology movement in Britain does not appear to be due to any want of enthusiasm among the British public (Fuchs and Rucht 1994) but is attributable instead to the fact that environmental campaigners in Britain, because they enjoy relatively favourable access to decision-makers, are constrained against action which might compromise that access (Lowe and Goyder 1983).

Environmentalists have found the mainstream political parties less accessible and less responsive. All the major parties have renovated their policies and loudly proclaimed their green credentials since 1988, but none has an interest in making the environment a central election issue because the polls suggest that it is the Green Party rather than any established party which stands to gain most from the highlighting of environmental issues (Flynn and Lowe 1991). Of the three major parties it is, not surprisingly, the Liberal Democrats who have pledged to make the environment an election issue; their environmental credentials, although poorly recognized by the electorate, are relatively good, but they might also have reckoned that, from their relatively weak competitive position, it is worth the gamble to try to capture the votes of people who might otherwise vote for an even weaker Green Party.

One peculiarity of the British case is the extent to which the environment issue has been identified with the protection of the countryside. The dependence of the Conservative Party upon rural and especially farming interest groups made it unusually attentive to the environmental lobby at least until 1979. This, and the historic neglect of urban environmental issues, helps to explain the Labour Party's former scorn for environmentalists. The countryside still has a prominent place in British conservative ideology and the traditional nature- and countryside-protection organizations still have a larger membership than Friends of the Earth or Greenpeace. These groups may have become more activist and relatively detached from the Conservative Party during the 1980s, but it is evident from the newsletters of the regional branches of the Council for the Protection of Rural England, for example, that they are scarcely about to embrace the 'dark green' programme of the Green Party.

If the ascendancy of right-wing populism in the Conservative Party has loosened the ties between traditional environmental protection organizations and the party, the efforts of socialist environmentalists have had some impact upon Labour Party policy, even though the classic dilemma of a social democratic party (how to square environmental protection with the economic expansion necessary to improve the lot of its supporters) remains. But while neither Conservative nor Labour now risks being accused of not taking the environment seriously, neither sees much competitive advantage in emphasizing environmental issues, particularly at a time when opinion polls show that other issues are more salient.

The net effect is that environmental lobbyists are constrained to be at least polite to all the mainstream parties and to offer advice when it is requested but, reckoning that manifesto commitments are taken lightly and that environmental issues transcend party political divisions, they see no advantage in attaching themselves to any one party and prefer to deal with the holders of decision-making power rather than with the contenders for political office (McCormick 1991: 41). For rather different reasons, environmental activists often regard the Green Party as something of an embarrassment whose existence may, by politicizing environmental issues, reduce the influence of environmental lobby organizations (McCormick 1991: 123–124). This may, however, have been more true of the brief period when the Green Party appeared to pose some electoral threat to the major parties; Green activists report that at other times environmentalist activists are grateful for the publicity the activities of the party bring to environmental issues.

This situation presents the more radical environmentalist organizations with a dilemma: by entering into dialogue with government they may well contribute to the protection of the environment in the short term, but only at the expense of neglecting the mobilization of the public upon which their influence in part depends. The moderation required to maintain their access to decision-makers may, however, be demoralizing and demobilizing for the average supporter of environmentalist movements who knows nothing of what goes on behind the closed doors of government.

The greater activism of traditional environmental organizations in recent years may have balanced this strategy somewhat, but British environmentalists have almost invariably had recourse to the politics of direct action out of tactical necessity rather than out of principled commitment to grass-roots democratic participation; when access has been achieved, they have quickly adapted to more conventional modes of activity. Only the Green Party has a strong value-commitment to democratic mass participation; the rest of the British environmental and ecology movement is more narrowly success-oriented and the likelihood is that it will, quite understandably, prefer to go on pushing at half-open doors rather than agitating outside closed ones. In effect, the institutional framework within which it operates tends to restrict British environmental activism to the conservationist and environmental reformist end of the continuum; radical ecologism is comparatively weak.[7]

The weakness of ecological activism, and the consequent weakness in the formation of collective identity through collective action, limits the ability of the environmental movement to contribute to the further democratization of what is, in many respects, a rather formal and non-participatory democracy. Reformist environmentalism has relatively little to contribute to the broader process of democratization simply because so much of its limited energy and resources is channelled into the process of institutionalized consultation and negotiation. It is not so much that, by entering dialogue with officialdom, environmentalists risk being co-opted, as that energies and resources channelled in that direction are unavailable for popular mobilization.

The one mobilization of recent times that did perhaps have larger potential was the campaign against the poll tax. Probably the most widespread campaign of civil disobedience in Britain this century, it had no closer connection with the environmental movement than the administrative accident that its implementation was overseen by the Department of the Environment. Yet, despite the best efforts of assorted Trotskyists and anarchists to represent it as the latest instalment in the class war, the campaign drew on some of the same sources of support as the environmental movement; it was moral outrage against the inequity of the tax rather than simple hardship that produced such widespread condemnation of the tax and resistance to its implementation. Whatever else it did, the campaign performed the first task in the formation of a social movement: the detachment of people, and especially young people, from 'normal' politics (McCrone 1991: 452). Clearly there was potential here, but for the development of a radical ecology movement it was an opportunity missed. As it was, the Anti-Poll Tax campaign proceeded in isolation from the environmental and ecology movement. The Green Party did declare itself against the poll tax but it did not unambiguously endorse non-payment. Some local Green parties and Green Party members were active, in various ways, but the party was not as prominent in the campaign as the numerically smaller Socialist Workers' Party.

THE LEFT, RADICALISM AND ENVIRONMENTALISM

The marginality of the Green Party during the Anti-Poll Tax campaign illustrates the extent to which radical leftist groups have remained within the orbit of the traditional, mainstream party of the left and have not been attracted to the Greens. Unlike the West German Social Democratic Party (SPD), which formally rejected Marxism in 1959 and subsequently expelled its student organization for excessive radicalism, the Labour Party has remained a 'broad church' encompassing Marxists and social democrats alike. The reasons for this are, in part, structural: an electoral system which is so closed to minority parties encourages radical groups to work within the Labour Party rather than put up candidates in their own names.

Contingent factors have, during the past decade, further concentrated the attentions of radicals upon the Labour Party. When Labour lost office in 1979, and especially after it was abandoned by a number of prominent social democrats in 1981, the battle for power within the party became a major preoccupation of leftists and Trotskyists who might in other circumstances have been encouraged to seek different outlets for their energies. Because the struggle for control of the 'mass party of the British working class' did not seem unwinnable, radicals were not, as were their German counterparts, compelled to rethink their political strategy, and so they continued to scorn an environmental movement they regard as 'middle class' and diversionary (Porritt and Winner 1988: 64).

Because it is such an inclusive party and because it was in opposition throughout the period of the revival of the peace and environmental movements in the 1980s, the Labour Party was well placed to act as vehicle for a variety of radical discontents. That it did so in the case of the peace movement is not surprising: the Campaign for Nuclear Disarmament (CND) was, from its inception in 1958, oriented mainly towards the Labour Party (Taylor 1988) and, since the 1960s, support for unilateral nuclear disarmament was a rallying point for the left within the party.[8] Environmentalists, however, did not find the Labour Party so hospitable. Even when they were not openly scornful of a movement they regarded as selfish and middle class (Porritt and Winner 1988: 63–71, 181–183; Carter 1992a), Labour leaders were locked into an ideology of human progress through material productivity and did not accord environmental issues high priority. With the exception of a few Labour-controlled local authorities (notably the Greater London Council before its abolition in 1986) and token manifesto commitments inserted at the insistence of members of the Socialist Environment and Resources Association (SERA), Labour failed to take up the environmental challenge until forced to do so by electoral competition from the Conservative and Liberal Democratic Parties.[9]

The permeability of the Labour Party to the radical left, the near institutionalization of the peace movement by CND and the Labour Party and the British left's traditional hostility to environmentalists, meant that in Britain conditions were unfavourable for the development of an alliance of leftists, pacifists and environmentalists such as had produced the Green movement and the Green Party in West Germany. Because the constellation of forces which elsewhere have favoured the development of radical left ecologism was absent in Britain, the environmental movement was largely left to its own devices and its moderation was never seriously challenged.

If the weak competitive position of the Green Party has been one factor discouraging infiltration of the party by the radical left, it has also been credited with generating within the party a 'fundamentalist'/'realist' dispute rivalling in intensity that within the German Greens (Doherty 1992). The British Green Party has as radical an ecological programme as any in Europe (Poguntke 1989), and is unusual in the extent to which it has been strongly influenced by holistic 'dark green' philosophy (Doherty 1992; Rüdig and Lowe 1986). The dispute within the party is not about matters of environmental policy but about organizational structure. 'Realists' like Jonathon Porritt and Sara Parkin assert that the party has squandered public sympathy by giving an impression of confusion and disorganization and argue for a formally elected leadership, while 'fundamentalists' regard all talk of leadership as anathema and argue for maximum decentralization within the party (Goodwin 1991). The realist argument prevailed at the 1991 conference and the organizational structure then proposed remains in place despite sharp criticism of the leadership's conduct in office, but decentralists not only remained strong in many local branches but swept the elections for the new party executive in 1992.

The British Green Party, like its European counterparts, appeals disproportionately to younger, highly educated professional people. In 1990, two-thirds of its members were university graduates or students and nearly half were employed in professional or technical occupations, with a notable concentration in teaching and the caring professions (Rüdig *et al.* 1991: ch. 3). Where the British party differs most from its European counterparts is that its membership base is not predominantly urban. Some 60 per cent of those who voted for the Greens in 1989 had previously voted for the Conservatives, Liberals or Social Democrats (Kellner 1989), but fewer than half of Green Party members could remember having voted for such parties in any general election since 1970. Of the 29 per cent of Green Party members who had previously been members of another political party, over half had been members of the Labour Party (Rüdig *et al.* 1991: 32, 38). This disparity between the previous political allegiances of members and of those who voted for the Green Party in 1989 suggests one reason why it was unable to capitalize upon its brief moment of popularity.

CONCLUSION

If the Green Party is virtually the sole standard-bearer for the radical ecology position in Britain, then radical ecology is a flag only weakly flown. The Green Party's membership peaked at nearly 20,000 in 1989–1990; it was reported to have fallen to about 10,000 by January 1992 (Brown 1992), to about 6,500 in September 1992 (Mitchison 1992: 25) and to 4,571 in July 1993 (Executive Report to Conference, September 1993).[10] As a national electoral force, it is, under present electoral laws, virtually irrelevant. Nor can it plausibly be claimed that by its mere existence the Green Party raises the profile of environmental issues. When, in 1989, it polled 15 per cent of the vote, the party was the beneficiary of the increasing environmental awareness of the public and the government; it was popular anxieties about environmental matters, fuelled in part by government initiatives, development pressures and food safety scares, which fed the stream of environmentalist concern which flowed to the Green Party. Even then, its spectacular result was only possible because of the extraordinary conditions of electoral competition which obtained in that election for the European Parliament. Although the Greens' relative success in 1989 did briefly provoke speakers for the mainstream parties into spasms of denunciation or patronizing dismissal, the greening of their programmes has been undertaken less in order to pre-empt electoral competition from the Green Party than to respond directly to environmental problems and to preserve the relative competitive balance among the major parties themselves.

Ironically, any short-term success at national level might deprive the Greens of the one thing upon which their long-term prospects depend – electoral reform – because the established party from which a resurgent Green Party would be most likely to take votes is the Liberal Democrats, the party which is not only the greenest of the major parties, but the only one committed to electoral reform. Without change in the electoral law, the Green Party is destined to remain marginal. In recognition of that, several prominent members of the Green Party, Jean Lambert foremost among them, have been active in Charter 88, the campaign for constitutional reform.

As long as the Green Party remains so marginal to the political process, the environmental movement will continue to tread the path of influence rather than that of power. As long as the major political parties remain keen to assert their environmentalist credentials that may appear consoling, but the decline of the environment in the public perception of salient political issues must ring alarm bells. One might be tempted instead to draw reassurance from such poll figures; if the public scarcely regards the environment as a political issue, it is perhaps a reflection of the fact that, in their public pronouncements, all the major political parties are now more or less green. The problem remains that, by the standards of the Green Party, none of the others is really very green at all.

NOTES

1 The best accounts of the development of the Ecology Party are Rüdig and Lowe (1986); McCulloch (1992, 1993). See also Byrne (1989); Frankland (1990); Porritt and Winner (1988: ch. 3); Parkin (1989: ch. 13); Kemp and Wall (1990: ch. 2). On the environmental movement and policy, see Lowe and Goyder (1983); Lowe and Flynn (1989); McCormick (1991).

2 The term 'division' is employed to distinguish the 78 British (i.e. English, Scottish and Welsh) constituencies for which members are elected to the European Parliament from the 650 'constituencies' for which members are elected to the United Kingdom Parliament at Westminster. The term 'seat' is used more generally to refer to seats both in parliament and on local government councils at both county and town or rural district level. Britain is alone in the EC in electing its members of the European Parliament not by proportional representation but by the same single-ballot, simple plurality method employed in elections for the national parliament. The main effect of this system is to reward parties which have substantial concentrations of support in a particular locality and to give no representation at all to parties which attract moderate support evenly spread geographically. The three members who represent Northern Ireland are elected by proportional representation (single transferable vote).

3 For more detail, see Rootes (1991: 291 n. 10). Eurobarometer data suggest that the trajectory of increase in approval of the ecology movement was very similar in Britain, the Netherlands, Italy, France and West Germany. The levels of strong approval of the ecology movement in Britain were very similar to those in France, somewhat lower than in Italy and The Netherlands, and rather lower than those found by a 1989 survey in West Germany (Fuchs and Rucht 1994).

4 The poll tax was introduced in Scotland in 1989 and in England and Wales in 1990 to replace the previous system of local property taxation.

5 Other survey data confirm this (Rüdig and Franklin 1992: 42).

6 Whether Dafis is thus Britain's first Green MP depends on how one counts the election of Stuart Syvret to the Jersey parliament in 1991.

7 Friends of the Earth and Greenpeace stop short of being wholly Green

because they are not, as organizations, explicitly committed to the fundamental social, economic and political changes implicit in the radical ecological critique (Dobson 1990: 14). Lowe (cited in McCormick 1991: 123) and Doherty (1992) claim that the Green Party has few links with the environmental movement. While this may be true at a formal, organizational level, it is less true at a personal level: a 1990 survey of Green Party members found that only 13 per cent were not members of any environmental group and 69 per cent belonged to more than one group, about half having joined Friends of the Earth and Greenpeace (Rüdig et al. 1991: 34). Nor was this simply a function of the influx of new members since 1988; long-standing members were more likely than newer recruits to be members of other environmentalist organizations.

8 In 1985, some two-thirds of CND members supported Labour (Byrne 1988: 61).

9 For discussions of the shifts in Labour policy, see Carter (1992a); Robinson (1992).

10 Given that most of the larger membership in the peak years of 1989–1990 was relatively passive (Rüdig et al. 1991: 40–41), this fall in membership is not necessarily indicative of a decline in vitality.

REFERENCES

Adonis, A. (1989) 'Great Britain', Electoral Studies 8: 262–269.

Breach, I. (1990) 'Green Vote Effect', Listener, 8 November: 4–5.

Brown, C. (1992) 'Party Aiming for "Visible Protest Vote"', The Independent, 16 January.

Burke, T. (1989) 'Green Europe: The Turning Tide', Marxism Today 33: 43–45.

Byrne, P. (1988) The Campaign for Nuclear Disarmament, London: Croom Helm.

—— (1989) 'Great Britain: The "Green Party"', in F. Müller-Rommel (ed.), New Politics in Western Europe, Boulder, Colo., San Francisco, Calif. and London: Westview, pp. 101–111.

Carter, N. (1992a) 'The "Greening" of Labour', in M. J. Smith and J. Spear (eds), The Changing Labour Party, London: Routledge, pp. 118–132.

—— (1992b) 'Whatever Happened to the Environment? The British General Election of 1992', Environmental Politics 1: 441–447.

Central Statistical Office (annually) Social Trends, London: HMSO.

Dobson, A. (1990) Green Political Thought, London: Unwin Hyman.

Doherty, B. (1992) 'The Fundi–Realo Controversy: An Analysis of Four European Green Parties', Environmental Politics 1: 95–120.

Flynn, A. and Lowe, P. (1991) 'The Party Politicization of the Environment in Britain', unpublished paper, Bartlett School of Architecture and Planning, University College, London.

—— (1992) 'The Greening of the Tories: The Conservative Party and the Environment', in W. Rüdig (ed.), Green Politics Two, Edinburgh: Edinburgh University Press, pp. 9–36.

Frankland, E.G. (1990) 'Does Green Politics have a Future in Britain?', in W. Rüdig (ed.), *Green Politics One*, Edinburgh: Edinburgh University Press, pp. 7–28.

Fuchs, D. and Rucht, D. (1994) 'Support for New Social Movements in Five Western European Countries', in C. Rootes and H. Davis (eds), *A New Europe? Social Change and Political Transformation*, London: UCL Press.

Goodwin, S. (1991) 'Greens Face Split Over Attempt to Change Leadership', *The Independent*, 19 September.

Heath, A., Jowell, R., Curtice, J. and Evans, G. (1990) 'The Rise of the New Political Agenda?', *European Sociological Review* 6: 31–48.

Inglehart, R. and Rabier, J.-R. (1986) 'Political Realignment in Advanced Industrial Society', *Government and Opposition* 21: 456–479.

Kellner, P. (1989) 'Decoding the Green Message', *The Independent*, 7 July.

Kemp, P. and Wall, D. (1990) *A Green Manifesto for the 1990s*, London: Penguin.

Lambert, J. (1992) 'Origins, Praxis and Prospective: The British Environmental Movement', in M.-P. Garcia-Guadilla and J. Blauert (eds), *Environmental Social Movements in Latin America and Europe*, *International Journal of Sociology and Social Policy*, 12(4–7): 204–215.

Lowe, P. and Flynn, A. (1989) 'Environmental Politics and Policy in the 1980s', in J. Mohan (ed.), *The Political Geography of Contemporary Britain*, London: Macmillan, pp. 255–279.

Lowe, P. and Goyder, J. (1983) *Environmental Groups in Politics*, London: Allen & Unwin.

McCormick, J. (1991) *British Politics and the Environment*, London: Earthscan.

McCrone, D. (1991) '"Excessive and Unreasonable": The Politics of the Poll-Tax in Scotland', *International Journal of Urban and Regional Research* 15: 443–452.

McCulloch, A. (1992) 'The Green Party in England and Wales: Structure and Development: The Early Years', *Environmental Politics* 1: 417–435.

—— (1993) 'The Ecology Party in England and Wales: Branch Organisation and Activity', *Environmental Politics* 2: 20–39.

Mitchison, A. (1992) 'Hugged out of Office', *The Independent Magazine*, 26 September: 24–27.

Niedermayer, O. (1990) 'Turnout in the European Elections', *Electoral Studies* 9: 45–50.

Parkin, S. (1989) *Green Parties: An International Guide*, London: Heretic.

Poguntke, T. (1989) 'The New Politics Dimension in European Green Parties', in F. Müller-Rommel (ed.), *New Politics in Western Europe*, Boulder, Colo. San Francisco, Calif. and London: Westview, pp.175–194.

Porritt, J. and Winner, D. (1988) *The Coming of the Greens*, London: Fontana.

Robinson, M. (1992) *The Greening of British Party Politics*, Manchester: Manchester University Press.

Rootes, C.A. (1991) 'The Greening of British Politics', *International Journal of Urban and Regional Research* 15: 287–297.

—— (1992) 'The New Politics and the New Social Movements: Accounting for British Exceptionalism', *European Journal of Political Research* 22: 171–191.

Rose, C. (1993) '"Green World" Local Election Results Report', 12 May 1993, London: Green Party.

Rüdig, W., Bennie, L. and Franklin, M. (1991) *Green Party Members: A Profile*, Glasgow: Delta.

Rüdig, W. and Franklin, M. (1992) 'Green Prospects: The Future of Green Parties in Britain, France and Germany', in W. Rüdig (ed.), *Green Politics Two*, Edinburgh: Edinburgh University Press, pp. 37–58.

Rüdig, W. and Lowe, P. (1986) 'The Withered "Greening" of British Politics: A Study of the Ecology Party', *Political Studies* 34: 262–284.

Taylor, R. (1985) 'Green Politics and the Peace Movement', in D. Coates, G. Johnston and R. Bush (eds), *A Socialist Anatomy of Britain*, Cambridge: Polity.

—— (1988) *Against the Bomb*, Oxford: Clarendon Press.

Watts, N. (1987) 'Environmentalism in Europe', D.Phil. thesis, Freie Universität, Berlin.

Young, K. (1987) 'Interim Report: The Countryside,' in R. Jowell, S. Witherspoon and L. Brook (eds), *British Social Attitudes: The 1987 Report*, Aldershot: Gower.

—— (1989) 'Interim Report: Rural Prospects', in R. Jowell, S. Witherspoon and L. Brook (eds), *British Social Attitudes: The 5th Report*, Aldershot: Gower.

Chapter 5

Belgium

Greens in a divided society

Benoît Rihoux

The Belgian Green parties are, in terms of durability, electoral performance, stability, presence in elected bodies and level of structural development, among the most successful Green parties in western Europe. This 'success' must however be defined and qualified. In this chapter, I shall focus on the relevance of two elements as explanatory factors in the rise and success of the Belgian Greens: environmental issues and, more fundamentally, party-political competition. I shall argue that the Belgian political system and institutional setting have strongly – and most often positively – influenced the fortunes of the Greens as autonomous newcomers on the political scene.

Several turning-points need to be identified in the emergence and development of the Belgian Green parties, the French-speaking Ecolo (founded March 1980) and its Flemish counterpart Agalev (founded February 1982). The rise of the Green *movement* in the 1970s and the development of the Belgian Green *parties* in the 1980s and 1990s will be analysed separately.

The existence in Belgium of two separate Green parties comes as no surprise once one knows that there are currently two distinct Belgian party systems, one French-speaking, the other Flemish.[1] From the late 1960s, the three national 'traditional' parties (Christian Democrats, Socialists, Liberals) split into six new parties: CVP and PSC (1968), PRL and PVV (1971), SP and PS (1978).[2] The evolution of the party system has since been one of ever-increasing fragmentation: in addition to the traditional national parties, there are the regionalist parties Volksunie (VU), Front Démocratique des Francophones (FDF) and the now defunct Rassemblement Wallon (RW), as well as the newcomers on the far right: Vlaams Blok (VB) and Front National (FN). The emergence of the Belgian Green parties can be better understood within this broader context.

THE FORMATIVE PERIOD

Ecolo was from the outset an unambiguously political formation. At the November 1971 legislative elections, the Walloon regionalist party, Rassemblement Wallon, obtained the highest vote in its short existence: 20.9 per cent.[3] Shortly thereafter, trouble arose in a local section of the party in Namur following the refusal of the party leadership to accept the election of a local president. The latter, along with some activists, left the party and created a 'movement of reflection and action' called Démocratie Nouvelle. Its manifesto (1973) stressed direct democracy, radical federalism, critical economic thought and environmental concern.

This movement presented a list at the March 1974 legislative elections in the two *arrondissements* of Namur province, achieving modest results. From then on, links were gradually established with other movements such as anti-nuclear groups, the Christian Youth Labour Movement (JOC) and the Christian Peace Movement (MCP). On Démocratie Nouvelle's initiative, these various movements presented a joint list, Combat pour l'Ecologie et l'Autogestion (CEA), for the October 1976 local elections in Namur. Another more environmentalist list was presented in Mons. Neither list obtained any seats and both were rapidly dismantled.

Away from the electoral arena, following early contacts in 1975, a Belgian section of Friends of the Earth (Les Amis de la Terre–Belgique) was founded in March 1976 by members of Démocratie Nouvelle, and emphasized both ecology and enhanced democracy, the themes that were later to form the frame of the early Ecolo doctrine. A few local sections were founded in 1977, most of them led by people who were to become 'founding fathers' of Ecolo.

Simultaneously, some key Green activists sought to come together to compete in the next legislative and provincial elections under a single banner. As a result, Green lists were fielded in eight Walloon *arrondissements* under the Wallonie-Ecologie (WE) label and in Brussels under the Ecolog label for the April 1977 legislative elections.[4] Results remained poor, ranging from 0.3 to 2.3 per cent.

In January 1978, WE was revitalized, this time as a permanent structure designed to co-ordinate the various subregional organizations. The WE programme, adopted in August 1978, stemmed directly from that of Les Amis de la Terre, with greater emphasis on environmental themes. Subsequently, in October 1978, after long and hard-fought internal struggles, Les Amis de la Terre split into two rival groups. A minority 'libertarian' group, advocating maximum autonomy for the local sections, named itself Réseau Libre des Amis de la Terre, while the majority 'institutionalist' group remained in control of Les Amis de la Terre. This split affected their next electoral performance in terms of geographic coverage: at the December 1978 legislative elections, WE competed in only six *arrondissements*, while two rival Green lists were fielded in Brussels: Ecolog (rather independent) and Ecopol (closer to the dissident 'libertarian' group). Les Amis de la Terre decided not to back any one list or individual candidate explicitly, but results were, on the whole, better than in 1977 (up from 1.1 to 3.7 per cent), though still not sufficient to obtain any seats.

The first real Green electoral breakthrough came with the June 1979 European elections. Earlier that year, following numerous formal and informal contacts, mostly among WE activists throughout Wallonia, a common programme was adopted; 13 of the 17 candidates were members of Les Amis de la Terre and the founder of Démocratie Nouvelle was top of the list. Despite internal conflicts, the joint Green list, Europe-Ecologie obtained 5.1 per cent of the French-speaking vote, the highest score of any Green list in Europe.[5] This surprising result meant that the French-speaking Greens became the fifth strongest political grouping in southern Belgium, although they still did not obtain any seats.

This success acted as a catalyst for the creation of a genuine Green political party in French-speaking Belgium. From mid-1979 to early 1980, the idea of forming such a party gained more and more support within the ranks of activists and leaders; not only were subregional and local Green groups becoming mature, but Green leaders felt, following the 1979 results, that they could rely on sufficient popular support to justify the creation of a new party. In fact the will to create a genuine political party had already been quite clear in the minds of Green leaders when WE became a permanent structure (January 1978).

The final decision was taken during two consecutive assemblies (*assemblées générales constitutives*) in March 1980, when Ecolo was officially created and its statutes adopted. It was defined as a 'permanent structure, organized in a federalist and self-governing way, aiming at the political expression of ecological demands in terms of the management of society'.[6] In terms of ideology, a clear line of descent can be traced back to Démocratie Nouvelle, through Combat pour l'Ecologie et l'Autogestion, Les Amis de la Terre, Wallonie-Ecologie and Europe-Ecologie (see Figure 5.1).

Unlike its French-speaking counterpart, Agalev's roots are not at all political. As early as 1970, a Jesuit priest and teacher in a secondary school in the suburbs of Antwerp set up a small group which was more of a spiritual and religiously inspired community than a political organization. The initial aim of this 'revival group' (*herlevingsgroep*) was the contemplation and implementation of three 'counter-values': solidarity, sobriety and silence. Until 1972, this rather counter-cultural 'self-improvement' group (*zelfverbetering*) remained inwardly oriented. Nevertheless, a small publishing house was founded in 1971, and the group took part in the revival of a nearby local primary school.

From 1973 on, the Anders Gaan Leven ('Live Differently') group (AGL) evolved from an insignificant counter-cultural organization to a genuine, albeit still quite small, social movement. The main action in which the movement took part was the opposition to a large-scale canal-building scheme near Antwerp (the *duwvaartkanaal*) alongside an *ad hoc* federation of environmental groups. In the wake of this environmental struggle, local 'action groups' (*aktiegroepen*) of the AGL movement sprang up, called the 'Green Cyclists' (Groene Fietsers) after their playful style of action involving bicycle demonstrations. Environmental issues – especially the anti-canal federation, but also several other more local issues – thus played a direct role in the further development of AGL from 1973 to 1975; in terms of personal contacts and organizational structure, they acted as a convergence point for the Flemish Greens (Walgrave 1988: 49–51).

In 1974, local AGL sections of another kind were set up alongside the action groups: the 'daily deeds' (*dagelijkse doeningen*) or 'reflection groups'. These groups became loci for incubating and maturing Green ideas in a more global society-critical orientation, going far beyond mere environmental concerns.

At the 1974 parliamentary elections and 1976 local elections, AGL chose not to compete in its own name, but rather to endorse 'green lists' of candidates running on the tickets of traditional parties. These candidates were to support the movement's demands, mainly on environmental issues. Both these attempts were

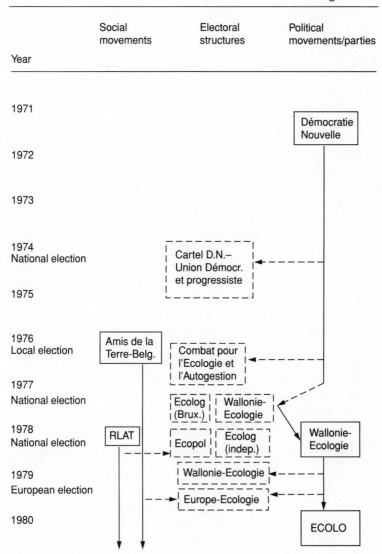

Figure 5.1 The emergence of Ecolo
Source: Rihoux 1991: 58.
Notes: Broken lines indicate *temporary* structures; continuous lines indicate
structures designed as *permanent* by their authors.
RLAT – Réseau Libre des Amis de la Terre.

entirely unsuccessful as the elected candidates did not deliver on their promises. It is clear that this failure accelerated the evolution towards the first genuinely 'political' stage in the development of the Flemish Greens. In the meantime, a 'national reflection group' was created in order to improve the movement's co-ordination.

In 1977, AGL decided to field its own list under the 'Agalev' name for the parliamentary elections in the Antwerp area; it achieved modest results (0.3 per cent).[7] At the 1978 legislative elections, the newly created 'national council' (*Landelijke Beraad*) of AGL decided to participate again. Results still remained low (0.7 per cent). That same year, however, the first specifically and explicitly *political* group was created within the movement: the 'Agalev working group' (*Agalev Werkgroep*). From then on, AGL began to attract activists from a broader range of 'new social movements', among them people with organizational experience and, in some cases, a political background.

At the 1979 European elections the Agalev list achieved its first electoral breakthrough, securing 2.3 per cent of the vote. This modest success led to an influx of activists and paved the way for the creation of a genuine Green political party. Conflicts between 'political' and 'movementist' activists began to develop, but the political branch of AGL became ever stronger, both in terms of membership and organizational developments, compared with the initial core of AGL activists. In May 1981, the Agalev working group was re-established as a permanent organ more and more auto-nomous of the AGL movement as a whole and with a clear political orientation.

At the November 1981 legislative elections, the Agalev list achieved an important if unexpected breakthrough with 4 per cent of the vote, obtaining three national seats (two in the chamber and one in the senate) and seven provincial seats. As a result, the Flemish Greens were confronted with a peculiar and uncomfort-able situation, being virtually compelled to form a genuine political party before having made an explicit decision to do so. In practical terms, this meant that the Flemish Greens now had three full-time professional politicians but no adequate organizational structure. As far as the newly elected representatives and their supporters were concerned, there were needs for finance and a small pro-fessional staff, and a need to elaborate more comprehensive programmatic proposals and to define the relationship between representatives and supporters. In short, there was a strong struc-

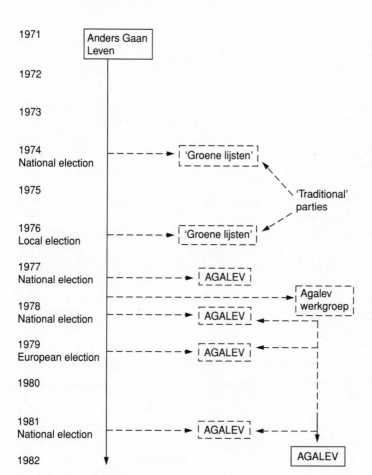

Figure 5.2 The emergence of Agalev
Source: Adapted from Rihoux 1991: 61.
Notes: Broken lines indicate *temporary* structures; continuous lines indicate structures designed as *permanent* by their authors.

tural pressure towards the formation of a real Green party. Thus, following intense and sometimes very conflictual debates, Agalev as a political party was officially created – and formally separated from the AGL movement – in February 1982.

The early histories of Ecolo and Agalev have several points in common. First, although environmental issues did play some part, the green movements and protoparties of the 1970s were by no means single-issue groups; indeed, although the environmental dimension was always present, it was not the major initial factor in the formation of either party. Ecolo's founding fathers did have close links with Les Amis de la Terre, but these did not directly lead to the constitution of Ecolo. In Agalev's case, environmental themes were of more direct relevance in the early 1970s: they created a convergence between the Anders Gaan Leven movement and other movements. Environmental issues were thus necessary but not sufficient conditions for the rise of the Belgian Green parties.

The primary explanation for the emergence of Ecolo and Agalev must be sought in the Belgian political system, which was – and still is, in some respects – quite favourable to the Greens.[8] In addition, the governmental instability of the late 1970s was itself a facilitating factor, for it gave the Greens numerous opportunities in the electoral arena; all the above-mentioned elections – including the decisive 1981 legislative elections – were anticipated. Second, the voting system is quite favourable to smaller lists: it is fairly proportional (d'Hondt system); moreover, the division of the country into *arrondissements* allows parties to field a list in even a single constituency. Finally, voting is compulsory for all elections (local, provincial, legislative and European), and from 1979 the minimum voting age was lowered from 21 to 18. Both the latter factors seem to have benefited the Greens.

In these circumstances, it is not surprising that the 1979 European elections played a catalytic role in the formation of Green parties. From 1974 on, the Greens had slowly gained political experience and structured themselves accordingly; the 1979 results were proof that Green parties were viable. In Agalev's case, the 1981 legislative elections played an even more direct role in the foundation of the party. However, in both cases, 1979 was clearly the turning-point in the slow maturing process: the Greens suddenly became aware of their potential. The European elections gave the Greens their first opportunity to field a list covering the whole country, and because only one list was needed, this was done at minimal organizational and financial cost.

Two other factors of party-political competition played a role in the rise of the Greens: first, there was, during this period, a decline in support for the regionalist parties, particularly in Wallonia; second, the traditional political parties failed to react to the newly emerging environmental agenda. Quite clearly, in the late 1970s the large political parties did not see the Greens as a major threat. The striking parallels in the timing of the emergence of Ecolo and Agalev give credence to the suggestion that the 'political opportunity structure' (as Kitschelt 1989 defines it) was the crucial factor.

THE POST-FOUNDATION YEARS: DEVELOPMENT AND CONSOLIDATION

Yet this does not explain why the Belgian Green parties gradually became significant political actors between the early 1980s and the early 1990s. Kitschelt (1989: 19) suggests that significant Green parties appear only when unresponsiveness of existing political institutions coincides with favourable opportunities to displace existing parties. However, for a more complete explanation, other elements must also be considered, among them the effects of the actions of the Green parties themselves within the party-political system.

The starting-point for an analysis of the development and consolidation of Ecolo and Agalev must be an evaluation of their electoral performance. Since their official foundation in 1980 and 1982 respectively, Ecolo and Agalev have competed in all elections (see Table 5.1).

The overriding feature of Agalev's and Ecolo's results is their relative stability. From 1981 on, the Greens have never fallen below the 5 per cent line; better still, for each given type of election (local, legislative, European), their results have consistently improved, Greens obtaining seats at each election. This clearly places the Belgian Greens among the most successful European Green parties in terms of electoral performance and penetration of the institutional political system.

In terms of structural development, the fact that Ecolo and Agalev gained seats in both houses as early as 1981 was a determining factor in their further development. Although the Belgian electoral system does not directly reward parties financially in

Table 5.1 Electoral results and seats, 1981–1991

Year	Level	Results (%)	Chamber	Senate	Provincial	Europe	Local
Ecolo							
1981	National	5.9	2	4	9		
1982	Local	7.1					75
1984	European	9.9				1	
1985	National	6.2	5	3	10		
1987	National	6.5	3	3	12		
1988	Local	8.4					117
1989	European	16.6				2	
1991	National	13.5	10	6	41		
Agalev							
1981	National	4.0	2	1	7		
1982	Local	6.2					43
1984	European	7.1				1	
1985	National	6.1	4	3	12		
1987	National	7.3	6	5	23		
1988	Local	6.9					108
1989	European	12.2				1	
1991	National	7.8	7	5	24		

Notes: 1 Two elections are not included here: the 1989 Brussels regional elections (eight Ecolo and one Agalev elected) and the 1990 German-speaking community council elections (Ecolo 15 per cent and four elected).

2 Results for national elections are for the Chamber; figures for Ecolo are per cent votes in Wallonia and among Francophone lists in Brussels; figures for Agalev are per cent votes in Flanders.

3 Results for European elections for Ecolo and for Agalev are per cent votes in the French- and Flemish-speaking *corps électorals* respectively.

4 Results for local elections are average results for those communes where the Greens fielded lists.

proportion to the votes cast for them as does the German one,[9] the election of representatives and senators in 1981 gave the Green parties a modest but sound financial basis and a permanent staff, and these provided the Greens with favourable circumstances in which to prepare for the 1982 local elections.

Three features of the evolution of the Greens' electoral results stand out. First, results are systematically better at European elections, most notably in 1989 when Ecolo once again achieved the highest score of the European Green parties (16.6 per cent of the valid vote). Many explanatory factors can be raised, such as the minimal organizational cost of these elections, the perceived lesser importance of the European Parliament for the average voter, the compulsory vote, the intrinsically more 'principled' and agenda-setting nature of the European elections and, finally, more contemporary factors such as the impact of the nuclear missiles debate (in 1984) and a probable post-Chernobyl effect (in 1989) (Rihoux 1992: 42–43).

Second, Ecolo and Agalev made little headway in legislative elections between 1981 and 1987. This is particularly clear in Ecolo's case, and partly could be due to the relatively high 1981 score: it can be assumed that Ecolo and Agalev conquered much of their potential core electoral public from the very start. Moreover, the establishment of local Green parties was very slow (Rihoux 1994b; Walgrave 1994). In Ecolo's case, during 1985 and 1986 severe internal conflicts played a major role. In particular, a major conflict developed between a 'reformist' majority and a more 'radical–libertarian' and more clearly left-wing minority. Following this conflict, many members – mostly radicals, including a high-profile national MP – left the party (Rihoux 1991: 110–112; Rihoux 1992: 4). This conflict received extensive and persistent media coverage and certainly had a negative impact on the image of the French-speaking Greens. Moreover, Ecolo had to face an unexpected opponent during the 1987 elections in the shape of a 'Christian left' protoparty, Solidarité et Participation.

Finally, from 1981 to 1987, both Agalev and Ecolo suffered from the fact that the Socialists (PS and SP) were in opposition. This had two implications. On the one hand, the Socialists were able to mobilize some segments of the 'new politics' electorate: for instance, both PS and SP joined the mass peace demonstrations of the early 1980s. On the other hand, party-political competition and the desire to cast an effective anti-majority vote to defeat the centre-right coalition diverted part of Ecolo's and Agalev's potential electorates towards the Socialists in 1985 and 1987.

From 1989 on, and even more since the November 1991 legislative and provincial elections, the Green parties have acquired a new dimension, not only in terms of electoral results but also in terms of power in a changing party-political system.

In the November 1991 legislative and provincial elections, Ecolo and Agalev for the first time experienced divergent electoral fortunes: a breakthrough for Ecolo and quasi-stagnation for Agalev. In order to explain the difference, it must be pointed out that the party-political systems of Flanders, Wallonia and Brussels have evolved in very different ways in the recent past. In Flanders, the Christian Democrats (CVP), until recently the dominant Flemish party, experienced a major defeat in 1991, for the first time in history falling below the 30 per cent mark (from 31.4 per cent in 1987 to 26.9 per cent in 1991). Similarly, the vote for Flemish Socialists declined from 24.2 per cent in 1987 to 19.6 per cent in 1991. On the other hand, the ultra-conservative Flemish nationalist party, Vlaams Blok, achieved a major breakthrough, polling more than 10 per cent and overtaking both the regionalist Volksunie and Agalev. Moreover, the newly created anarcho-libertarian and 'anti-politics' Rossem list attracted more than 5 per cent of the vote. Conversely, the political balance did not shift so dramatically in Wallonia or in Brussels, where Ecolo was the main winner, and neither the far right nor any other 'non-traditional' lists achieved significant results.

It can thus be assumed that Agalev – unlike Ecolo – was stripped of most 'protest voters' in 1991; according to a simulation based on recent survey material, the most important vote shift in Flanders from 1987 to 1991 was that from Agalev to Rossem. On the other hand, whereas Agalev gained few voters from the SP, Ecolo gained more than 80,000 voters from the PS. Finally, it is evident that Agalev received the votes of only about 10 per cent of new voters (those less than 21 years of age), while the corresponding figure for Ecolo was above 30 per cent (Aish and Swyngedouw 1992). Ecolo's increased share of the vote can, in fact, be linked with a substantial proportion of 'protest voters' in the 1991 Ecolo electorate (Frognier 1992; Rihoux 1993a). Further confirmation can be found in the fact that, between 1987 and 1991, Ecolo's results evolved less favourably in the few urban areas where the far right (Front National and 'Agir') achieved encouraging results.

This recent development is clearly important for the Greens: for the first time, a contrasting north–south evolution of the party-political balance has been translated into very different electoral fortunes for the two parties. This has been aggravated by the fact that the Green electorate is more volatile than that of the traditional parties: no fewer than 45 per cent of those who voted for Agalev in 1987 (and 30 per cent of those who voted for Ecolo) voted differently in 1991 (Swyngedouw et al. 1992). It should nevertheless be remembered that, despite such a high level of electoral volatility, since 1981 neither Agalev nor Ecolo has ever experienced electoral defeat at any level.

There remain three further factors concerning the emergence and relative success of the Belgian Green parties which merit consideration. The first concerns the nuclear power issue and the extent to which it was a relevant factor in the rise and consolidation of the Greens. There has never been any mass mobilization against nuclear energy in Belgium; the largest demonstration (some 20,000 participants, including a large proportion of Dutch demonstrators) took place in Doel (near Antwerp) in 1982. Clearly, the Belgian experience has been very different from that of countries such as Germany. However, although the nuclear issue was never very salient on the political agenda, and the nuclear debate never had a major and direct implication in purely electoral terms, in the late 1970s and early 1980s, because the nuclear issue was a meeting-point for activists of various 'new social movements', it played a key role in the formation of the Green (proto) parties. It was during this period that some elements of the Green movement became more radicalized and politicized (Rihoux 1991: 42–46). Thus, the nuclear issue acted as a catalyst in the formation of Green parties. Finally, it is quite clear – though difficult to quantify – that the Chernobyl accident had a positive impact on the electoral performance of the Belgian Greens at the 1989 European elections. Other factors, such as the high visibility of other environmental issues (acid rain, climate change), may also have had a positive influence on their results.

The second question concerns the extent to which competition between Greens and other political parties about particular issues (such as the environment or disarmament) influenced the fortunes of the Green parties, both in terms of electoral results and structural development. There are at least three reasons why Belgium's traditional parties have found it difficult to take on the green agenda. First, the Belgian political system has often – and rightly – been described as 'pillarized': three subcultural 'pillars' (*zuilen*) have developed, each revolving around one political party family (Catholic, socialist, liberal). The pillars consist of tightly knit inter-organizational networks of interest groups, social service organizations and political parties. This is why Belgium has often been defined as a 'partycracy': the major political parties, linked to their respective strongly structured and hierarchical pillars, play a dominant role in the policy-making process. Radically new demands are not easily assimilated by pillars, and this is an important factor not only in the emergence and durability of the Greens, but of the regionalist parties (though the latter are being more or less successfully swallowed by the established parties).

This analysis must however be tempered, for the established parties have at times been able to take on the 'new social movements' agenda at the expense of the Greens. For example, while in opposition, both Socialist parties supported the demands of the peace movement and, especially in Flanders, some fractions of the traditional parties have always been quite close to aspects of the 'new politics' agenda: peace (SP and VU), local environmental concerns (VU), Third World (CVP and SP). That said, the overriding picture remains that the traditional Belgian political parties, structurally tied to their large and monolithic interests groups, have not consistently reacted or dynamically adapted to the demands of the green agenda. Hence they have not been able effectively to counter most of the moves of the Green parties.

The third question concerns the extent to which the actions of the Green parties themselves have played a role in their relative success and stability. Ever since their entry on to the political scene, Ecolo and Agalev have been active participants in party-political competition. In terms of image and attractiveness, their action has been beneficial in at least two respects. First, Ecolo and Agalev have not only been carrying a new agenda; they have also advocated and in many ways put into practice a new political behaviour. For example, the Greens have been quite uniquely able to co-operate constructively across the linguistic divide: as early as 1981, Ecolo and Agalev formed a single group in parliament. Other formal arrangements such as regular joint meetings and a 'co-ordination bureau' ensure close co-operation between the French-speaking and Flemish Greens. Indeed, the Greens have always kept a good image with the broader public by giving practical effect to slogans such as 'politics with clean hands' which contrast sharply with practices such as clientelism, 'political' nominations, not to mention more dubious financial practices associated with more traditional parties.

Second, both Green parties have been able to expand their pragmatic scope of action far beyond mere environmental concerns, and this makes it increasingly difficult for their competitors to counter all their moves. For example, it is assumed that Ecolo attracted new voters in 1991 by skilfully exploiting issues salient during the campaign, such as the non-profit sectors and education. In any case, a close look at the parliamentary activity of the Greens proves that purely environmental issues are not at all dominant: in quantitative terms, a majority of the Greens' activities and interventions focus on social problems, the economy, the budget and institutional reform (Speelman 1986; Uyttenhove 1986).

CONCLUSION

An overriding feature emerges from our analysis. The political opportunity structure, both institutional and party-political, has been the most important factor in the relative success of the Belgian Greens, during both the emergence and development of Ecolo and Agalev. Other factors, among them (and increasingly) the initiatives of the Greens themselves, have also played a part, but this should not be overrated, for the Greens have seldom really held the balance of power, even at local level, and they have not always been very visible, whether politically or in the media.

What, then, can be said about the future of the Belgian Green parties? The Greens were able to maximize their strengths and minimize their weaknesses throughout the 1980s, but the 1990s will pose new challenges. At least five issues are potentially problematic for the Greens in the years to come.

The first concerns the financial stability of the Green parties. Until now, they have been able to use their (comparatively small) financial and human resources in an optimal way. The problem is that both Ecolo and Agalev remain extremely dependent on external (public) funds, strongly linked with their electoral performance and number of seats in elected bodies. A single electoral defeat could cause major structural problems for the parties, in the same way that defeat in the Bundestag elections in 1990 caused severe problems for the German Greens.

Second, the base of members and activists on which the Greens can rely is narrow: the ratio between the numbers of members and voters is very low (less than 2 per cent) compared with the more established parties (from 10 to 15 per cent). This lack of human resources is the source of numerous structural problems, problems which will multiply if the Greens obtain more seats in elected bodies (Kitschelt 1989; Kitschelt and Hellemans 1990).

Third, since the Green electorate is on average younger and more highly educated, it may be assumed that it is more volatile than others. In other words, the Greens cannot rely on a relatively stable electoral base. Nor do they have the resources which would allow them to secure an electoral 'clientele', something to which they are in any case opposed on principle.

Fourth, the Greens have not tried to build a 'green pillar'. No social movement is explicitly, unilaterally or structurally linked with the Green parties. As a result, the Greens cannot rely on the support of organizations which could act as useful channels (both top-down and bottom-up) between them and society.

The fifth issue builds on the other four. Until now, although Greens have already held office in a few places at local level,[10] they have not been in office at national or regional level. The main question is: how will they cope if they join a coalition in years to come? The paths of continued opposition and power will both be tricky.

The latest events suggest that the Greens are moving closer to power. From April 1992 to July 1993 both Ecolo and Agalev joined the ruling majority (Socialist/Christian Democrat) in support of the institutional reform of parliament (federalization);[11] they have also been able to bring the question of 'green taxes' to the negotiation table (Rihoux 1994a). The most likely scenario is that in the short to medium term the Greens will join some sort of coalition at the regional and/or federal level. In any case, it is likely that the number of instances of Greens participating in office at the local (*commune*) level will increase after the October 1994 local elections. In the medium term, such experience could prove valuable for the Greens. Any short-term Green participation at regional and/or federal level would, however, clearly be risky, but it is hard to imagine that the Green parties will not submit to the perilous 'test of power' if they really want to translate some of their programmatic demands into concrete policies.

NOTES

1 French-speaking parties field lists in Wallonia and Brussels, while Flemish parties field lists in Flanders and Brussels.
2 Christian Democrats: Christelijke Volkspartij (CVP) and Parti Social-Chrétien (PSC); Socialists: Socialistische Partij (SP) and Parti Socialiste (PS); Liberals: Partij voor Vrijheid en Vooruitgang (PVV) and Parti Réformateur Libéral (PRL). The PVV (Flemish Liberal Party) was dissolved in November 1992 and currently forms the core of a new party, Vlaamse Liberalen en Demokraten (VLD).

3 Unless otherwise indicated, election results refer to votes cast for the Chamber, the lower house of the national legislature.

4 There are thirteen electoral *arrondissements* in Wallonia, each divided into smaller units (*cantons*) covering one or several *communes*.

5 For the European elections, Belgian voters are split into two subgroups: the French-speaking and Flemish-speaking electorates.

6 Its exact name was – and still is – Mouvement Ecolo though it clearly is a political party.

7 The acronym 'Agalev' (a contraction of *Anders GAan LEVen*) was deliberately chosen to sound confusing: half-way between a Turkish immigrant group and a Russian dissident organization.

8 And to other smaller parties, such as the regionalist parties which reached their peak electoral level in the late 1960s and early 1970s.

9 A new law was passed in 1993 which plans greater financial support to the parties, partly with a fixed sum and partly in proportion to the votes cast for them, and partly conditional upon the presence of the party in both houses.

10 Although few, these experiences of local office include, in the case of Ecolo, large cities such as Liège (1982–1988) and Brussels (since 1988).

11 Institutional reforms involving modification of the constitution require a two-thirds majority vote in both houses. Belgium became a 'federal' state on 14 July 1993.

REFERENCES

Aish, A.M. and Swyngedouw, M. (1992) *Les élections législatives du 24 Novembre 1991. Analyse de la stabilité et du changement de l'électorat Wallon*, Louvain-la-Neuve: UCL, PIOP.

Frognier, A.P. (1992) *Le vote écologiste et d'extrême-droite en Wallonie*, Louvain-la-Neuve: UCL, cahier du PIOP.

Kitschelt, H. (1989) *The Logics of Party Formation: Ecological Politics in Belgium and West Germany*, Ithaca, NY and London: Cornell University Press.

Kitschelt, H. and Hellemans, S. (1990) *Beyond the European Left: Ideology and Political Action in the Belgian Ecology Parties*, Durham, NC: Duke University Press.

Rihoux, B. (1991) 'Emergence et institutionalisation des partis écologistes. Etude de politique comparée: Die Grünen (RFA), Les Verts (France), Ecolo et Agalev (Belgique)', Louvain-la-Neuve: UCL (unpublished).

—— (1992) 'Résultats électoraux d'Ecolo, 1981–1991', *Courrier Hebdomadaire du C.R.I.S.P.* 1371–1372: 1–62.

—— (1993) 'Emergence et développement des deux partis écologistes belges: Ecolo et Agalev', Barcelona: ICPS working paper.

—— (1994a) 'Les écotaxes – produits sur la scène politique belge', *Courrier Hebdomadaire du C.R.I.S.P.*

—— (1994b) 'Le parti Ecolo aux élections communales de 1982 et 1988. Stratégies, résultats et perspectives', *Actes du Colloque Les élections communales et leur impact sur la politique belge, Spa, 2–4 Septembre 1992*, Brussels: Crédit Communal de Belgique.

Speelman, M. (1986) 'De Vlaamse groene partij Agalev. Voorstelling en situering a.d.h.v. een analyse van haar parlementaire aktie in de Kamer van Volksvertegenwoordigers tijdens de periode november 1981– oktober 1983', Leuven: KUL (unpublished).

Swyngedouw, M. *et al.* (1992) *Van waar komen ze, wie zijn ze? Stemgedrag en verschuivingen op 24 november 1991*, Leuven: KUL, ISPO paper no. 1992–3.

Uyttenhove, I. (1986) 'De plaatselijke werking Agalev in het arrondissement Antwerpen', Gent: RUG (unpublished).

Walgrave, S. (1988) 'Agalev. Van beweging tot partij', Leuven: KUL (unpublished).

—— (1994) 'Agalev en de Gemeenteraadsverkiezingen van 1982 en 1988', *Actes du Colloque Les élections communales et leur impact sur la politique belge, Spa, 2–4 Septembre 1992*, Brussels: Crédit Communal de Belgique.

Chapter 6

The Netherlands

Losing colours, turning green

Gerrit Voerman

In September 1989 a new political formation, Green Left (Groen Links), took part in the Dutch national elections. Under this banner the Communist Party of The Netherlands (CPN – Communistische Partij van Nederland), the Pacifist–Socialist Party (PSP – Pacifistisch–Socialistische Partij), the Political Radical Party (PPR – Politieke Partij Radikalen), the Evangelical People's Party (EVP – Evangelische Volkspartij) and a group of independents joined hands. Though Green Left won six parliamentary seats out of 150, double the number held by the constituent parties before the election, the increase in its share of the vote was not impressive: 4.1 per cent in 1989 compared with 3.3 per cent in 1986. Nevertheless, Green Left was more successful than its ecological rival, The Greens (De Groenen), who scored only 0.4 per cent. After the election, CPN, PSP, PPR, EVP and the independents decided to continue their co-operation and Green Left was officially founded – without The Greens – on 24 November 1990.

This chapter will examine the origins and development of the Green political movement in The Netherlands. It will focus upon two paradoxes (Voerman 1992). The first is the failure of a strong pure Green party to develop despite favourable social and political conditions. Despite the low electoral threshold (a party requires only 0.67 per cent of the vote to obtain a seat in the national parliament) and the presence of a large electoral reservoir in the shape of relatively strong new social movements in the 1970s and early 1980s, a Green party did not enter the Dutch parliament. The reason lies in the second paradox: the *rapprochement*, under a 'green' label, of initially totally different parties – the PPR (founded as a progressive Christian party), the pacifist PSP and the orthodox Stalinist CPN.[1]

Despite their variety, co-operation among these parties started in the 1970s, stimulated by the introduction of New Left ideas and the rise of new social movements, combined with the declining electoral fortunes of the parties themselves. In the course of its transformation, the PPR took the initiative to pick up the environmental issue, the PSP overcame its reluctance to work together with the other parties and the CPN lost its rigid Stalinist traits. The result was growing electoral co-operation and eventually fusion.

Not everyone within CPN, PPR and PSP believed that their merger was inevitable or desirable. In the 1980s, intense debates took place within the parties, but eventually all ended in victory for the 'co-operators'. Finally, Green Left was formed as an electoral combination in 1989, and as a new political formation in 1990. Because of its plural origins, it had real difficulties in framing a coherent ideology, and in its manifestos Green Left hesitates between red and green. This ambiguity is reflected in the ideological preferences of the middle-level élite, as the findings of a survey held at the November 1990 constituent congress will demonstrate.

DE GROENEN: THE STILL-BORN GREEN PARTY

In the course of the 1960s, the 'pillarized' social and political system of The Netherlands changed fundamentally. Continuing economic growth was accompanied by the construction of the welfare state. Partly as a result of increasing secularization, individualization and the rise of television, the traditional pillars, in which various religious and ideological sections of the population were organized, started to crumble. Political attitudes and values came under pressure; patience and docility made way for activism and politicization. Attention shifted from material concerns to 'post-material' issues such as the environment, self-realization and women's liberation. New social movements grouped themselves around these themes, drawing most of their adherents from the new middle class (Van der Loo *et al.* 1984; Van Deth 1985; Kriesi 1986; Duyvendak *et al.* 1992). These new social movements prospered in the 1970s and early 1980s. Both the environmental and the anti-nuclear movement protested against the construction of the fast-breeder reactor in Kalkar (Germany) and against the enlargement of a uranium enrichment plant in The Netherlands, and the peace movement's campaign against the stationing of

American Cruise missiles on Dutch soil culminated in several large demonstrations.

Under these circumstances, the soil seemed very fertile for a Green party. At the end of 1982, two prominent members of the PPR registered the Green Party of The Netherlands (GPN – Groene Partij Nederland) with the Electoral Council. It was not, however, a serious attempt to create a real, viable ecological party; both founders simply hoped by this device to prevent possible abuse of the name 'green' by the extreme right. So GPN existed mainly on paper; in practice, it was called Green Platform because it intended to offer a platform for parties left of Labour. At the European elections of 1984, CPN, PPR, PSP and the Platform came to terms on a so-called Green Progressive Accord (GPA – Groen Progressief Akkoord), but the Radical attempt to add an ecological tinge to the Accord ran up against the combined opposition of Pacifists and Communists. In practice, the GPA programme was simply the sum of the demands of the different partners with regard to international security, unemployment and environmental pollution – in that order.

The electoral agreement of 1984 led to a split within the Green Platform. Regional Green parties, which had been formed earlier in preparation for provincial elections, feared being engulfed by the small left parties and wanted, in particular, to keep aloof from the CPN. Some of them left the Platform and founded a new party called The Greens (De Groenen) in December 1983. This newcomer focused on the political centre of progressive Christian Democrats and left–liberals. It also decided to take part in the 1984 European elections as European Greens. It was not very successful. The European Greens – recognized by most other Green parties within the European Community – got only 1.3 per cent of the popular vote, compared with 5.6 per cent for GPA which, supported by the West German Greens, won two seats in the European Parliament (Parkin 1989: 176–185, 257–265).

After this disappointment, the European Greens went downhill. As Federative Greens (as they renamed themselves in 1985) they took part in the national elections of 1986, but received only 0.2 per cent of the vote. The Federative Green platform was highly holistic and ecologistic – humankind, earth and universe were considered one interdependent whole – and demanded an integrated approach to politics and policy based on decentralization, recycling, small-scaleness, basic democracy and basic income. In

1988 the Federative Greens merged with a local ecologist party, Green Amsterdam, to form De Groenen – the name first used at the start of the Green Party formation five years earlier.

The Greens did not participate in the European elections of 1989, but a joint list of CPN, PPR, PSP and GPN, this time reinforced by the EVP and independents, and calling itself Rainbow, attracted 7 per cent of the votes. The failure of The Greens by comparison with Green Left at the national elections of 1989 suggests that voters preferred Green Left's diluted ecologism to the dark green, holist platform of The Greens.

So, slowly but surely, the only genuine Green Party in the Dutch political landscape faded away electorally and organizationally. In 1992, divergences of opinion resulted in several splits. At the party congress at the end of that year voices were heard suggesting dissolution. Though it did not come to that, The Greens' prospects are rather gloomy. In essence, the Green Party never had a real opportunity to develop. The ground was cut from under it at the outset by the greening of the PPR. The Radicals had already taken part in the Coordination of European and Radical Parties in 1979, in which Die Grünen, the Belgian parties Agalev and Ecolo, the French Mouvement d'écologie politique and the British Ecology Party worked together (Parkin 1989: 257). The ensuing *rapprochement* in The Netherlands among Radicals, Pacifists and Communists, which assumed greener colours in the course of time, then delivered the final blow to the pure green experiment.

GROEN LINKS – GREEN LEFT

At the beginning of the 1970s, there were no signs of imminent co-operation, let alone fusion among the 'small-left' parties; Radicals, Pacifists and Communists marched separately at the national level (Voerman 1990). However, the differences between PSP and PPR were not great. Profoundly influenced by New Left ideas (Lucardie 1980), both Radicals and Pacifists thought society should become much more democratic and that the predominant mentality had to be changed by actions 'from below'. The PSP, emanating from the peace movement during the Cold War in 1957, was in favour of extra-parliamentary activism and was not willing to get 'dirty hands' by participating in government. Basking in splendid isolation, the PSP emphasized issues like non-violent defence, anti-imperialism, socialization of production and workers' self-management. The Radicals, who left the Catholic People's Party (KVP – Katholieke Volkspartij) in 1968, were more governmentally inclined and considered actions at the grass roots to be supplementary. They made eyes at Labour and participated in a coalition cabinet led by the Social Democratic Prime Minister Den Uyl (1973–1977). The Radicals never became socialist, however, but focused on peace, environment, welfare and democratization.

The mutual differences between PSP and PPR paled in significance compared with the differences between them and the Communists. Although the CPN did not formally maintain relations with Moscow, it did adhere to the Soviet type of communism (Voerman 1993). The party was still part of the old left tradition and gave top priority to the socio-economic demands of the workers; 'post-materialist' issues were hardly discussed. Moreover, there were enormous organizational divergences among the parties: PSP and PPR were democratic, whereas the CPN was organized on centralist and Stalinist lines. These 'small-left' parties each acted independently at the national level, and with relative success, until 1977. The parliamentary elections of that year proved disastrous; of 16 seats which they held between them, they retained only six (see Table 6.1). Labour, by contrast, gained the largest electoral victory in its history.

This dramatic outcome led to the call for national co-operation among the three parties. It was thought that a joint list might stop their electoral decline and perhaps even attract more voters, and

Table 6.1 Membership and parliamentary seats of CPN, PSP and PPR, 1971–1989

Year	CPN	Seats	PSP	Seats	PPR	Seats	Total Members	Seats
1971	?	6	4,000	2	4,300	2	?	10
1972	10,000	7	4,600	2	3,800	7	18,400	16
1977	15,300	2	6,500	1	13,400	3	35,200	6
1981	14,400	3	9,600	3	10,500	3	34,500	9
1982	13,900	3	10,000	3	10,000	2	33,900	8
1986	8,500	0	6,500	1	6,300	2	21,300	3
1989	5,700	–	4,100	–	6,000	–	18,400*	6**

Notes:* Membership Green Left, consisting of membership of CPN, PSP, CPN and EVP (1,500) and the direct members of the Association Green Left (VGL – Vereniging Groen Links) (1,100).
** Total Green Left.

that a new united party might draw Labour more to the left. Moreover, it was pointed out that at local and provincial level PPR and PSP were, during the 1970s, increasingly co-ordinating their efforts, despite the Radicals' national predilection for Labour. Though the CPN was not involved in these concerted actions, its electoral set-back triggered a large-scale process of ideological and organizational renewal. By taking its leave of Stalinism, the CPN became acceptable as a partner to the Pacifists and Radicals (Voerman 1993).

Another factor which influenced the national *rapprochement* was the rise, in the course of the 1970s, of the new social movements. PPR and PSP joined with these movements in extra-parliamentary actions, and party members came across one another in blockades of nuclear plants or in the large peace demonstrations of the early 1980s (Schennink *et al.* 1982; Van der Loo *et al.* 1984). Consultations between the executives of PSP and PPR and the new social movements became more institutionalized. Initially, the CPN acted independently and organized several actions on its own, but after 1977 it gradually started to participate with the others.

In these combined actions of political parties and social movements, old dividing-lines tended to fade. As a consequence, activists pressed for more collaboration between PSP, PPR and CPN. It was thought that 'small-left' unity could give better parliamentary voice to the demands of the new social movements and at the same time put greater pressure on Labour. In 1983 a manifesto, 'In favour of a left breakthrough' ('*Om een linkse doorbraak*'), was published. About 1,000 subscribers – among whom were many non-party social activists – protested in this way against the 'small-left' diaspora.

Beside this organizational pressure, the new social movements seem to have contributed to the ideological convergence of PSP, PPR and CPN (Brinkman *et al.* 1990). Initially, the three parties assumed completely different attitudes towards these movements. The PSP was very receptive, partly as a consequence of the emphasis it had traditionally put upon direct action and, in 1983, the party congress considered the social movements 'the most important force for social change'. PSP saw its task as being 'to explain the links between the different forms of resistance against capitalism, patriarchy and militarism and to make connections between the different social movements'.

For its part, from its foundation in 1968, the PPR regarded itself as 'an action-party which want[ed] to change mentality as well as social structures', but saw extra-parliamentary action as complementary to parliamentary activities. Unlike the PSP, which stressed direct action, the PPR considered each to be of equal value. However, in the 1980s, with prospects of participation in government diminishing, the Radicals moved closer to the Pacifists; parliament was no longer looked upon as the initiating or leading actor in the process of social change, but as a coping-stone.

Unlike PSP and PPR, the CPN stood firmly in the tradition of Marxism–Leninism which left its mark upon its orientation towards social organizations. The Communists considered themselves to be the conscious vanguard of the working class in the class struggle. This leading role implied that social movements such as trades unions or the peace movement were regarded as 'transmission belts' between party and working class. The activities of these movements were partial struggles within the framework of the all-embracing struggle between labour and capital. After 1977, this traditional position faded during the process of party renewal (Voerman 1991); indeed, the new party programme of 1984 officially declared party and movements as equivalent and rejected any hierarchical relationship. The notion of the class struggle as the sole engine of history was abandoned; instead several social antitheses were acknowledged: man and nature, man and woman, north and south, hetero- and homosexuality and, of course, labour and capital.

One by one, the three parties opened themselves to the new social movements and, in the course of the 1970s and 1980s, developed very similar opinions on the issues of peace, environment, anti-nuclear power and gender. The social movements may have supplied new issues to the parties, but a more autonomous and simultaneous emergence of such concerns should not be discounted. In any case, an ideological *rapprochement* took place and was welcomed by the social movements.

On most of the new issues, Pacifists and Radicals had long been agreed, but the Communists had to undertake a conversion. They were, for instance, the last to acknowledge the seriousness of environmental pollution. Traditionally, the CPN linked pollution with the 'anarchic' capitalist mode of production, rejecting restraint of economic growth because growth was regarded as essential for the material well-being of the workers. In the 1980s, this old left dogma also disappeared from the set of Communist principles, as the party started to advocate an 'ecologically justified policy'.

The PSP was one of the first Dutch parties to become conscious of environmental problems. The Pacifists rejected the necessity of economic growth even before the publication of *Limits to Growth* (Meadows *et al.*) in 1972. The PSP did not, however, develop into a real ecology party. It was thought that environmental pollution could be solved only in a socialist society, where social needs rather than the pursuit of gain would determine production. In this way – though less rigid than the CPN – the PSP put socialism above ecologism: society had to turn 'red' before it could become 'green'.

In a way, the PPR was 'green' *avant la lettre*. From their foundation, they faced up to the increasing impairment of the environment, borrowing the concept of 'selective growth' from *Limits to Growth* and making it one of their key themes. After a short period of ambiguity, the Radicals rejected nuclear power and, together with the PSP, were among those who initiated the opposition against nuclear energy. The PPR acquired a clear ecologist image by increasingly stressing environmental issues, even toying with the idea of dissolving itself in order to found a new, broader green political formation. In 1983, the party congress defined the PPR as 'radical, solidary, non-conformist, ecologist and libertarian'.

The traumatic elections of 1977, collaboration in municipal councils and provincial states, common experiences in extra-parliamentary actions and ideological convergence all seemed to point in the direction of more national co-operation among the 'small-left' parties. Yet they hesitated. The issue of co-operation led to serious intraparty debates in the early 1980s. Within the PPR, the wing of the party that traditionally looked to Labour dropped out. The Pacifists were also divided. The protagonists of splendid isolation and the 'co-operators' were kept in balance for years, but in 1985 the balance of power shifted in favour of the latter. As a consequence, some hundreds of 'purists' left the PSP.

The strife within the CPN was especially linked to the shift from a traditional 'proletarian left' stance to an 'ecological left' orientation and was only indirectly related to the theme of 'small-left' co-operation. The Moscow-oriented orthodox wing, in favour of an independent Marxist–Leninist CPN, was challenged by a group of renovators who wanted to get rid of Leninism. In 1984, the orthodox wing was defeated and the party congress renounced democratic centralism and adopted a new constitution in which feminism replaced Leninism as a source of inspiration.

Thus, in the middle of the 1980s, the intraparty debates were all settled in favour of the 'co-operators'. The road to merger seemed to be clear but, though the CPN, PPR and PSP acted together in the European elections of 1984, they could not reach agreement during the national elections of 1986. Consequently, the parties were thrown on their own resources, with disastrous results. CPN (and EVP) lost all their seats and the PSP lost two of its three (see Table 6.1, p. 113). Only the PPR maintained its position. To make matters worse, the decline in membership accelerated.

Against this background, it was not surprising that the parties reached an understanding for the national elections of 1989 (they had already decided to join again for the European elections). Early in 1989 an open letter was published in which activists from trades unions, the women's and the environmental movements pressed for a 'strong, left-green formation'. Negotiations among the parties soon reached deadlock but, because of the fall of the cabinet and the imminence of an election, they came to an understanding. On 19 May 1989, it was decided to take part in the national elections as Green Left. Twelve years after the trauma of 1977, CPN, PPR and PSP had overcome their reservations and agreed upon a common programme and a joint list of candidates. The EVP and independents who were invited to participate also joined the co-operative electoral body.

The baptism of Green Left at the national elections in September 1989 was less convincing than had been hoped. Opinion polls suggested that the newcomer could count on 10 parliamentary seats, but in the event Green Left gained 4.1 per cent of the vote and six seats. Green Left made some progress thereafter: at the municipal elections in 1990 it received 4.6 per cent of the vote, and at the provincial elections in 1991, 5.2 per cent, but at the 1994 national elections its support fell to 3.5 per cent.

After the 1989 elections, the new political formation tackled the problem of its organizational structure. October 1989 saw the founding of the Association Green Left (VGL – Vereniging Groen Links) which organized the direct members of the co-operative body. Party representatives, affiliated organizations and research bureaux were in due course combined. In the summer of 1990 dual membership of the constituent parties was introduced and members of all four massively acceded to Green Left. The conclusion of this process was the official constitution of Green Left as a political party on 24 November 1990 in The Hague. In 1991, PSP, PPR, EVP and CPN disbanded.

From the beginning, Green Left has struggled with its ideology. This is not surprising, given its diverse antecedents. Radicals have put forward ecological elements, while the Communists (and Pacifist–Socialists) have brought in their socialist heritage. The first Green Left manifesto was a cocktail of pacifist, Marxist, progressive Christian, libertarian socialist, ecologist and feminist ideas.

As the party's name indicates, the ideological content of Green Left is dualistic. Until now, the party has tried to compromise between a red Scylla and a green Charybdis. On the one hand, it advocates the ideal of social equality and more equal income distribution – the electoral platform of 1989, for instance, demanded complete compensation for the cuts in social benefits implemented in the 1980s; on the other, it advocates ecological sustainability and pleads for taxation on polluting products.

This ambiguity between environmental and social ideals was somewhat resolved in the manifesto adopted at the second party congress in December 1991. It accepted that ecological considerations should determine economic policy, but insisted that people on lower incomes should be financially compensated in the event of their economic position deteriorating in consequence. At the congress, another compromise was reached with regard to the socio-economic role of the state: Green Left accepted the principles of the free market economy and planning, aspiring to a 'democratically and ecologically managed economy with market elements'.

With these statements, Green Left is shifting slowly but surely in a more ecological direction. In 1993 its parliamentary group unequivocally opted to prioritize the environment ahead of socio-economic issues such as income and employment. People on lower incomes were to be compensated if the ecotax was implemented, but would face a decrease in buying-power if they continued consuming polluting products. The socialist wing of the party, which had organized itself in a so-called 'Left Network', seems unable fundamentally to alter this ecological profiling of Green Left.

SOCIAL BASE AND POLITICAL ORIENTATION OF GREEN LEFT

At the constituent party congress in November 1990 a survey was conducted into the social and political backgrounds of those present. The respondents have been classified according to party membership: CPN, PSP, PPR and the VGL, the group of 'direct' members of Green Left.[2]

A theory of merger processes seems scarcely to have been developed in political science, but it seems reasonable to suppose that party mergers will often originate in response to (perceived) threats, especially to electoral prospects, from other forces in the political environment. This seems to have been the case with the parties which fused into Green Left (Lucardie *et al.* 1991). Furthermore, one might expect that parties will fuse more quickly and smoothly when the participating organizations are more homogeneous in their organizational cultures, social backgrounds and ideology. In the case of Green Left, this latter aspect is especially important because the party is positioned at the junction of the green (ecological) and left (socialist) traditions. This ideological diversity is to some extent balanced by a degree of social homogeneity in that Green Left appears to have a common base in the new middle class.

As far as age is concerned, the Green Left congress was rather heterogeneous (see Table 6.2). About half the PSP and CPN contingents were in their 30s, compared with 30 per cent of the Radicals. The average age of Green Left's direct members (VGL) was 35, of PSP and CPN members 39 and of PPR members 43. VGL drew more of its strength from the very young than did the constituent parties, and the most recent recruits were also the youngest.

One in three congress delegates was female, the largest number of women (37 per cent) belonging to the PPR. With the exception of the PPR (24 per cent of Radicals identified themselves as Protestant), the majority of respondents did not consider themselves to be members of a religious denomination; Catholics appeared to be a small minority in every group (from 1 per cent among CPN members to 11 per cent among PPR members).

Table 6.2 Age (percentages)

Born	VGL	CPN	PPR	PSP	Total
Before 1940	9	15	27	12	18
1940–1949	18	20	26	23	22
1950–1959	42	47	30	51	40
1960 or later	31	19	17	14	19
Total	100	101	100	100	99

Note: N = 474.

Table 6.3 Education (percentages)

	VGL	CPN	PPR	PSP	Total
Elementary	0	0	1	1	1
Lower secondary/vocational	5	12	7	5	7
Higher secondary	13	10	12	13	12
Higher vocational	34	32	39	23	33
University	47	47	41	60	48
Total	99	101	100	102	101

Note: N = 478.

In general, Green Left congress delegates were well educated: 33 per cent had followed some form of higher vocational education (polytechnics, teacher's college, etc.), and 48 per cent held a university degree or were still studying (see Table 6.3). In all, over 80 per cent of respondents appeared to have attended some form of higher education, a high figure by comparison with the middle levels of other parties. Among the highly educated, social scientists were best represented (42 per cent), with the arts in second place. This predominance of the social sciences and related disciplines is in line with the hypotheses of Goul Anderson (1990) and Lucardie (1980, 1989) who detect an affinity between the phenomenon of 'communicative workers' and 'logocrats' (well-educated persons who derive influence from their rhetorical and psychological skills), on the one hand, and New Left or Green parties, on the other. Less than a third of respondents held no paid job (i.e. worked less than 20 hours a week, or ran the household, were

Table 6.4 Occupations (percentages)

	VGL	CPN	PPR	PSP	Total
Agriculture, fishery	1	0	1	1	1
Industry	8	5	7	2	5
Trade, transport	4	3	6	2	4
Service	20	23	28	27	24
Profession	7	5	3	11	6
(Semi-) public service	26	30	24	28	26
Teaching	9	10	16	7	11
Student	5	5	5	3	5
Other	21	21	12	17	17
Total	101	102	102	98	99

Note: N = 390.

handicapped or retired). Even fewer were unemployed. This hardly supports the theories of Bürklin (1985) and Alber (1989) that young, well-educated people become Green party activists out of frustration at their unemployment.

The professional activities of Green Left delegates reflected this pattern of education (see Table 6.4). Of the 70 per cent in employment (i.e. working at least 20 hours a week), a third worked in the (semi-) public and educational sectors and a quarter in the service sector. The constituent parties hardly differed in this respect. Green Left attracted few delegates from agriculture and fishing. The industrial sector was hardly better represented, even among Communists only 5 per cent had an industrial or blue-collar background. These results confirm the view that the adherents of Green Left are concentrated in the new middle class employed in the expanded government and service sector (Lucardie 1989).

Judging by their extra-parliamentary activities, respondents attached much value to social movements. The potential influence of these organizations is exemplified by the fact that more than half (56 per cent) of congress delegates were active members of a trades union, an action committee or a 'new' social movement; indeed, nearly a quarter (23 per cent) were active in two or more of these. Environmentalist groups and peace movements were most popular, closely followed by trades unions. Almost 40 per cent of women delegates were members of feminist groups.

This relatively high degree of social participation by Green Left delegates might point to the role of new social movements as a meeting place of CPN, PPR and PSP party activists. However, this social activism coincides to a certain extent with party membership. Nearly 30 per cent of Communists were active in trades unions, about twice as many as among members of other parties. PPR and PSP members participated in the environmental and peace movements to the same degree, the Radicals especially in the former and Pacifists in the latter. The CPN brought up the rear, especially in the environmental movement. There was hardly any difference between CPN, PPR and PSP with regard to the feminist movement.

The older members of the CPN, founded in 1918, and of the PSP, which dates from 1957, did not play any role at all in the founding congress of Green Left; over half the PSP, CPN and PPR delegates had joined in the 1970s, part of the wave of students and social workers which flooded these parties during that decade. Roughly

Table 6.5 Motives for merger (percentages)

	VGL	CPN	PPR	PSP	Total
Independently no future	27	36	35	39	35
Together more influence	65	59	76	53	64
Ideological renewal	61	51	47	50	51
No mutual ideological differences	29	16	29	31	25

Notes: N = 481.
1 Because more than one motive could be mentioned, totals sum to more than 100 per cent.

one-third of respondents became members in the 1980s and were naturally less attached to the traditions and culture of the parties than was the old guard.

Not surprisingly, respondents were nearly unanimously in favour of merger. The motive most often mentioned was the strengthening of the political position of the new party; nearly two-thirds thought that 'together we will be able to exert more influence than separately' (see Table 6.5). Most delegates did not perceive an electoral threat to their parties; only a third believed that 'the individual parties will not be able to survive very long electorally', and in this the delegates of CPN – which had lost its parliamentary representation in 1986 – were no more pessimistic than the delegates of other parties. Apart from the pursuit of political influence, the main motive for merger was ideological renewal. Half the respondents expected that 'a new party will be accompanied by a renewed ideology'. This was especially the hope of 'direct' Green Left delegates (VGL) and Communists who had to cope with a discredited ideology after the East European revolutions of 1989.

If Green Left's 'middle level élite' share a reasonably homogeneous social background, its ideological complexion is rather more diverse. Three issues demonstrate the continuing tension between 'red' and 'green': the role of government, the income of minimum wage-earners in relation to environmental policy and the introduction of a basic income.

In the 1990 survey, a bare majority of respondents (51 per cent) agreed that 'important large companies should become public enterprises' (see Table 6.6). The majority was largest among PSP members (78 per cent) and somewhat smaller among CPN members (64 per cent); VGL respondents were divided, whereas a majority of the PPR members clearly disagreed with the statement.

Table 6.6 Nationalization of major corporations (percentages)

	VGL	CPN	PPR	PSP	Total
Strongly in favour	13	23	4	26	15
In favour	31	41	24	52	36
No opinion	15	15	17	9	15
Opposed	39	20	49	12	31
Strongly opposed	2	0	6	1	3
Total	100	99	100	100	100

Note: N = 468.

Table 6.7 Financial sacrifices for the environment (percentages)

	VGL	CPN	PPR	PSP	Total
Strongly in favour	3	0	1	1	1
In favour	20	4	31	14	19
No opinion	12	6	7	6	7
Opposed	55	48	45	53	50
Strongly opposed	10	43	17	27	23
Total	100	101	101	101	100

Note: N = 471.

Opinions did not differ much as to whether minimum-wage-earners should contribute to environmental protection – the classical red/green dilemma (see Table 6.7). In the election campaign of 1989 The Greens (De Groenen) had argued in favour of this, while in 1990 the matter was debated within Green Left. The Greens' position was not greeted with much enthusiasm at this conference: only 20 per cent of delegates agreed that 'protection of the environment requires that even the lowest incomes should not be raised'; over 70 per cent rejected the proposition. As expected, it found most acceptance within PPR (31 per cent) and least among Communists (4 per cent).

The high level (72 per cent overall) of agreement about a guaranteed basic income was surprising (see Table 6.8), the endorsement of PSP and VGL members especially so; even 38 per cent of Communists were in favour of a policy which sits awkwardly with Marxist principles.

Finally, respondents were asked which political problem they ranked highest: the environment, unemployment, Third World poverty, democratization or something else. Generally, the environment came first, especially among PPR and VGL members (72 and

Table 6.8 Introduction of basic income (percentages)

	VGL	CPN	PPR	PSP	Total
Strongly in favour	25	12	45	21	27
In favour	52	27	46	50	44
No opinion	9	19	7	11	11
Opposed	12	32	1	15	13
Strongly opposed	3	11	1	4	4
Total	101	101	100	101	99

Note: N = 470.

65 per cent respectively) compared with CPN and PSP members (47 per cent and 53 per cent respectively). Communists mentioned unemployment most often (27 per cent), and it was they who attributed most importance to democratization (17 per cent). Nevertheless, 60 per cent of CPN members thought the environment of greater significance than unemployment, whereas 27 per cent thought the reverse. Even more PPR members (85 per cent) ranked the environment higher than unemployment; only very few ranked the problems the other way around (8 per cent).

Ideologically, the diversity among Green Left members is still relatively large, but it is already small compared with the 1970s when, especially between Communists, on the one hand, and Radicals, on the other, there were substantial differences. Such differences were reflected in the left–right self-placement of congress delegates: CPN members considered themselves more left-wing than PPR members, while PSP and VGL often took an ideological middle position. Under the surface, however, a kind of 'greening' of the 'reds' could be detected. There was, however, no corresponding 'reddening' of the 'green' Radicals; the Radical dislike of the old socialist demand of nationalization, for instance, remained fully in line with the traditional PPR stance. In general, these findings were confirmed by surveys held at the last conventions of PPR, PSP and CPN (and EVP) in 1991 (Lucardie *et al.* 1994).

CONCLUSION

In The Netherlands an exclusively Green party was unable to establish itself as a major political actor, despite auspicious conditions such as a permissive electoral system and a large reservoir of potential followers. The reason for this paradox lies in the fact that such favourable factors contributed to the foundations on which Green Left would later build. Thanks to the low electoral threshold of the Dutch political system, small left-wing parties like PSP, CPN and PPR were represented in parliament long before the appearance of Green parties elsewhere in Europe. Besides, PSP and PPR were, as New Left parties, natural allies for the emerging social movements in the 1970s. These movements in their turn contributed to the ideological convergence in the 1980s of PPR, PSP and – later – CPN.

In this way the first paradox – the failure of a Green party – was created by the resolution of another paradox – the *rapprochement* and eventual merger, under a green label, of three initially substantially different parties. This latter paradox, however, is not yet completely resolved. Green Left is still boxing with its historical shadows when it tries to reconcile environmental and social ideals. In the cross-pollination of the old party standpoints, however, classical socialist dogmas such as unlimited confidence in social engineering seem to have perished. Gradually, ecological articles of faith are gaining higher profiles.

Nevertheless, despite its increasingly strong ecological characteristics, Green Left is still a shallow Green party. Considering its origins and composition, development in a biocentric direction is hardly to be expected, since this would jeopardize its unity and hence its existence. In theory, then, there remains room in the political landscape of The Netherlands for a deep Green party. In practice, it has been demonstrated that such a party will not grow in the present Dutch electoral climate.

NOTES

1 The EVP, a small party drawn into the Green Left formation only in the final stage (Nieboer and Lucardie 1992), remains outside the scope of this chapter.

2 This survey was conducted by Dr W. van Schuur and Dr J. van der Knoop (Department of Sociology, University of Groningen) and Dr A.P.M. Lucardie and Dr G. Voerman (Documentation Centre on Dutch Political Parties, University of Groningen). Seven hundred and sixty questionnaires were distributed; 482 were completed and returned (62 per cent). Of these 482 respondents, 30 per cent were members of PPR, 23 per cent of PSP, 23 per cent of CPN, 20 per cent of VGL and 4 per cent were EVP members. One respondent did not answer the question about party membership. The EVP respondents are not

mentioned in the results of the survey because of their low number, but they are included in the total.

REFERENCES

Alber, J. (1989) 'Modernization, Cleavage Structures, and the Rise of Green Parties and Lists in Europe', in F. Müller-Rommel (ed.), *New Politics in Western Europe*, Boulder, Colo.: Westview, pp. 195–210.

Brinkman, M., Freriks, B. and Voerman, G. (1990) 'Klein links en de nieuwe sociale bewegingen', *Jaarboek 1989*, Groningen: Documentatie-centrum Nederlandse Politieke Partijen, pp. 163–188.

Bürklin, W. (1985) 'The German Greens: The Post-Industrial Non-Established and the Party System', *International Political Science Review* 6: 463–481.

Duyvendak, J.W., Van der Heijden, H.A., Koopmans, R. and Wijmans, L. (eds) (1992) *Tussen verbeelding en macht. 25 jaar nieuwe sociale bewegingen in Nederland*, Amsterdam: SUA.

Goul Anderson, J. (1990) 'Environmentalism, New Politics and Industrialism: Some Theoretical Perspectives', *Scandinavian Political Studies* 13: 101–118.

Kriesi, H. (1986) *Nieuwe sociale bewegingen: op zoek naar hun gemeenschappelijke noemer*, Amsterdam: University of Amsterdam.

Lucardie, A.P.M. (1980) *The New Left in the Netherlands (1960–1977): A Critical Study of New Political Ideas and Groups on the Left in the Netherlands with Comparative References to France and Germany*, Kingston, Ontario: Queen's University.

—— (1989) 'The Liturgy of the Logocrats. New Left Politics and New Middle Class Interests', paper presented to the ECPR, Paris, 10–15 April.

Lucardie, A.P.M., Van der Knoop, J., Van Schuur, W. and Voerman, G. (1994) 'Greening the Reds or Reddening the Greens? The Case of Green Left in The Netherlands', in W. Rüdig (ed.), *Green Politics Three*, Edinburgh: Edinburgh University Press.

Lucardie, A.P.M., Van Schuur, W. and Voerman, G. (1991) 'De oprichters van Groen Links. Voorlopig verslag van een enquête onder de leden van het congres van Groen Links op 24 november 1990', *Jaarboek 1990*, Groningen: Documentatiecentrum Nederlandse Politieke Partijen, pp. 167–185.

Meadows, D.H. *et al.* (1972) *The Limits to Growth*, London: Earth Island.

Nieboer, M. and Lucardie, A.P.M. (1992) '"Aanschuren tegen het CDA" of aansluiten bij klein links?', *Jaarboek 1991*, Groningen: Documentatie-centrum Nederlandse Politieke Partijen, pp. 149–167.

Parkin, S. (1989) *Green Parties: An International Guide*, London: Heretic.

Schennink, B., Bertrand, T. and Fun, H. (1982) *De 21 november demonstranten: wie zijn ze en wat willen ze?*, Nijmegen: Jan Mets.

Van der Loo, H., Snel, E. and Van Steenbergen, B. (1984) *Een wenkend perspektief: nieuwe sociale bewegingen en culturele veranderingen*, Amersfoort: De Horstink.

Van Deth, J.W. (1985) *Politieke waarden: een onderzoek naar de politieke waarde-orientaties in Nederland in de periode 1970 tot en met 1982*, Amsterdam: CT Press.
Voerman, G. (1990) 'Hoe CPN, PSP en PPR van kleur verschoten: van klein links naar Groen Links', *Namens* 5(2): 34–39.
—— (1991) 'A Drama in Three Acts: Communism and Social Democracy in The Netherlands since 1945', in M. Waller, S. Courtois and M. Lazar (eds), *Comrades and Brothers. Communism and Trade Unions in Europe*, London: Frank Cass, pp. 103–123.
—— (1992) 'The Netherlands' Green Paradoxes', *Capitalism, Nature, Socialism. A Journal of Socialist Ecology* 3(3): 19–27.
—— (1993) 'Premature Perestroika: The Dutch Communist Party and Gorbachev', in D. Bell (ed.), *Western European Communists and the Collapse of Communism*, Oxford: Berg, pp. 157–171.

Chapter 7

Sweden

The rise and fall of Miljöpartiet de gröna[1]

Martin Bennulf

Environmental problems were salient in most western countries during the late 1980s (Hofrichter and Reif 1990), and Sweden was no exception. Downs (1972), however, suggests that the 'heated' environmental debate is unlikely to continue because a process of satiation influences the attention-cycle of all political issues. But while the *intensity* of environmental concern may wax and wane, there are good reasons to suppose that ecology will continue as a politicized issue in most countries. The environment, like taxes and defence costs, will become an ingrained fixture of politics. Viewed this way, the green breakthrough of the 1980s will be permanent in the 1990s.

In Sweden, the connection between the saliency of the environmental issue and support for the Green Party (Miljöpartiet de gröna) is very clear. The proportion of citizens who regard the environmental issue as one of the most important has decreased from its late 1980s peak (Bennulf and Holmberg 1992), and the fortunes of the Green Party have fluctuated accordingly, the electoral breakthrough of 1988 being followed by failure in 1991.

In Miljöpartiet's first attempt at the polls in 1982, environmental concerns were not salient (the issue was mentioned by only 7 per cent of voters). Miljöpartiet faced an impossible task because the election campaign was almost exclusively focused on left–right issues, primarily the wage-earners' fund issue (Gilljam 1988). The story of its second attempt, in 1985, was much the same – low saliency of the environmental issue and low support for Miljöpartiet.

In 1988 the situation was very different. In the general election of that year (the 'environmental election'), the environmental issue was top of the political agenda. Indeed, never has a political issue so dominated an election campaign as the environmental issue did in 1988 (Esaiasson 1990). Miljöpartiet received 5.5 per cent of the vote and gained 20 seats in parliament, the first party in 70 years to break into a party system often, until recently, considered the most stable in the west (Affigne 1990; Bennulf 1990, 1994; Vedung 1989, 1991).

The Greens' success in 1988 was not as big a surprise as some suggested. The figures in Table 7.1 show that support for Miljöpartiet had grown substantially between the 1982 and 1985 elections. The poor result in 1985 notwithstanding, the Green Party was slowly and quietly gaining momentum. A larger proportion of voters had the Greens as their second choice in 1985 (4.5 per cent) than in 1982 (2.7 per cent).

The saliency of the environmental issue peaked in 1988 and has since decreased (see Figure 7.1). In 1991 only half as many citizens considered environmental problems an important issue as in 1988. Miljöpartiet not only failed to retain its parliamentary status, but suffered a decline in the number of second preferences it attracted (see Table 7.1).

I shall return to the question of the 1991 failure and the future prospects of the Green Party towards the end of this chapter, but first let us consider the party's historical development, the characteristics of its voters and whether a cross-cutting green cleavage exists in Swedish politics.

THE GREEN PARTY

Miljöpartiet de gröna is not an entirely new actor on the Swedish political scene. The catalyst for its foundation in 1981 was the

Table 7.1 Electoral support for the Green Party in Sweden, 1982–1991 (percentages)

	1982	1985	1988	1991
Vote share in parliamentary elections	1.6	1.5	5.5	3.4
Proportion of eligible voters with the Green Party as first preference ('best party')	2.6	1.8	5.4	3.3
Proportion of eligible voters with the Green Party as second preference ('second best party')	2.7	4.5	10.8	4.0
Proportion of eligible voters with the Green Party as first or second preference	5.3	6.3	16.1	7.3

Note: Based on data from the Swedish Election Studies 1982–1991, Gilljam and Holmberg (1993).

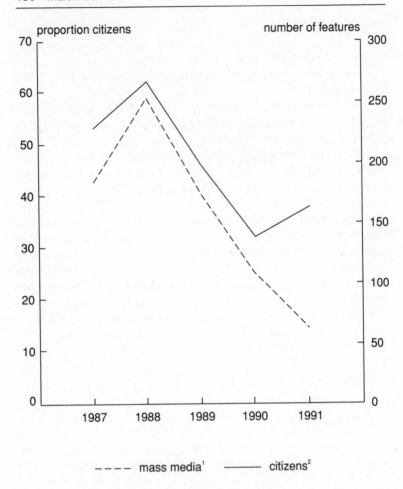

Figure 7.1 The saliency of the environmental issue in Sweden, 1987–1991

Notes: 1. The number of features on the environment in Rapport (TV news programme).

2. The proportion of citizens who state that the environment issue is an important societal problem (percentages).

The figure is taken from Bennulf and Holmberg (1992).

Figures for citizens are based on the SOM studies. The media data are from the Election Studies day-by-day coding of the TV news programme.

outcome of the 1980 referendum on nuclear power. At that referendum, the moderate, compromise option outpolled the option most antagonistic to nuclear power (Holmberg and Asp 1984). Naturally, the leaders of the anti-nuclear forces – 'The People's Campaign Against Nuclear Power' – were disappointed, but disappointment was mixed with optimism because the anti-nuclear alternative had attracted almost 40 per cent of votes. Surely, some of the leaders of the People's Campaign thought, with such a large base of potential supporters the ground must be fertile for a new political party.[2]

The roots of Miljöpartiet can also be traced in earlier Swedish social movements and environmental organizations. So-called 'new social movements' were formed in the late 1960s and early 1970s, often with foreign groups as models. Many of the earliest were dedicated to the protection of the environment: movements were mobilized around the protection of a river, or directed against the building of a motorway through previously untouched countryside, or as a protest against heavy traffic in inner cities. Many such groups were temporary; when the problem was solved, the group was often dissolved. However, some groups and organizations formed then exist even today (Bennulf 1993).

Environmentalism has a long tradition in Sweden. Even prior to the publication of Rachel Carson's *Silent Spring* in 1962, the Swedish feminist Elin Wägner showed great concern for the environment, and in her 1941 book *Alarm Clock* warned against the exploitation and poisoning of nature. Another landmark book in the history of environmentalism, the Club of Rome report, *The Limits to Growth* (Meadows *et al.* 1972), also had a forerunner in Sweden, Professor Georg Borgström having published articles and books with the same message in the 1950s and 1960s (cf. Lundqvist 1980; Jamison *et al.* 1990). If, such pioneers apart, the Swedish environmental movement can be regarded as a slow starter, at the national and international level Sweden was involved at an early stage in protecting the environment; the Swedish government was, for instance, one of the major actors behind the UN's 1972 Stockholm conference on the global environment.

As the name Miljöpartiet (the Environmental Party) indicates, the party is not only an anti-nuclear party. It has a much broader scope, both as regards ideology and the issues the party addresses. Ecological balance, local self-rule, decentralization, small-scale production, reduced or no economic growth and quality of life are some of the party's most important ideological catchwords. In terms of concrete issues, Miljöpartiet pushes for tougher measures on all kinds of environmental problems. Such is the party's profile and original *raison d'être* in Swedish politics, but the party is also highly active on many non-environmental issues. For example, the Greens are in favour of cutting defence costs, against Sweden joining the European Community, against wage-earner funds, in favour of more equal income distribution and against state-owned businesses. As the examples indicate, the Green Party tends to straddle the left–right divide with some positions to the left and some to the right.

The semi-official position among Green leaders is that the left–right dimension has been surpassed and is no longer relevant in Swedish politics. However, when pressed, Green Party representatives tend to acknowledge that the party is located in the middle or slightly to the left. Green voters tend, on average, to locate themselves slightly to the left. In a study of Swedish members of parliament, including the newly elected Green members, more members placed the Greens to the left than to the right, although a majority placed the party in the middle (Gilljam and Holmberg 1990).

The environment and a rather broadly defined ecological ideology apart, another prominent feature of the Green Party's profile is its opposition to the professionalization of politics. The Greens believe in amateur politicians who do not lose touch with everyday life. They try to practise what they preach through the principle of rotation and division of office-holding; Green office-holders are supposed to hold only one position of power at a time and they are expected not to retain it for more than two parliamentary terms. When it comes to leadership, the Greens think modern politics is too much centred on party leaders. Hence the Green Party has no leader, but instead has two spokespersons – always one man and one woman – who have been rotated at more or less regular intervals (Bennulf 1990; Lundgren 1991).

GREEN VOTERS

As one might expect of a new party, in the 1988 and 1991 parliamentary elections the Green Party received its strongest support among voters who are traditionally the most volatile – young voters, people in big cities, professionals and people with occupations in the public sector (mostly in health care and education). The party was least successful among the oldest voters and among farmers, industrial workers and people with little education. Contrary to pre-election expectations, the Greens did not attract particularly strong support from women or from first-time voters (see Table 7.2).

Two points concerning the results are especially noteworthy. First, the Green following has a distinctly middle-class or even upper-middle-class flavour. This does not mean that Green workers are yuppies: most yuppies do not work in health care or in the public sector. Rather, the Green vote is concentrated among the new middle class of public sector, white-collar, well-educated, city-dwellers (cf. Poguntke 1993). Second, the Green Party cannot take its voters for granted. Green voters tend to be drawn from those sections of the population who have proven to have a high propensity to switch parties. Thus, the probability is rather high that Green support will be fairly unstable in forthcoming elections. This prediction is further strengthened by the fact that Green voters have the lowest degree of party identification among Swedish voters: in the elections of 1988 and 1991 only about 30 per cent of Green Party supporters had any form of identification (strong or weak) with their party, compared with 69 per cent of Social Democratic and 58 per cent of Conservative voters (Gilljam and Holmberg 1990, 1993). The electoral support for Miljöpartiet was somewhat different in 1991 than 1988; young first-time voters, students and women appeared as strong bases of support much more clearly than previously.

Traditional socio-economic variables are essential when it comes to characterizing a party's voters, but they go only so far. Looking at lifestyles and what people do when they are not working may, especially with the relative increase in leisure time, be as important for political behaviour as work experiences have been. In their spare time, Green voters tend to be somewhat more active than other people in most leisure activities (Bennulf and Holmberg 1990). They also tend to be relatively more involved in cultural activities (playing musical instruments, reading books, going to museums), and less engaged than others in activities such as watching videos, reading weekly magazines and gambling on horses, football pools or the stock market. Members of environmental organizations show very much the same pattern of activities as Green Party sympathizers (Bennulf 1993).

To characterize the differences in lifestyles between Green and

Table 7.2 Socio-economic characteristics of Green Party (mp) voters 1988 and 1991, and proportion of voters in different groups who voted for the Green Party (percentages)

Socio-economic group	Proportion mp Votes 1988	1991	Difference 1991 – 1988
Gender			
Men	6	2	−4
Women	6	5	−1
Age			
18–21 (first-time voters)	4	7	+3
21–30	7	6	−1
31–40	10	4	−6
41–50	6	3	−3
51–60	6	3	−3
61–70	2	4	+2
71–80	1	0	−1
Occupation			
Workers in manufacturing	3	1	−2
Workers in service sector	6	4	−2
Lower white collar	5	3	−2
Middle white collar	7	5	−2
Professionals/managers	8	5	−3
Small entrepreneurs	6	1	−5
Farmers	2	4	+2
Students	8	11	+3
Type of work			
Farming, fishing, forestry	3	5	+2
Manufacturing	4	2	−2
Trade, transport	5	2	−3
Health care, education	11	6	−5
Public and private administration	5	3	−2
Occupational sector			
Public	8	6	−2
Private	5	3	−2
Education			
Low	4	2	−2
Middle	5	3	−2
High	10	7	−3
Place of residence			
Countryside	8	4	−4
Smaller built-up area	6	4	−2
City or larger built-up area	4	3	−1
Stockholm, Göteborg or Malmö	10	6	−4
Union membership			
LO (workers)	5	3	−2
TCO (white-collar)	7	5	−2
SACO (university graduates)	12	10	−2
Farmer or employers' organization	4	4	0
Non-members	4	2	−2

Note: Based on data from the 1988 and 1991 Election Studies. For classification principles, see Gilljam *et al.* (1991).

other voters, Inglehart's concepts of post-materialism and materialism seem appropriate; the spare-time activities of Green voters reflect more of a post-materialistic value orientation than a materialist one. The correlations are not impressive (around 0.10), but high scores for cultural activities are associated with post-materialistic attitudes while high scores for video-watching, gambling and so on are related to materialist views (Bennulf and Holmberg 1990; Inglehart 1990; Reimer 1989; Bennulf 1994). Further evidence of the post-materialism of Green voters is given in Table 7.3, which shows the proportion of post-materialists and materialists, based on Inglehart's four-item scale, among voters for each party in 1988 and 1991.

The association between the post-materialism/materialism scale and party choice is modest; comparable correlations for various left–right scales are much higher (Bennulf and Holmberg 1990). But the Green Party and the Left Party stand apart as the only parties whose voters comprise more post-materialists than materialists: among Green voters in 1988, 33 per cent were post-materialists and 22 per cent materialists. In 1991, the distinctiveness of the Greens was even more marked: 41 per cent of Greens expressed post-materialist preferences and only 7 per cent materialist ones. In comparison, the new party, New Democracy, had a clear materialistic voter profile.

Socio-economic variables, different lifestyles and different value orientations each contribute to the characterization of Green voters, albeit in a rather limited way. Relevant correlations and differences are fairly small. If we really want to find what distinguishes Green voters from others we have to look at issue positions and questions of distrust in government and politicians. Issue positions are especially important since we know that policy opinions are strongly connected with party choice among Swedish voters and have tended to become more so in recent elections (Gilljam and Holmberg 1990). Most of the correlations are quite high, much higher than with socio-economic background, lifestyles and value orientations.

As far as Green voters are concerned, the results reveal a very clear and systematic pattern. On left–right issues, Green Party voters tend to have opinions to the middle or slightly to the left of the spectrum. The slight leftward tilt among Green voters is also noticeable in their second party preferences. In 1988, almost half (48 per cent) of those who named Miljöpartiet as their first

Table 7.3 Party voted for in the 1988 and 1991 elections and Inglehartian value types (percentages)

Party choice	1988 Value type					1991 Value type				
	Pm[1]	Mixed	Mat[2]	Total	Diff.: pm–mat[3]	Pm	Mixed	Mat	Total	Diff.: pm–mat
Left Party (v)	37	42	21	100	+16	32	48	20	100	+12
Social Democracy (s)	16	56	28	100	–12	15	56	29	100	–14
Centre Party (c)	13	54	33	100	–20	12	49	30	100	–18
Liberals (fp)	18	60	22	100	–4	16	63	21	100	–5
Conservatives (m)	11	68	21	100	–10	13	57	30	100	–17
Christian Democrats (kds)	8	51	38	100	–36	11	51	38	100	–25
Green Party (mp)	33	45	22	100	+11	41	52	7	100	+34
New Democracy (nyd)	–	–	–	–	–	10	63	27	100	–17
Total	17	57	26	100	–9	16	56	28	100	–12

Notes: Based on data from the 1988 and 1991 Election Studies' pre-election surveys. The interview questions used are Inglehart's four-item battery, see Inglehart (1990).

1 Pm = post-materialist.
2 Mat = materialist.
3 Diff. pm–mat = percentage of post-materialists minus percentage of materialists.

preference gave a leftish party as their second preference compared with 36 per cent who named a non-socialist party. This difference was even more visible at the 1991 election: 55 per cent of Miljöpartiet had a socialist party as second preference and 37 per cent a non-socialist one. No Miljöpartiet sympathizer surveyed gave New Democracy as second preference (Gilljam and Holmberg 1990, 1993; Bennulf 1994). On environmental issues the pattern was totally different: Green voters were no longer middle-of-the-roaders but had attitudes towards the extreme green end of the continuum on all the environmental issues considered.

Green attitudes, however, do not tell the whole story of why Green voters supported Miljöpartiet in 1988. Distrust towards established parties and politicians also played a role, Green voters tending to be more distrustful of politicians than the average citizen. With the help of multivariate analyses it has been shown that political distrust had an effect on the Green vote independent of the effect of environmental attitudes, but it was relatively modest compared to that of ecological opinions (Bennulf 1990). The importance of this analysis is twofold. First, it shows that the Green vote of 1988 contained a measure of protest; it was not just a green vote. Second, the protest component was clearly only secondary; support for the Green Party was motivated more by environmental concerns than by distrust of established politicians. The clear implication of this is that Miljöpartiet had a green mandate. To label it just a protest party is clearly wrong.

Nor can Miljöpartiet's losses in 1991 simply be attributed to competition from a newer protest party, the right-wing populist party, Ny Demokrati (New Democracy). Only about one-tenth of the votes Miljöpartiet lost between 1988 and 1991 went in that direction (Gilljam and Holmberg 1993). Looking forward, Miljöpartiet is the only party apart from the Left Party which officially opposes Swedish membership of the European Community, a position shared by a majority of Swedish citizens (Gilljam and Holmberg 1993). Popular opposition to Sweden's joining the EC might therefore prove beneficial to Miljöpartiet, just as it was for the Centre Party in the 1993 Norwegian parliamentary election.

One dilemma for Miljöpartiet, and one which it shares with other Green parties, is the tension between the party leadership and the grass roots of the party. In order to conduct a modern national election campaign, a party needs national guidelines, but the national direction or co-ordination of campaigns is a potential source of conflict between the central and local levels of the party, particularly because the desire of local activists to conduct the campaign in their own way is entirely consistent with the party's principles.

If Miljöpartiet has so far had difficulty gaining sufficient support to secure representation at national level, it has been more successful at subnational levels, mainly due to regional variations in support for the party and because there is no formal threshold obstructing representation on local councils. Miljöpartiet gained several council seats at its first attempt in 1982, and in 1985, although it failed to improve its vote in the election for the national parliament, the party increased its tally of local seats. Since the 1988 election, Miljöpartiet has been represented on most local councils. In some places, its representatives are in a pivotal position, and sometimes they have even been included in local coalition governments. In most cases Miljöpartiet has found its political partners towards the left of the party system, but there are also cases of co-operation with the non-socialist parties.

THE GREEN DIMENSION IN SWEDISH POLITICS

Since 1982, respondents in Swedish election surveys have been asked to state the issues which they consider to be assets and burdens for the various political parties. Before Miljöpartiet's success in 1988, voters did not see environmental issues as a major asset for parties. Historically, the Centre Party and the Left Party had a somewhat positive profile on environmental issues; Social Democrats, Liberals and Conservatives, on the other hand, were not perceived as 'green' (Gilljam and Holmberg 1990, 1993). Hence there was some discussion in 1988–1991 of the possibility of creating in the Riksdag a green bloc consisting of the Green Party, the Centre Party and the Left Party, and there is some empirical evidence of a green coalition pattern in legislative behaviour (Gaiter 1991). However, the pattern is not valid for all issue areas.

On left–right issues, attitudes of Swedish voters are highly constrained. Opinions on questions about government influence over private business, income distribution and social justice tend to be correlated with one another in ways one would expect on logical or ideological grounds (Granberg and Holmberg 1988); the level of inter-item correlation is sufficiently high to make it reasonable to talk about the existence of an ideological left–right dimension among Swedish voters.

The advent of a new political cleavage in western countries has been widely proclaimed (for example, by Inglehart 1990; Müller-Rommel 1989). The reasons and possible consequences have been much discussed (Hildebrandt and Dalton 1978; Dalton 1988; Jahn 1993). The burning question for researchers is whether there really exists a new cleavage (or perhaps two new cleavages) in western party systems. Are we dealing with a new cleavage based on changing values ('post-materialism') or another phenomenon more broadly or more narrowly defined? It is not clear that any such generalizations apply to Sweden, which, together with Finland, is sometimes considered a deviant case in the 'new politics' debate (Gundelach 1992).

How then has the 'new' cleavage been defined and measured by Swedish political scientists? First it is necessary to consider Inglehart's post-materialism/materialism scale. As was shown in Table 7.3 (p. 136), the pattern of correlation between party support and value orientation is the expected one but it is too modest to be taken as conclusive evidence of the existence of a new cleavage (Bennulf 1994). Further, it can be shown by the use of panel analyses that the individual-level stability of value orientation over a three-year period (1988–1991) is low ($r = 0.40$), whereas the stability of orientations towards most political issues is more stable (r between 0.40 and 0.72), and self-placement on a left–right scale is very stable ($r = 0.72$). Thus it appears that in Sweden deep-rooted values are not measured by the value scale (Bennulf 1994).

Two other strategies have been tried to measure a more narrowly defined green dimension relating to the conflict between ecology and growth. One strategy has been to make respondents place parties and themselves on a scale of 'green-ness'. The result appears to be a nice ordering of Swedish political parties (Bennulf and Holmberg 1990), but, beneath the surface, there is much confusion: respondents commonly place their own party closer than in fact it is towards the ecology end of the spectrum, a 'mistake' actually more pronounced among members of parliament than among voters. Thus the attribution of 'green-ness' to a party is difficult to separate from a simply positive general attitude towards the party (Gilljam and Holmberg 1990; Bennulf 1994).

The second strategy in the search for a green dimension is to analyse attitudes to survey questions on environmental issues. How do orientations on these matters correlate with one another and with other matters, such as left–right issues? Westholm (1990), using factor analysis, has shown that among élite groups in Sweden, attitudes on environmental issues are best viewed as part of the left–right dimension. Left and environmentalist opinions tend to go together. In the Swedish Riksdag Study of 1988, the correlation between the members' self-placement on a left–right scale and on an environmental scale was 0.44 (Pearson's r). Available data suggest a similar situation among the electorate (Bennulf and Holmberg 1990; Bennulf 1994). All the evidence points in the same direction: a coherent green dimension structuring attitudes on different kinds of environmental issues does not seem to exist in the minds of the Swedish public.

THE 1991 FAILURE AND AFTER

For a Green party – if no position on the left–right spectrum is 'free' – the best strategy is to be perceived as having no position (or a position towards the middle) on the left–right dimension. In the 1991 election, however, Miljöpartiet's proclamation that it would not support the Conservative Party leader, Carl Bildt, if he were to be appointed Prime Minister led voters to perceive Miljöpartiet as a party of the left, and so voters with right-of-centre attitudes did not support it in 1991 to the same extent as they had in 1988.

Table 7.4 Self-placement of Green Party sympathizers on left–right spectrum, 1986–1991 (percentages)

Left–right position	1986	1987	1988	1989	1990	1991
Far to the left	10	3	4	4	6	16
Somewhat to the left	18	18	36	21	16	35
Neither left/nor right	59	56	46	54	54	41
Somewhat to the right	13	18	12	20	24	8
Far to the right	0	5	2	1	0	0
Total	100	100	100	100	100	100
Number of respondents	77	121	119	99	67	49
Difference: left–right (Overweight left)	+15	–2	+26	+4	–2	+43

Note: Data are from the SOM studies, a mail questionnaire sent to a representative sample of 2,500 Swedish citizens every autumn, see Holmberg and Weibull (1992).

Miljöpartiet's proclamation did not mark a change in policy; its policy has always been to support the prospective government, socialist or non-socialist, which has the best environmental programme, but, according to Miljöpartiet spokesperson Birger Schlaug, that has in practice always ruled out the Conservatives. What was new in 1991 was that this was clearly reported in the mass media.

The transformation of Miljöpartiet into a left-wing party in the eyes of the public is evident in the data presented in Table 7.4, which shows the self-placement of Miljöpartiet sympathizers on a five-point left–right scale for the years 1986 to 1991. Most Green Party sympathizers (41 to 59 per cent) place themselves at the mid-point of the left–right dimension (neither left nor right). However, on four occasions, there have been more Greens placing themselves to the left than to the right; this is most clearly the case in 1991, with 51 per cent to the left and only 8 per cent to the right.

Another, probably important, explanation for the party's problems in 1991 was the lack of a popular party leader, a factor avidly discussed in political debate. Support for this thesis can be found in election survey data (Gilljam and Holmberg 1993). Respondents in the 1991 survey also expressed disappointment with Miljöpartiet's parliamentary record and stated that, knowing from opinion polls that the Green Party would not be able to repeat its 1988 success of crossing the 4 per cent threshold to gain representation in the Riksdag, they did not want to waste their votes. The loss of these tactical votes was compensated by the gaining of others: some people did not vote for their preferred party purely and simply in order to ensure Miljöpartiet's parliamentary survival (Gilljam and Holmberg 1993).

Although their saliency has declined markedly since the 1988 peak, environmental issues have not completely vanished from public debate and are not likely to do so. Environmental problems can be seen as a valence issue (Stokes 1963): almost everybody wants a better environment. Therefore, given the seriousness of the threat to nature, environmental matters will remain among the most important – and most debated – societal problems, but their position of primacy will be challenged by other issue areas such as economic policy and foreign policy (Bennulf 1994).

From the standpoint of environmental concerns, this is good news. Ecological issues will be part of politics in the future. It is not, however, certain that environmental concerns will ensure the long-term survival of the Green Party. When environmental issues become permanent ingredients of politics, the chances increase that the old established parties move in, adjust their policies and capitalize on the subject. It might seem a paradox, but if the Greens are too successful in promoting and politicizing environmental issues, they may find themselves out-competed on their own turf by the other parties. Increased attention to environmental issues means higher electoral stakes for everybody, forcing all parties to articulate their own green claim. At the same time, the Green Party would still do best to maintain its ecological profile; the left-wing profile of Miljöpartiet in the 1991 election proved disastrous.

The long-term survival of the Swedish Greens seems threatened and, in Sweden, it is a matter of much speculation. There are four dimensions to the problem. First, one obvious problem for any small party is the number of parties. The achievement of parliamentary status by New Democracy and the Christian Democrats in 1991, and the formation of the new Women's Party, have substantially sharpened the competition for the 4 per cent needed to surmount the parliamentary threshold.

Second, the Green Party has had its newcomer's honeymoon with the public. It is not likely that future elections will turn, as the 1988 election did, almost exclusively on environmental issues. Almost certainly, some of the perennial left–right issues of Swedish politics (economy, taxes, income distribution) will remain in focus and such a focus will clearly be disadvantageous to the Greens. Most voters – including Green Party voters – appreciate the party's environmental policies but know little of or dislike the party's economic policies. This may be a problem for Miljöpartiet since the saliency of environmental issues is even lower than before: data from the 1992 SOM survey (cf. Figure 7.1, p. 130) point to a sharp decline, the environment being mentioned as an important societal problem by only 19 per cent of the Swedish people compared to 62 per cent in 1988.

Third, the problem is compounded by the fact that many Green voters belong to groups known to be among the most volatile in the Swedish electorate, and results from election surveys show that few have developed any sense of identification with the Green Party. Consequently, party loyalty is not an asset upon which the Greens can draw.

Fourth, the Greens have to face many different issue-publics on environmental matters. A coherent green dimension structuring people's opinions on environmental issues is to a large extent an élite phenomenon, and even here it is empirically difficult to distinguish between the green and the left–right dimensions. Although environmental issues have made what is likely to be a permanent breakthrough in Swedish politics, it is questionable whether a distinct ecological dimension to political choice exists. The Green Party made a breakthrough in the election of 1988 but failed to capitalize upon it in 1991. Even though a poll in December 1993 indicated that Miljöpartiet was winning back support, it will be difficult to regain the lost votes in the 1994 election.

NOTES

1 The data for this chapter were collected by the Swedish National Election Studies Programme, Department of Political Science, University of Göteborg (project leaders Mikael Gilljam and Sören Holmberg). The main results from the 1988 and 1991 voter surveys are reported in Gilljam *et al.* (1991) and Gilljam and Holmberg (1993). Data from the SOM (Society Media Opinion) surveys from the University of Göteborg are also analysed; see Holmberg and Weibull (1992). The Election Studies Programme surveys with members of the Riksdag are presented by Esaiasson and Holmberg (1993). I would like to thank Sören Holmberg, Chris Rootes and Anders Widfeldt for comments on previous versions of this chapter.
2 On the founding of Miljöpartiet, see Vedung (1989, 1991); Bennulf (1990).

REFERENCES

Affigne, A. (1990) 'Environmental Crises, Green Party Power: Chernobyl and the Swedish Greens', in W. Rüdig (ed.), *Green Politics One*, Edinburgh: Edinburgh University Press, pp. 115–152.

Bennulf, M. (1990) *Grönt ljus. Väljarna och miljöpartiets valframgång 1988*, Göteborg: University of Göteborg: Department of Political Science.

—— (1993) 'Einstellung bei Mitgliedern von Umweltorganisationen: Veränderung und Stabilität in "Neuen Europa" am Beispiel Schwedens', *Forschungsjournal Neue Soziale Bewegungen* 4: 33–41.

—— (1994) 'Miljöopinion i Sverige', University of Göteborg: Department of Political Science (manuscript).

Bennulf, M. and Holmberg, S. (1990) 'The Green Breakthrough in Sweden', *Scandinavian Political Studies* 13: 165–184.

—— (1992) 'Förbättras eller försämras miljön i Sverige?', in S. Holmberg and L. Weibull (eds), *Trendbrott?*, SOM-rapport 8, Göteborg: University of Göteborg: Department of Political Science.

Dalton, R. (1988) *Citizen Politics in Western Democracies*, Chatham, NJ: Chatham House.

Downs, A. (1972) 'Up and Down with Ecology – The "Issue Attention-Cycle"', *Public Interest* 28: 38–50.

Esaiasson, P. (1990) *Svenska valkampanjer 1866–1988. Studier i opinions-bildningens historia*, Stockholm: Allmänna förlaget.

Esaiasson, P. and Holmberg, S. (1993) 'Parliamentarians. Members of Parliament and Representative Democracy in Sweden', Göteborg: University of Göteborg: Department of Political Science (manuscript).

Gaiter, P. (1991) *The Swedish Green Party. Responses to the Parliamentary Challenge 1988–1990*, Stockholm: International Studies.

Gilljam, M. (1988) *Svenska folket och löntagarfonderna*, Lund: Student-litteratur.

Gilljam, M. and Holmberg, S. (1990) *Rött Blått Grönt. En bok om 1988 års riksdagsval*, Stockholm: Bonniers.

—— (1993) *Väljarna inför 90-talet*, Stockholm: Norstedts.

Gilljam, M., Holmberg, S. and Bennulf, M. (1991) *Valundersökning 1988. Teknisk rapport*, Stockholm: SCB.

Granberg, D. and Holmberg, S. (1988) *The Political System Matters. Social Psychology and Voting Behavior in Sweden and the United States*, Cambridge: Cambridge University Press.

Gundelach, P. (1992) 'Recent Value Changes in Western Europe', *Futures* 24: 301–319.

Hildebrandt, K. and Dalton, R.J. (1978) 'The New Politics: Political Change or Sunshine Politics?', in M. Kaase and K. von Beyme (eds), *German Political Studies*, vol. 5, Beverly Hills, Calif.: Sage.

Hofrichter, J. and Reif, K. (1990) 'Evolution of Environmental Attitudes in Western Europe', *Scandinavian Political Studies* 13: 119–146.

Holmberg, S. and Asp, K. (1984) *Kampen om kärnkraften. En bok om väljare, massmedier och folkomröstningen 1980*, Stockholm: Liber.

Holmberg, S. and Weibull, L. (eds) (1992) *Trendbrott?*, SOM-rapport 8, Göteborg: University of Göteborg: Department of Political Science.

Inglehart, R. (1990) *Culture Shift in Advanced Industrial Society*, Princeton, NJ: Princeton University Press.

Jahn, D. (1993) 'The Rise and Decline of New Politics and the Greens in Sweden and Germany', *European Journal of Political Research* 24: 177–194.

Jamison, A., Eyerman, R. and Cramer, J. (1990) *The Making of the New Environmental Consciousness. A Comparative Study of the Environmental Movements in Sweden, Denmark and the Netherlands*, Edinburgh: Edinburgh University Press.

Lundgren, Å. (1991) 'Miljöpartiet – en alternative partiorganisation?', *Statsvetenskaplig tidskrift* 94: 55–76.

Lundqvist, L.J. (1980) *The Hare and the Tortoise. Clean Air Policies in the United States and Sweden*, Ann Arbor, Mich.: Michigan University Press.

Meadows, D.H. *et al.* (1972) *The Limits to Growth*, London: Earth Island.

Müller-Rommel, F. (1985) 'The Greens in Western Europe: Similar But Different', *International Political Science Review* 6: 483–499.

—— (ed.) (1989) *New Politics in Western Europe. The Rise and Success of Green Parties and Alternative Lists*, Boulder, Colo.: Westview.

Poguntke, T. (1993) *Alternative Politics. The German Green Party*, Edinburgh: Edinburgh University Press.

Reimer, B. (1989) 'Postmodern Structures of Feeling. Values and Life Styles in the Postmodern Age', in J.R. Gibbins (ed.), *Contemporary Political Culture*, London: Sage.

Stokes, D.E. (1963) 'Spatial Models of Party Competition', in A. Campbell, P.E. Converse, W.E. Miller and D.E. Stokes (eds), *Elections and the Political Order*, New York: John Wiley & Son.

Vedung, E. (1989) 'Sweden: The "Miljöpartiet de gröna"', in F. Müller-Rommel (ed.), *New Politics in Western Europe. The Rise and Success of Green Parties and Alternative Lists*, Boulder, Colo.: Westview.

—— (1991) 'Miljöpartiet, nedfrysningsteorin och den järnhårda oligarkilagen', in B. Gustafsson (ed.), *Människa, Miljö, Samhälle: Ett antal uppsatser författade av forskare inom samhällsvetenskapliga fakulteten och utgivna i anslutning till fakultetens jubileumsår 1989–1990*, Uppsala: Uppsala University, Samhällsvetenskapliga fakulteten, pp. 165–219.

Wägner, E. (1941) *Väckarklocka*, Stockholm: Bonniers.

Westholm, A. (1990) 'Maktéliten', *SOU*: 44, Stockholm: Allmänna förlaget.

Chapter 8

Switzerland

Greens in a confederal polity

Clive H. Church

Thus far the history of the Swiss Green Party (GPS) has belied assessments of it as an unpromising deviation from the New Politics model of ecological politics (Church 1992a; Poguntke 1989: 189). However, this does not mean that it has been able to carve out an unchallenged position for itself in Swiss politics. Because the Swiss political system charges a much higher price for consolidation than it does for entry, the GPS has experienced difficulties in five key areas:

- competition with other mainstream parties;
- its distance from the environmental social movement;
- its limited influence on the political agenda;
- its reticent use of the instruments of direct democracy;
- its vulnerability on the issue of Europe. (Its inability to reshape cleavage lines over Europe has raised new questions about the party's internal balance, strategy and unity.)

If it is still true that 'the party is here to stay' (Steiner 1991: 62), it is clearly the case that the Swiss system of political competition has done more to change the GPS than the latter has done to change the system. Ecology has not emerged as the decisive cleavage some expected, and while the Swiss Greens have successfully run the first laps of their competitive race, they have yet to cross the finishing line.

The fact that the party now faces questions about its future direction should not obscure its achievements. The rise of the GPS has been analysed in detail elsewhere (Laver and Schofield 1990: 242; Church 1991; Ladner 1989; Walter 1990), but it is worth stressing a few facts here. The history of environmentalism in Switzerland long predates the emergence of specifically ecological parties. As a result there has been a good deal of environmental legislative activity, both locally and nationally. This has involved a large number of *votations*,[1] some of which have written environmental protection into both the federal constitution and the statute book.

This partly reflects the environmental pressures from which Switzerland suffers, both those generated locally like the forest crisis, and those originating at a distance such as the impact of Chernobyl. During the 1970s and early 1980s reaction to these pressures involved a wide variety of parties, usually cantonally based, and often reflecting different attitudes to politics. However, attempts to turn these groups into a German-style 'rainbow' party failed because of both the variety of parties concerned and the overriding preoccupation of leading Greens with ecological issues.

Out of this long tradition of concern and activity came early and significant achievements. In 1979, the Vaudois Party was one of the first to achieve national parliamentary representation. Then, following the development of more co-ordination between groups and the creation of a fully fledged party in 1986, the GPS made major gains in the national elections of 1987. This meant that it became the major vehicle for political ecology, forcing rival movements first into ineffective competition and ultimately into merger. Environmental legislation continued to grow, as did the electoral strength of the party.

The GPS became the fifth largest party, first cantonally and then nationally, following the 1991 general elections (Church 1992c). By the summer of 1991 it held 154 seats in cantonal parliaments, a gain of 35 since 1987. Nationally, it won 14 seats in October 1991, with 6.2 per cent of the popular vote. Of the 16 cantons which it contested, its highest score was 11 per cent, in Basel Landschaft. The electoral base continued to hold up well into 1993. All this was quite striking, given the gains then made by the populist far right.

By then the party had a successful, flexible organization, a developed programme and representation at various levels of Swiss politics and government. It saw itself as having developed a coherent posture without having sacrificed its independence. Equally, it saw itself as the political voice of the many environmental lobbies which continued to be very active in Switzerland (GPS 1991c). The country had become noted for its strong stand on environmental issues, both domestically and internationally.

POLITICAL COMPETITION

Clearly the GPS of the early 1990s had not established a monopoly of environmentalism. Other parties, small and large, continued to make use of environmental themes. Moreover, even though it had absorbed the old Grüne Bündnis (GBS), the GPS was still quite distinct from both the many organized lobbies and the many activist social movements in the field. This tended to limit its influence on the political agenda and process.

Competition from established parties was, at first, limited. While the GPS was pursuing its upward course, potential rivals on the far left found it very difficult to compete. Thus the old front runner, the Progressive Organizations (POCH), evaporated, giving way to a new Alternative Green alliance which itself had difficulties developing a coherent strategy. Although from the late 1960s POCH had been the most dynamic New Left force in Swiss politics, it was a protean body with a chequered history. While it won two seats at the 1987 general election, its members and supporters were increasingly turning to environmental issues as they did in Basel and Bern, where they merged with the old Democratic Alternative wing of the GPS. Retaining a meaningful cantonal presence only in Basel Stadt, the party became almost wholly a parliamentary one. Even in Basel its MPs sought to move towards the Social Democrats (SPS) or the Greens (APS 1989, 1990). Doubts as to whether the party would survive until 1991 proved well founded. Although a new left-wing umbrella of a very flimsy kind, Die Andere Schweiz (DACH), did emerge for the general elections, this made much less impact, even though it stood with Alternative Greens in Fribourg and Zug. This was, in turn, a reflection of the fact that the Alternative Green movement had far more problems than academic critics were aware.

The increasing interest in green politics on the Swiss far left had led, in 1987, to the formation of a loose federation, the Grüne Bündnis, to fight the elections that year. This was led by radical Greens from Luzern although the strongest of its 10 member parties was that in Zug. Cantonally there were other member parties in Basel Landschaft, Bern, Fribourg, Graubunden, Schaffhausen, St Gallen and Vaud, together with three local parties in Fribourg and Zurich.

Although it won two seats in 1987, held a symposium in Luzern in 1988 and set up a mail-box office, the GBS had considerable difficulty in consolidating its position (Vonmoos 1990). Sympathizers in Aargau that year preferred to join the GPS and the member parties were divided, when they met on 28 January 1989, between those who wanted to develop a separate left/green force and those who wanted to co-ordinate activities with the GPS. The GBS also rejected the idea of a comprehensive programme, preferring to concentrate on case by case actions. With other parties seeking observer status on the GPS as part of a dual-track strategy, the problems of the GBS intensified. So, when they met again, in March 1990, they opted for fusion with the GPS, sketching out their view of what the new, combined party should look like. This included making allowances for minority positions on all policy matters and stressing women's rights, social issues and anti-militarism more than the GPS did.

The GPS view had always been that it was perfectly willing to collaborate (GPS 1989b). However, while it did not seek to dictate to newcomers, there had to be agreement on policy and single membership and positions. Given the very different demands of the GBS, the GPS decided in 1990 that the basis for a merger did not exist, and that other forms of collaboration would have to be sought. In the event another Alternative national MP joined the GPS parliamentary group. Thomas Baerlocher of the by then isolated Basel Stadt POCH also applied but, since he wished to turn the group into a 'rainbow' formation, was turned down.

With more parties being accepted into the GPS in 1990–1991, either as members, as was the case with the Luzern GB, or as observers as with the Solothurn Greens, the question of fusion became less meaningful. Hence in 1991, in a demonstration of growing confidence, the GPS accepted joint lists in Vaud and Zurich with the Alternative Greens, something it had refused to do in 1987. This may have helped to ensure that the GPS held the seats gained by transfers from the GBS; it brought the Alternatives little electoral profit. So, by 1992, for Green voters there was no real alternative to the GPS. The competitive elements in Swiss politics had clearly worked in its favour.

However, if the GPS has upheld 'deep green' ecological politics over those of leftist environmentalism, it has not been able to establish a monopoly of environmental concern either in parliament or outside. On the parliamentary front, most parties have, in response to obvious public concern, included the environment as one of their policy planks. However, they do not always give it great prominence. Nor do they share the GPS's specific policy prescriptions, usually preferring to follow the government's lead.

The independent Landesring (LdU) is unusual in having made
the environment a central plank of its policy, seeing environmental
protection as a prior condition for all long-term developments. It
has, for example, come out strongly in favour of ecological farming.
In Basel Landschaft the party at one time formed a joint group with
the Greens in the cantonal parliament. It also mounted a joint list
there, and in St Gallen, Solothurn and Thurgau, in the 1991
general elections. However, this stress does not seem to have
helped it electorally as it has been losing votes on a large scale in
recent years. The GPS has also refused to consider closer ties
because, as a small non-establishment party, it finds itself competing with the LdU and others for the 'opposition' vote.

Of the mainstream parties, the Christian Democrats (CVP) argue
that the environment is more than an ensemble of resources to be
exploited, and call for more research. The party also favours
environmental taxation and penalties for polluters. The SPS takes
a similar line, but goes further, urging a legal code on the
environment. Having campaigned on its pro-environmental voting
record in 1987, the party is widely regarded as the most environmentally concerned after the GPS and collaborated with the latter
in several constituencies in 1991. It also worked with the Alternative
Greens in Zug. The Communist Party (PdT) was willing to stand
on joint lists with the GPS in Geneva, Neuchâtel and Vaud.

This clearly contrasts with views on the right where the environment is seen more as part of the quality of life. However, the
Radicals (FDP), the Liberals (LPS) and the agrarian Peoples' Party
(SVP) all believe that, as the country has higher standards than
most, there is already enough legislation on the statute book. Their
prescription is to enforce it more effectively, perhaps by creating a
special ministry, as the SVP once wanted. For the rest, the market
can be used to solve problems with a greater chance of success than
simple legislative prohibitions.

In other words, there is competition between the GPS and other
parties of the centre-left for the ecological vote. At the same time
there are policy disagreements between the GPS and both the
centre-right and centre-left. The centre-right stands very much for
what has been called 'managerial environmentalism' and points up
contradictions in the GPS stance, such as their opposition to the
new alpine rail tunnels while claiming to defend rail and public

transport. The GPS has thus to fight on a number of fronts to put its ecological case across to other parties and their voters (Seiler 1987b: 186). Indeed, one view of ecological politics in Switzerland is that they have been absorbed by the conventional left–right division (Finger and Sciarini 1991).

SOCIAL MOVEMENTS AND LOBBIES

A second, more significant and certainly less-well-known[2] aspect of political competition, is the extent to which the Green Party has remained at arm's length from much grass-roots environmental activity in Switzerland. Although the party recently claimed to be the 'articulating instrument for manifold ecological grass-roots groups and movements' (GPS 1991a), the evidence does not substantiate this. Environmental lobbies very much predate the GPS, as do many social movements in the field, and both seem to have their own autonomous life cycles.

Formal pressure groups in defence of the national heritage go back to the beginning of this century, with the foundation of the Schweizerische Vereinigung für Heimatschütz in 1905 and the Schweizer Bund für Naturschütz in 1909 (Walter 1991). Other major lobbies are the Schweizerische Gesellschaft für Umwelt-schütz, the Swiss Committee for the Protection of Birds, the Animal Protection Society, the Swiss Energy Forum, the Anti-Noise Society and the Alpine Club. By the mid-1970s at least 25 such bodies were reported (Walter 1990). The Naturschütz numbered 100,000 members in 1980 and was strong enough to press the government for policy changes. The Umweltschütz was a notable influence on parliament in the 1970s, being consulted on environmental legislation. The Federal Council took the views of well over 70 such bodies into account when drafting what became the 1983 law on environmental protection.

Perhaps the most significant body in this field, however, is the Swiss branch of the World-Wide Fund for Nature. Founded in 1961, it now has over 110,000 members and is an energetic campaigning body. Its role at the forefront of protests against the industrial despoliation of the Valais has made it the target of a certain amount of violence there, and, in trying to distinguish itself from the nominal environmentalism of mainstream parties and lobbies, it does not refrain from confrontational action. Despite this it clearly carries credibility with the government; its director, Philippe Roch, was selected as the new head of the Federal Office of Environment and Forests in 1992.

Greenpeace and the Association for Transport and the Environment are other campaigning bodies happy, if need be, to resort to direct action as in 1990–1991 with the St Gotthard motorway and with blockades of trains carrying toxic waste. In 1993 Greenpeace activists hang-glided into Besnau to protest about nuclear developments. Such bodies obviously have much in common with the Green Party, but their targets are much more precise and are seen as too pressing to wait for political change. Nevertheless, such lobbies are still consulted by the authorities.[3] So, while press opinion assumes that the GPS is closely involved with both the WWF and the ATE, there is also some suggestion that the lobbies see the GPS as a rival for public support. Their uneasy relationship was typified by the dismissal of Laurent Rebeaud MP, one of the founders of the GPS, from his job with the WWF in Geneva.

For many years Switzerland has also seen a large number of less structured social movements active in the environmental field (Epple-Gass 1992). The anti-nuclear and pro-environmental social movement was one of the strongest in the 1970s (Bassand 1990: 29). The campaign against the proposed nuclear power station at Kaiseraugst was one of the longest and most successful examples of environmental direct action. Such movements remained active in the early and mid-1980s when other movements, such as those for peace and urban autonomy, faded. They are often fairly institutionalized in order to exploit the direct democratic process (Giugni and Kriesi 1990). Some, however, prefer to concentrate on non-electoral activities rather than risk being weakened by the constraints of the direct democratic process (Giugni 1991). The use of direct democracy in environmental politics goes back to the campaigns of Uri and Graubünden peasants to protect pastures from power companies in the 1940s. Such movements can be very spontaneous and fluid (like the movement of protest against the search for sites for storing nuclear waste), are usually carefully targeted and have their own portfolio of activities and their own supporters.[4] Such protests do not need the GPS to make themselves felt and they may have no interest in politics (Sorensen 1988: 163–165). Certainly, for example, there seems little contact between the youth movement and Greens (Gros *et al.* 1991).

Conversely, the GPS has shown a certain ambivalence about some social movements, whereas it has been willing to co-operate with formal lobbies and is involved with proposals to set up a Green Cross corps to be the environmental equivalent of the Red Cross. All this reflects the fact that the GPS has not been able to attract all the ecologically inclined voters in Switzerland. At the same time, the assumption that the Greens are simply part of the broader environmental movement (Eyerman and Jamison 1991: 108) is not the whole truth. The truth is that, while no party can ignore the environmental issue, no single body can comprehend it all (Gruner 1991: 381). What the GPS did was to help put ecological issues on the agenda and to encourage action to resolve them. It did not, in fact, replace other parties and movements, if this had ever, indeed, been its aim.

POLITICAL INFLUENCE

If the GPS has clearly not been the determining factor in Swiss politics, especially on policy-making, it has not been insignificant. Its weaknesses have been those of all small parties in Switzerland, but the party has been less active in using the devices of direct democracy that conventionally compensate small parties for their exclusion from much of the decision-making process.

The GPS has potential for influence at all three levels of Swiss politics: the communal, the cantonal and the confederal. On the first two the party and its sympathizers have shown little reluctance to accept the responsibilities of power and have held executive and legislative posts. Indeed, in cantons like Bern, possession of two seats on the executive led to new legislation on policing and higher education. The impact of the Frei Liste was, in fact, sufficient to encourage the LdU and the SVP to launch a successful move to reduce the size of the cantonal executive from nine to seven so as to destroy the Greens' chances of retaining power. The resulting loss of the two Bernese seats in 1990 was partly balanced by the victory of a sympathizer in Neuchâtel the previous year, while the Alternatives also gained a seat in Zug. Greens also hold seats in Lausanne and other communes, exercising a certain influence on decision-making at the micro-level. However, for the most part, the Greens have been little more than a contributory element in local politics.

This is even more the case at the confederal level. The fact that the Greens, along with all other members of parliament, take part in the election of the Federal Council does not imply that they can influence government policy. In December 1991, they proposed, unsuccessfully, that the election of the Federal Council should be delayed until after parliament had debated the broad policy lines it wished to be followed over the next four years. Of course, even the major parties represented in government can exercise only very limited influence on 'their' ministers, and policy clashes between parties and federal councillors drawn from their ranks are not uncommon. Moreover, the previous Christian Democrat Minister for the Environment, Flavio Cotti, was attacked by the SVP for his environmentalism, even though the SVP is represented in the 'Magic Formula' coalition.[5]

The GPS is involved in the complicated consultation process and is assiduous in communicating its views to various expert and other committees. Because its voice is merely one among many, for the most part the GPS uses parliamentary channels. This partly explains why it has consistently argued for an increase in the constitutional role of parliament. The party has exerted influence in parliament in three main ways. To begin with, both the group and its individual members have been very active in tabling questions and motions. Second, the GPS has made full use of its places on the standing committees of the Nationalrat. It has also been represented both on the Conference of Presidents of Groups, which organizes the business of the house, and on emergency committees such as those which investigated the behaviour of Elizabeth Kopp and the Military Department. Whereas some formations are excluded from such bodies, the GPS has often been treated as a full member. It has not, however, penetrated control committees, parliamentary delegations nor the committee which decides whether proceedings should be secret. As a party which sees itself as the only force independent of the 'cartel of power' it has been vigorously pursuing such parliamentary rights. Third, the Greens have used the chance to speak and vote in major debates. Immediately following the last elections they spoke on such matters as forest legislation, entry to the International Monetary Fund (IMF) and the creation of a meaningful alternative to the existing system of compulsory military service for men. On some issues, including the budget, they were part of the majority, but on others they were in a minority.

Continued pressure for more monitoring, controls and enforcement of environmental norms has clearly brought results. The GPS secured the outcome it wanted over the investigation of the

Kopp affair and on the need for a report on European integration. Pressure from the GPS was one reason why conservative
parliamentary interests moved, in 1989, to drop the Kaiseraugst
nuclear power station project by buying out the promoters. The
government's recent criticism of the party's statements on energy
policy suggests that the GPS has some influence on their activities
(Bôhlen 1992).

GPS influence on the broader political agenda has been mixed;
while other parties have, on occasions, taken up their themes and
vocabulary (Linder 1987: 182) this has not always been the case. On
a number of major public issues the party has supported winning
causes, such as the Rail 2000 project and the maintenance of
reduced speed limits on motorways. In other areas, for instance, tax
reform, where the party urged the extension of the polluter-pays
principle and evolved a detailed project for an ecologically acceptable fiscal system, it very much lost the argument (GPS 1991b).

The experience of the GPS is probably no different from that of
any other small party limited by such facets of the Swiss political
system as the maintenance of small cantonal constituencies. More
importantly, strict separation of powers and massive electoral
stability have prevented any real change in the so-called 'Magic
Formula' government over many years (Papadopoulos 1991). Small
parties have little hope of coming to power through the ballot box
and it is only very rarely that they can exercise any sort of veto
on policy.

Because of this, the GPS, like other small parties, has had to use
other channels. To a limited extent it can use the consultation
process, but given the Swiss tendency to create the largest possible
coalition in order to sustain consensus, this can involve both lowest
common denominator decisions and greater marginalization in
case of defeat than would be likely in majoritarian systems. Participation in demonstrations is also possible but, such is the com-
plexity of decision-making processes in Switzerland, it rarely has
much effect. However, all this ignores the potential of Swiss
traditions of direct democracy.

DIRECT DEMOCRACY

Many small parties use direct democracy as their main channel for
influencing strategic decisions because these offer greater possibilities of success. First, they can launch a challenge to legislation

of which they disapprove. Second, they can put forward positive proposals of their own, but only in the shape of constitutional amendments, a somewhat constraining framework which requires 100,000 signatures rather than the 50,000 needed for a challenge. Third, a small party may also take positions on others' initiatives and challenges and attempt to get their supporters to vote appropriately (Linder 1987: 184).

Perhaps surprisingly, given its strong views on democracy, the GPS has, in contrast to far right parties, been somewhat timid in its use of direct democracy. The GPS leadership is aware that it needs to be able to put forward suggestions of its own, but they have not yet really been able to manage it (Stauffer 1991). Only twice, and very recently, has the GPS launched a challenge. Its first challenge – an attempt to block the commitment to new alpine rail tunnels – proved something of an embarrassment because of its unpopularity, especially in French-speaking Switzerland. Hence the GPS and the organizing committee found it very hard to collect the necessary 50,000 signatures. Indeed, it looked at first as if the effort had failed; it only scraped through after some reassessment of the signatures collected not just by the GPS but by local interests and by a pro-motorist campaign against the tunnels. This link ought to have been anathema to the Greens, especially as both the SPS and the ATE were in favour of the tunnels. Perhaps because of this the GPS was also excluded from the action committee opposing the tunnels.

Nor has the GPS ever attempted on its own to launch a positive national initiative for constitutional reform. Much as it would like to be able to do so, it is aware that it lacks the necessary resources. However, it was involved, with the LdU, the EVP and the WWF, in the May 1990 initiative 'for an agriculture in accordance with nature'. This proposed a complex reworking of Article 31 *bis* to lay down aims and policies – technical, processual and fiscal – by which peasant agriculture might be preserved. It has also been very close to the organizers of the initiative to set constitutional limits to traffic in the Alps. In 1993 the party sought to launch an initiative to insist on a quota of women in public office.

The direct democratic channel the GPS has most frequently used has been that of acting in support of ideas put forward by others. As well as supporting the alpine initiative, the party backed unsuccessful initiatives to prevent the purchase of 34 F/A18 planes for the air force, and to introduce a co-ordinated transport policy. It also lost a whole raft of anti-motorway challenges. Equally, it has campaigned against successful *votations* launched by its opponents, such as those in 1992 on Swiss entry to the IMF and the new alpine rail tunnels. The party did find itself on the winning side, however, in recent *votations* on a 10-year moratorium on new nuclear installations and a new energy act.

As a result of its relative caution, the GPS has so far avoided the kind of crushing defeats that the SPS has sometimes suffered and which led it, in December 1988, to adopt a more cautious policy on supporting leftist ideas. However, for several reasons the GPS has not gained the advantage from direct democracy that one might have expected. Launching popular initiatives requires a good deal of organization and money, and the GPS, unlike the big lobbies, lacks the structures and funds to mount the kind of publicity campaigns which really affect votes. Moreover, the party is uncomfortable about dictating to its own supporters, and to public opinion at large, even when it can manage to do so. The challenge to the tunnels shows how difficult that can be.

The party is also aware that direct democracy can be flawed. *Votations* often favour anti-environmental interests while reducing the leverage of political parties and parliament. Moreover, with low turnouts and cantonal vetoes, they can play into the hands of conservative blocking minorities, often known as '*neinsager*'. Equally, there is evidence to suggest that public opinion is not always inclined to live up to its professed environmental beliefs: a 1991 poll in *L'Illustré* showed that, while a majority accepted that the environment was being degraded, only 19 per cent saw cars as being partly responsible and only 5 per cent were willing to accept higher petrol prices. In any case, deep ecological issues may not lend themselves to the necessarily simple form of questions asked in a referendum.

As a result, few popular initiatives are successful. Ecological ones may be even more at risk. The GPS's caution about testing its support and its preference for supporting challenges rather than initiatives is understandable, but it has led to criticism that it always takes a negative and unpopular stance. While the GPS has succeeded in making the public more aware of environmental problems, it has not convinced them that it has the requisite solutions or the means of implementing them. The party has therefore accepted that it needs to be more professional in its attitudes to popular initiatives and to develop more positive policies rather than simply urging zero growth.

None the less, direct democracy does have a place in the party's armoury (Laver and Schofield 1990: 242). As Papadopoulos (1991) has suggested, the value of direct democracy to small parties is variable but not negligible: it can keep the party's image before the public, help to bring people back into the political arena and, sometimes, it can even offer a veto. Thus direct democracy helps the GPS to achieve its major end, ensuring that the issues it espouses are kept high on the agenda and are not overlooked (Kreuzer 1990: 25). In other words, the GPS's influence is more on the policy agenda than on specific decisions.

ECOLOGICAL AND EUROPEAN CLEAVAGES IN SWISS POLITICS

The final evidence that the GPS has not radically transformed the Swiss political landscape comes from the rise of far right forces, something very visible in the European debate. Environmental issues have declined in salience while European policy has become the most divisive question now facing the Swiss. This has had a marked effect on political competition.

At one stage, with Green forces playing a major part in the rise of the Auto Partei (AP) with its visceral opposition to 'red ecological dictatorship', it looked as though the environment could become a major cleavage. However, the Swiss electoral system, which allows voters to mix party lists in a variety of ways, also makes such clear divisions hard to achieve. Examination of election results confirms this: in the late 1980s there was no simple pattern of gains in cantonal elections, let alone GPS gains from the Social Democrats (Church 1992c); often the GPS won seats in elections where the AP also won, and the same happened with the SPS.

In the general election of 1991, as befits a situation in which the GPS shared lists with centrist, social democratic and far left formations, the pattern was equally complex. The GPS, along with far right parties, gained seats from the FDP, SPS and the SVP. Since then the mixture has continued. Immediately after the elections the GPS won four seats in Fribourg from the centre-right parties, but in 1992 the party lost seats both to the AP and the SPS while winning seats in Basel Stadt, Schaffhausen and St Gallen. In 1993 it conceded a seat in Solothurn to the Social Democrats. The Green sympathizer on the cantonal government of Neuchâtel was also defeated.

What this shows is a continuing switch away from the main parties, with the CVP being the greatest loser. The great gainers have been the AP and the GPS. Since the latter's gains at cantonal level do not correlate simply with losses by the Socialist Party any more than they do at national level, the case is strengthened for seeing this as partly a matter of protest votes rather than the Greens winning over leftish voters (Kreuzer 1990: 17, 20). Equally the claim, made by the AP and others, that the Greens are identical with and simply 'carried' by the left does not hold up.

The fact that both the GPS and the AP have made gains suggests that there is a body of peripheral electoral support which does take ecologism and the party's claim to represent it increasingly seriously (GPS 1991a). Indeed, some may well have switched from the big parties to the AP because the former were too environmentally inclined. However, where the electorate as a whole is concerned, the environment has become somewhat less salient than it was in the late 1980s: fewer people have been involved in pro-ecological activity, the index of concern declined from 68 to 58 between 1987 and 1991 (Longchamp 1991: 63) and ecology was not a major theme in the 1991 general election.

One reason is the declining interest of the media. With a great deal of environmental legislation coming into force and further changes demanding considerable commitment and sacrifice, mainstream opinion appears to be satisfied with what has been achieved. For other interests, such as the new canton of the Jura which feels cut off by its lack of good road connections with the rest of Switzerland, environmental protection clashes with other urgent needs.

However, the success of the AP also clearly draws on other factors than its opposition to ecology. Increasingly inclined to call itself 'die Freiheitlichen', in line with growing public concern about migration and national identity, it has come out in favour of deregulation and against unlimited entry of asylum-seekers. The electorate, in October 1991, rewarded not just the AP but other far right formations such as the Swiss Democrats, the Lega dei Ticinesi and the fundamentalist Confederate Democratic Union (EDU).

As well as reflecting rising, and often violent, hostility to immigration and asylum-seeking in a period of increasing unemployment (Church 1993), the far right has also taken a significant part in prosecuting the divisive European issue. The GPS has been hostile to Europeanization, thereby aligning itself with figures like

Christoph Blocher, the industrialist SVP MP from Zurich, leader of the anti-European Association for a Neutral and Independent Switzerland. Clearly the cleavage over Europe is both deeper and more complicated than that on the environment.

Previously a secondary theme in foreign policy, itself a minor element in Swiss political debate, relations with Europe have moved dramatically to the top of the public agenda (Church 1992b). The consensus in favour of the 'Third Way', avoiding both marginalization and EC membership, began to fade in 1990–1991 because of the ending of the Cold War and new developments inside the EC. By October 1991 opinion polls were reporting 50 per cent in favour of entering the EC. At the same time the Federal Council began to 'Europeanize' Switzerland's neutrality and security policies. Then, finding the European Economic Area (EEA) agreement flawed, it made EC entry its long-term policy, and presented its formal application on 26 May 1992 (Conseil Fédéral 1992).

This fundamental policy switch by the foreign policy establishment caused immense soul-searching because direct democracy and other political principles, which might be changed by the EEA and the EC, are essential components of Swiss national identity. The reservations and divisions this soul-searching created appeared all too clearly on 6 December 1992 when, by a very small majority, the Swiss voted not to enter the EEA. The country divided along language lines, mainly between French- and German-speakers (Kriesi 1993), as well as between town and country, between those who wanted an open rather than a closed Switzerland and, especially, between those who trusted the political establishment and those who did not. Concern for the sacrifices that Europeanization would involve crossed party lines. Because the GPS was concerned about the environment, valued Swiss tradition and distrusted the élite, it found itself in the 'no' camp, along with the far right (Stauffer 1991: 17).

The Green Party feels very strongly about these issues partly because its members see the EC as exemplifying the evils besetting modern Europe and its environment. Hence the GPS has found itself forced to devote increasing attention to Europe. Rather than ecology determining the agenda on Europe, it is the European issue which is challenging the Greens.

The pressures of Europe testify to the distance the GPS has yet to go to establish itself in Swiss political competition. It has recently been claimed, admittedly by the Social Democrats, that the Greens are using Europe as an issue to avert electoral decline and programmatic changes (SPS 1991). Europe, it is claimed, has replaced capitalism as the source of all ills for the Greens. Turning ecological concerns into practical legislative form requires concrete programmatic adaptations and painful compromises, neither of which appeal to such a deep green party. A negative and essentially anti-European stance on issues like the IMF, the new alpine rail tunnels and the EEA, puts the GPS in the same camp as the new right, whose attitudes on issues like asylum-seekers and migrants it abhors. This has also allowed critics to talk of Greens being 'neo-conservatives and neo-patriots' (Stauffer 1991: 17).

While there is an element of truth in such claims, the situation is actually more complicated. The GPS shares with many others a belief in the value of Swiss institutions and practices. They also wish to export some of them to the rest of Europe. The GPS's views on Europe do not derive simply from electoral expediency. While the Greens have consistently argued against what they see as the anti-Third World, growthist and great power orientations of the Brussels technocracy, they have claimed that they are not anti-European. Instead they seek a pacific, social, culturally diverse and environmentally respectful Europe. This might be sought through the Council of Europe or some kind of European federation involving both Council and Community. Switzerland could thus offer Europe higher environmental standards, a model of cultural diversity and more grass-roots democracy. While the GPS has normally seen the EC as much less attractive than voluntary or autonomous co-operation between nation-states, the EEA did not commend itself to the majority of the party either, despite the fact that it did not involve supranationality. At a special Congress in November 1992 the GPS decided to oppose the EEA because this too would tie Switzerland to a productivist organization at the cost of Swiss identity and environmental interests.

After the 6 December defeat of the EEA, the deep divisions in the party over the issue prompted a rethink. Many French-speaking Greens supported ratification, suggesting to some observers that there was a growing divide between German-speaking *fundis* and French-speaking *realos*. Moreover, the GPS found itself being cast as a spear-carrier for the far right. Worse, hopes that a 'no' vote on 6 December 1992 would lead to more acceptable socio-economic policies were rudely shattered. The government and big business moved towards more deregulation, while the budget deficit and Switzerland's new marginalization conspired to call into question some of the environmentally friendly policies in which the party believes.

The problems encountered since the defeat of the EEA have forced the party to reconsider its European stance. There are now hints of a new flexibility. Despite fears that entry would be a disaster for Swiss direct democracy, environmental standards, neutrality and small farms, it is not wholly ruled out. If there are reforms at home and if the hard core of the Swiss *acquis* is defined and defended, entry could, in certain circumstances, be tolerated. Entry would at least give the country a voice where environmental decisions are taken.

In all this the GPS has been responding to a pressing situation and not just to political competition. In any case, the Swiss political system does not demand the kind of panicky competitive response implied by socialist criticisms. GPS views have a very different motivation from those of most right-wing views on Europe and the tone in which they are expressed is very different from that of Christoph Blocher or the Lega dei Ticinesi.

DIFFICULTIES, DIVISIONS AND THE FUTURE

Adapting both to new issues and to its changing position in the political arena is proving a challenge for the Swiss Greens. Evolving a strategy which will handle both the paradoxes of their ultimate commitment to deep green policies and the need, imposed on them by the Swiss political system, to remain a real party, will not be easy (Hoffman-Martinot 1991).

In its handling of the EC issue, the GPS should be seen not as desperately seeking a new policy lifeline but as coming to terms with a pressing new issue facing Switzerland and one which has to be confronted within the special conditions of party competition in Switzerland. Some authorities have suggested that Green parties do best when social democratic parties have been in power because, especially in periods of economic crisis, socialist parties have to look to the interests of their working-class constituents and are precluded from developing environmental legislation and new political styles (Müller-Rommel 1991; Rüdig 1991: 30). However, this does not apply in Switzerland because of the autonomous and multi-party nature of government. The Swiss party system is multi-dimensional (Hug and Finger 1992: 298–299) because it is so fragmented, with 15 parties now represented in Parliament (Seiler 1987a: 137). With increasing dealignment, issue-voting and the breaking down of religious and social cleavages, no party can afford to compete simply with one other force; each has to fight on as many fronts as possible in order to win votes and cannot always afford too much differentiation (von Beyme 1985: 293). Hence parties can be rightish on some issues, leftish on others and isolated in their ecological concerns on others. Apparently odd alliances, usually of a very transient kind, are thus quite common.

Kreuzer (1990) lays great stress on this, suggesting that the way the Swiss political system disperses political power means that there is a limited opposition deficit. Hence the GPS is not forced into conflictual stances and self-defeating protests but has become a 'responsible pro-system opposition' (Kerr 1987: 115). It has preserved its autonomy and has been able to influence constructively. By concentrating on the ecological issue it is able to attract voters.

While some opinion claims that the GPS is on the left, perhaps even that it forms a red–green coalition, there is evidence that the two can also be rivals. Because the relatively low levels of class conflict in Switzerland keep the system open to new forces and movements (Müller-Rommel 1989: 13), the GPS can compete with the SPS on ecological and social issues yet participate in some SPS *votations* and other ventures. This is not a coalition but merely the adoption of similar stances in legislative and public debate. Equally, because the GPS does not yet fully participate in either the consultative or the selectorate roles of the major parties, it is forced to remain a campaigning party save when the electorate gives it executive authority (Kerr 1987: 112, 168).

Real coalitions are only found on municipal and cantonal executives. However, such is the autonomy of individual executives, both from other executives and parties, that coalition is usually only on an issue-by-issue basis; it does not spring from the kind of agreed policy programmes found in majoritarian countries. Even so, things can be difficult as they have been in Lausanne, Neuchâtel and in the Zurich Parliament. In the latter, Greens and the SPS together have a majority but have not found collaboration easy. Nevertheless, in the canton of Bern between 1986 and 1990, the GPS was able to co-operate with the SPS on education, energy conservation, nuclear and transport policies. A similar municipal alliance emerged after the city elections of late 1992.

Co-operation is made easier by the fact that élites tend to take the left–right division much more seriously than does public opinion (von Beyme 1985: 258, 286). New Swiss voters, in particular, can integrate ecology on the left–right axis (Finger and Sciarini 1991). The environmental issue has polarized politics in two ways: it has become clear that there is only room for one Green party now that the GPS has secured the benefits of accepting the 'system' and other parties have taken up environmental themes. Equally, those who violently oppose this new dimension have been presented with a vehicle in the AP.

Conversely, no Swiss party can afford to be a single-issue party. Difficulties in elections and with collecting signatures for the tunnels challenge have led to a questioning of what some people see as fundamentalism, perhaps influenced by the arrival of members from the old far left. Voices are now being raised in favour of a much more active but moderate prosecution of environmental protection at the expense of grand gestures (Gruner 1991: 390). This is a response to the lack of comprehension when Greens like Rebeaud argue that Switzerland should accept a much higher level of unemployment as the price of restricting growth. It also reflects the compromises forced on parties by the Swiss political system (Stauffer 1991: 18–19).

In facing up to the demands of behaving as an orthodox party in the highly complicated political geography of contemporary Switzerland, the GPS has some difficult and very Swiss problems to face. On the one hand, it needs to decide whether to keep the purity of its deep green ideas even if this lessens its effectiveness inside the political system. On the other hand, especially if environmental issues regain their salience, it will need to keep in touch with an ecologically aware public which goes well beyond the GPS (Hug and Finger 1992). Equally, it will have to come to terms with Seiler's argument that the key to the Swiss party system, its 'Magic Formula', is to open itself to change in order to change as little as possible.

It will also need to decide what stress it should put on the peculiarities of Swiss political life if these have to be reformed or abandoned in order to achieve environmental and other gains inside the EC. The GPS's future will depend on how it performs in relation to the defeats and difficulties that these and new issues throw up (Church 1992a). The clash between the requirements of political dynamics and the pull of political culture means that, in the changing political scene, the GPS will find it difficult to maintain its position as a party which is both pure Green and a real party. The way the GPS reacts is likely to continue to challenge conventional wisdom on the nature of Green parties.

NOTES

1 The term '*votation*' comes from the French and is here used instead of referenda, after the suggestion by Christopher Hughes, to mean the whole range of popular votes in Switzerland, many of which are not technically referenda. The German term is *abstimmung*.

2 Less well known because, as in Britain, intellectual concentration has been on the party at the expense of a significant environmental movement (Rootes 1992).

3 This is because, since 1989, major environmental organizations have enjoyed a statutory right of appeal against proposed building development likely to be harmful to the landscape. This has not merely forced builders to take environmental concerns on board, but has also brought bodies like WWF more into the political arena and hence into contact with the GPS.

4 Examples are the recent occupation of the French consulate in Geneva in protest against the reopening of the Super-Phoenix nuclear plant at Creys-Malville, and that in the Bollwerk in Bern, against the levels of lead in the air.

5 The term is used to describe the composition of the Federal Council which, since 1959, has consisted of two Social Democrats, two Radicals, two Christian Democrats and one representative of the Swiss Peoples' Party. This means that the four largest parties are represented in government more or less in line with their share of votes cast.

REFERENCES

APS (annually) *Année politique Suisse*, Bern: Forschungszentrum für SchweizerischePolitik.

Bassand, M. (1990) *Urbanization: Appropriations of Space and Culture*, Pro Helvetia Lecture 7, New York: CUNY Graduate School.

Bôhlen, B. (1992) 'Vingt ans au service de l'OFEFP', *Protection de l'environment en Suisse* 2/92: 3–18.

Church, C.H. (1991) 'The Consolidation of Green Politics in Switzerland', workshop paper, ECPR Essex Joint Sessions, Colchester: ECPR.

—— (1992a) 'The Development of the Swiss Green Party', *Environmental Politics* 1(2): 252–282.

—— (1992b) 'Swiss Foreign and Security Policy: The Emergence of a New Paradigm', SEMLS Occasional Paper, Canterbury: University of Kent.

—— (1992c) 'The Swiss Election of 1991', *West European Politics* XV(4): 184–188.

—— (1993) 'Switzerland: Recent History and Politics', in *Western Europe 1994*, London: Europa, pp. 547–551.

Conseil Fédéral (1992) *Rapport du CF sur la question de l'adhésion de la Suisse à la Communauté*, Bern: Federal Chancellery, May.

Epple-Gass, R. (1992) 'Effects of Social Movements: The Example of the Bauern und Arbeiterbund, Baselland', workshop paper, ECPR Limerick Joint Sessions, Colchester: ECPR.

Eyerman, R. and Jamison, A. (1991) *Social Movements. A Cognitive Approach*, Cambridge: Polity.

Finger, M. and Sciarini, P. (1991) 'Integrating New Politics into Old Politics', *West European Politics* XIV(1): 98–112.

Giugni, M. (1991) 'Les impacts de la démocratie directe sur les nouveaux mouvements sociaux', *Schweizerisches Jahrbuch für Politische Wissenschaft* 31: 173–186.

Giugni, M. and Kriesi, H. (1990) 'Nouveaux mouvements sociaux', *Schweizerisches Jahrbuch für Politische Wissenschaft* 30: 79–100.

GPS (1989a) *L'Europe a Besoin des Verts*, Bern: GPS.

—— (1989b) *Prise de position du PES face à l'Alliance Verte Suisse*, Bern: GPS, 16 December.

—— (1991a) *GPS Info*, 3, September.

—— (1991b) *Pour un régime écologique des finances*, Bern: GPS, 14 May.

—— (1991c) *Zur GPS Programmplattform – eine Lesehelfe*, Bern: GPS.

Gros, D. *et al.* (1991) *Les jeunes en Suisse*, Zurich: Pro Helvetia.

Gruner, E. (1991) 'L'écologie arrivera-t-elle à s'imposer?', in F. Masnata *et al.* (eds), *Le Pouvoir Suisse, 1291–1991*, Lausanne: L'Aire, pp. 383–391.

Hoffman-Martinot, V. (1991) 'Grüne and Verts: Two Faces of European Ecologism', *West European Politics* IX(4): 70–95.

Hug, S. and Finger, M. (1992) 'Green Politics in Switzerland', *European Journal of Political Research* 21(3): 289–306.

Kerr, H. (1987) 'The Swiss Party System', in H. Daalder (ed.) *Party Systems in Denmark, Austria, Switzerland, the Netherlands and Belgium*, London: Pinter, pp. 107–84.

Kreuzer, M. (1990) 'Beyond New Politics: Just Post-Materialist?', *West European Politics* XIII(1): 12–30.

Kriesi, H. (1993) *Analyse des votations fédérales du 6 décembre 1992*, Adliswil and Geneva: GfS and University of Geneva.

Ladner, A. (1989) 'Switzerland', in F. Müller-Rommel (ed.), *New Politics in Western Europe: The Rise and Success of Green Parties and Alternative Lists*, Boulder, Colo.: Westview, pp. 155–175.

Laver, M. and Schofield, N. (1990) *Multiparty Government*, Oxford: Oxford University Press.

Linder, W. (1987) *La décision politique en Suisse*, Lausanne: Réalités sociales.

Longchamp, C. (1991) 'Politisch-Kultureller Wandel in der Schweiz', in F. Plasser and P.A. Ulram (eds), *Staatsbürger oder Untertanen?*, Frankfurt: Lang, pp. 49–101.

Müller-Rommel, F. (1989) 'New Political Movements and New Politics Parties', Lüneburg University: Arbeitsbericht des Fachbereichs Wirtschafts-und Sozialwissenschaften, 52.

—— (1991) 'Explaining Green Party Electoral Success', unpublished paper, Lüneburg University.

Papadopoulos, Y. (1991) 'Quel rôle pour les petits partis dans la démocratie directe?', *Schweizerisches Jahrbuch für Politische Wissenschaft* 31: 131–150.

Poguntke, T. (1989) 'The "New Politics" Dimension in European Green Parties', in F. Müller-Rommel, *New Politics in Western Europe: The Rise and Success of Green Parties and Alternative Lists*, Boulder, Colo.: Westview, pp. 175–194.

Rootes, C.A. (1992) 'Political System, the Green Party and the Environmental Movement in Britain', *International Journal of Sociology and Social Policy* 12 (4–7): 226–229.

Rüdig, W. (1991) 'Green Party Politics Around the World', *Environment* 33(8): 7–32.

Seiler, D. (1987a) 'Enjeux et parts politiques', *Pouvoirs* 43: 115–138.

—— (1987b) 'Postscript' to Kerr, 'Switzerland', in H. Daalder (ed.), *Party Systems in Denmark, Austria, Switzerland, the Netherlands and Belgium*, London: Pinter, pp. 185–186.

Sorenson, R. (1988) 'Civic Action Groups in Switzerland', in K. Lawson and P. Merkl (eds), *When Parties Fail*, Princeton, NJ: Princeton University Press.

SPS (1991) *Manuel Electoral*, Bern: SPS (August), p. 22.

Stauffer, P. (1991) 'La fuite dans le passé', *Hebdo* 28 March : 18–19.

Steiner, J. (1991) *European Democracies*, 2nd edn, London: Longman.

von Beyme, K. (1985) *Political Parties in Western Democracies*, Aldershot: Gower.

Vonmoos, R. (1990) 'Auf dem Wef zur Fusion', *Grüne Tribune Verte* 1: 4–5.

Walter, F. (1990) *Les Suisses et l'environnement*, Geneva: Zoé.

—— (1991) 'Nature and Nationality', *Passages* 11 August: 6–8.

Chapter 9

Italy

Greens in an overcrowded political system

Martin Rhodes

Italy's Green movement presents the political analyst with a paradox. On the one hand, the limited national electoral success of its national political wing – the Liste Verdi – and the abysmal record of environmental protection in Italy would suggest that ecologism has had little effect, either on public opinion or government policy. On the other hand, there is substantial evidence of a diffused and sporadic impact of both protectionist–conservative and social–political ecologism on Italian politics and society. Such evidence includes the growing role of ecologists in local and regional government, the cancellation of Italy's nuclear energy programme via popular referendum, the collapse of a governing coalition which tried partially to reverse that decision, the closure or relocation of a large number of polluting industrial plants, a proliferation of environmental laws and decrees, the creation of a new Environment Ministry in the mid-1980s, an acceptance of environmentalist principles by large parts of the trades union movement and a redefinition of politics on both the 'old' and the 'new' Italian left (Ceri 1990).

This chapter aims to explore this paradox by examining the forces behind the emergence of a Green movement which, while sharing many of the attributes of new social movements elsewhere in Europe, has a distinctive character, shaped both by the unique Italian political opportunity structure of the 1970s and 1980s and by the specific relationship forged between 'new' and 'old' middle-class activists. By the early 1990s, the Italian Green movement had succeeded in creating a united political force, in forging a position for itself within a highly competitive party system and in gaining some access to political decision-making, either through Green MPs or via the lobbying influence of environmental associations.

Nevertheless, the movement has found it difficult to sustain a distinct identity, separate from its roots in both 'old' and 'new' left parties. As Paolo Ceri (1988: 89) has commented, its 'right to claim for itself the primary representation of the marriage between the "red" (Marxism) and the "green" (ecology)' has always been problematic, 'especially since it is now unclear what the red stands for and what the green can become'. It now faces a new challenge: the discrediting of the political establishment by the *tangentopoli* ('bribe city') scandals has boosted the fortunes of new parties of protest and triggered a radical transformation of Italian politics. In the 1990s the Greens must defend an already indistinct and contested identity against two concurrent developments: a further redefinition of both the 'red' and the 'green' by changes on the Italian left; and a majoritarian revision of Italy's proportional electoral system.

THE NATURE OF THE ITALIAN GREEN EXPERIENCE

Green politics in Italy, as elsewhere in Europe, is characterized by an emphasis on post-materialist values, a significant shift away from a traditional left–right definition of politics and the emergence of both the 'old' and 'new' middle classes as sources of activism and support for a more politicized form of environmentalism. Although Italy was a relatively late modernizer, a post-industrial context conducive to ecologism began to emerge from the late 1960s: individuals with higher levels of education and exposure to new forms of political information began to break their links with traditional parties, women became more politically active and post-material values began to spread in response to greater economic security (Inglehart 1988: 444–445). The creation of a political wing occurred rather later than elsewhere (the Greens first contested national elections in 1987) but it has encountered the dilemmas of left–libertarian parties everywhere in trying to reconcile the logic of core constituency representation with the logic of party competition: while the first prevents the attraction of a broad spectrum of moderate sympathizers, pursuing the second may lead to the loss of core support or absorption by competitor parties (Kitschelt 1990: 199). As elsewhere, this dilemma has produced a constant debate between 'realists' and 'fundamentalists' over issues of organization, leadership and strategy (Doherty 1992: 108–110).

Yet the Italian Green experience has been unique in many ways.

This has much to do with the country's 'political opportunity structure' (Kitschelt 1986). The specific features of that structure – the electoral system, the recent evolution of party competition and cleavage structures, and the nature of the policy-making process – have simultaneously constrained and facilitated the emergence of Italian ecologism and determined the extent of its impact on Italian society. As Diani (1988, 1989b: 27–33) has pointed out, a favourable evolution of the 'political opportunity structure' has helped create one of the most distinctive characteristics of the Italian movement – a productive relationship between originally very different and conflicting sectors (and between 'new' and 'old' middle-class elements) – in contrast to the separatism between protectionist and political ecologism which persists in most other European countries. Convergence between these camps was encouraged by two factors: the failure of apolitical environmental lobbies to make an impact on a clientelistic political system; and by the crisis of traditional ideologies in Italy which propelled many new social movement activists away from partisan politics towards an issue-oriented form of political participation (Diani 1989b: 25). This alliance has not been free of tensions: Green activists with roots in the neo-Marxism of the late 1960s and early 1970s continue to think globally (in terms of the links between man, society and nature) while 'pure Greens' (the *verdi doc*) maintain a single-issue approach. Nevertheless, the Italian Greens have been distinguished by their capacity to combine political ecologism with a flexibility and pragmatism on institutional issues which sets them apart from both the moderation of the British movement and the alternative, oppositional stance of the German Greens (Biorcio 1992: 39–40).

The rules of the political system have clearly helped advance the aims of the movement. Once the Greens had decided to contest elections at local, national and European levels, they were greatly assisted by a pure form of proportional representation (based on the *imperiali* largest-remainder formula for distributing seats) and, once elected, by relatively generous state funding (Pridham 1991: 80–81). At the same time, a fragmented party system and fierce electoral competition from other parties contesting the left–libertarian political terrain (the Radicals and Proletarian Democracy) have limited their electoral success, even if the decline of the dominant political subcultures of Communism and Christian Democracy has liberated a growing number of 'opinion voters' (Mannheimer and Sani 1987) and competition for the environmental vote from larger parties has been weak (Diani 1989a: 114). However, Italy does provide alternative mechanisms for influencing policy, the most important of which are referendums (which can be held on request by 500,000 voters). Those held on nuclear power in 1987 not only terminated the Italian nuclear power programme but also helped forge an unprecedented degree of unity in the Green camp (Ceri 1988). Nevertheless, although such mechanisms make the Italian political system relatively 'open' to influence by new social movements (encouraging an 'assimilative' rather than 'confrontational' strategy), such influence is counteracted by the importance of clientelistic relationships with lobby groups and business interests and by the Italian state's weak capacity for policy implementation (Kitschelt 1986: 61–66). Thus, while the impact of the Green movement on policy has sometimes been dramatic, it has also been sporadic and often inconsequential. This in turn has limited its national electoral appeal beyond the small core of committed Green voters.

FROM ENVIRONMENTAL LOBBYING TO POLITICAL ACTION

Although Italian ecologists began to contest local and regional elections from the late 1970s onwards, their first experience of national politics was the 1987 general elections, following the creation of the first Green national structure – La Federazione delle Liste Verdi (Federation of Green Lists) – in October 1986. This relatively late entry on to the national political stage was due to political, cultural and generational divisions in the Green camp (ranging traditional environmentalists against political ecologists) and to the single-issue and local nature of many environmental groups. Resistance to a national Green project came from three main sources: traditional associations dedicated to their lobbying function; former New Left activists who, having abandoned party politics, were reluctant to return to it; and those who wanted to continue working within the ranks of existing parties, primarily the Italian Communist Party (PCI), the Radical Party (PR) or Proletarian Democracy (DP) (Biorcio 1992: 18–19).

These divisions had to be overcome before a national Green party could be formed. The strength of the traditional lobby groups within the environmental movement can be explained by the dominance of traditional cleavages in Italian society during the

1950s and 1960s – those between classes, state and church and between centre and periphery. An establishment/anti-establishment cleavage began to appear in the late 1960s, but was complicated by the persistence of a 'proletarian ethos' in the Italian New Left (Accornero 1992) and by the presence of a significant left-wing terrorist movement. Under these circumstances, there was little hope of building an alliance between the conventional associations and radical political activists. Thus, organizations like Italia Nostra (1955), Federazione Pro Natura (1959), the Italian World Wildlife Fund (WWF) (1966), LIPU (the bird protection organization) (1966) and LAC (the League for the Abolition of Hunting) (1978) acted largely as pressure groups, supported by MPs representing the Socialist Party or the so-called lay centre parties – the Social Democrats, Liberals and Republicans. Grass-roots participation or activism was virtually non-existent (Diani 1989b; Farro 1991).

The first signs of a shift towards left-oriented political action occurred in the early 1980s. The formation of the Lega per l'Ambiente (Environmental League), which is affiliated to the Socialist/Communist cultural organization Arci, the forging of close links between Amici della Terra (Friends of the Earth) and the Radical Party and the participation of many conventional environmental groups in the conferences of the Arcipelago Verde (Green Archipelago) – a national information co-ordinating body – all helped politicize traditional environmentalists and forge links between them and both the old and the new, libertarian, left (Diani 1988; Biorcio 1992: 20–21). Inspired by the experience of the German Greens, a meeting of the Arcipelago Verde in October 1984 proposed a national co-ordination of the various Green Lists which had emerged at the local and regional levels in the early 1980s, and the first official national assembly of the Green Lists took place in Florence in December 1984. Two further conferences were held in Florence – in February and May 1985 – prior to the creation of the national Federation of Green Lists in Finale Ligure in October 1986 (Lodi 1988: 23–25).

This movement towards participation in national politics was driven by several developments. First, the success of other European Green parties in the 1984 European elections was critical in convincing the more traditional environmentalists of the value of political participation, as was the role of radical intellectuals in calling for a new synthesis between political and social change. The positive results for the Green lists presented in the 1985 regional elections also confirmed the utility of electoral politics. Second, other parties had been instrumental in mobilizing grass-roots support for radical demands, most notably the Radical Party of Marco Pannella – which had pioneered the anti-establishment use of referendums on issues like abortion and divorce (Panebianco 1988) – and the New Left Proletarian Democrats. Their success opened up new possibilities for political action. Third, these same parties had also mobilized public opinion on environmental issues, the nuclear power debate assuming particular importance in both uniting and politicizing environmental groups. In the process, the membership of groups like the WWF and the Lega per l'Ambiente expanded, assisted by other developments, including a growing disenchantment with traditional parties, a crisis on the New Left and the defeat of terrorism which, together, released a large number of grass-roots activists for new forms of political activity. A 1985 survey found that only 15 per cent of ecological activists in the mid-1980s had been involved in the movement 10 years earlier (Biorcio 1992: 10–11).

In the background, environmental issues were becoming more salient. Environmental consciousness in Italy had increased markedly after an accident in July 1976 when large amounts of dioxin gas escaped from the Icmesa factory in the small town of Seveso, north of Milan. However, conventional groups were reluctant to join in the radical campaign which Milanese ecologists tried to launch in response. It was raised further by the announcement in 1977 of a plan to build 20 nuclear power stations across Italy. However, the protest campaign which it provoked was not united and support from ecological groups was only weak: the conventional associations did not yet oppose nuclear power in principle (Diani 1989b: 14). The anti-nuclear campaign of the late 1970s did, however, have important local successes: 20,000 people marched on Montalto di Castro (the site of a planned power station) in March 1977 and 50,000 people demonstrated against the national energy programme in Rome in May 1979. These early protests were important for developing the first links between the leftist new and moderate old middle-class activists (Diani 1988, 1989b: 15–16).

However, public opinion remained ambivalent on environmental issues: surveys revealed that while they were seen as important, the priority given to them was relatively low. Some

45 per cent of Italians were pro-nuclear in the late 1970s and only 25 per cent against (Biorcio 1988c: 33). Among political parties, only Proletarian Democracy had fully declared itself against nuclear power. But the April 1986 accident at the Soviet nuclear plant in Chernobyl – which caused substantial damage to food production in Italy – proved to be a catalysing event, transforming public opinion and uniting the ecological movement. One hundred and fifty thousand people marched against nuclear power in Rome on 10 May 1986 in a demonstration organized by the Lega per l'Ambiente, and new and firm alliances were struck between traditional and radical groups in the ecological movement. Two referendum campaigns were launched that year – against hunting and against the nuclear power programme – and although the Radicals and Proletarian Democrats were the prime movers, they were backed by the entire range of environmental associations. The impact of the campaigns on public opinion and other political parties was immense: although the turnout for the three anti-nuclear referendums in November 1987 was only 65 per cent (previous referendums on issues like divorce, abortion, life imprisonment and wage indexation had attracted between 78 and 88 per cent of the electorate), opposition to the nuclear programme was overwhelming: 80.8 per cent voted against the siting of nuclear stations, 79.7 per cent opposed subsidies to local governments permitting nuclear power and 71.8 per cent opposed Italian participation in nuclear programmes abroad (Hine 1993: 155–156). The Communist Party was rapidly converted to the anti-nuclear cause, and by the time of the referendums, all parties of the governing coalition (except the Republicans) had distanced themselves from the pro-nuclear vote – primarily to detract from the success of the Greens, Radicals and Proletarian Democrats. The Socialist leader, Bettino Craxi, even attempted to hijack the campaign for his own political purposes.

THE GREENS AT THE POLLS, 1985–1992

The mid-1980s proved to be a turning-point for the Italian Green movement. Not only had a coalition of New Left and ecological forces obliged the government to abandon its nuclear power programme, but a new environmental awareness began to permeate public opinion and other political parties. Recognizing the political saliency of the issue (and the potential for winning new votes), 'old' left parties like the Socialists and Communists began to open their own lists to ecological candidates. At the same time, there was evidence of a more general impact on government policy: in 1985, the wide-reaching 'Galasso Act' set strict limitations on environmental damage, allowed citizens to take polluters to court and provided mechanisms enabling the government to comply with EC environmental legislation (Alexander 1991: 101). In 1986, the creation of a new Ministry for the Environment (following several earlier unsuccessful attempts to do so) gave a new official status to environmental policy, even if its actual impact on policy was to be slight (Lewanski 1993).

Despite the dramatic victory of the anti-nuclear campaign, the Green movement had still to assert its own identity and establish its credibility as an electoral force. Its involvement in electoral politics prior to 1987 had been limited to the local level. The first experiment had been in 1978 in Trentino–Alto Adige with the formation of Nuova-Sinistra and Neue Link lists which subsequently became the fourth most important political force in Alto Adige–Südtirol (Biorcio 1992: 20) and evolved into Green/Alternative lists in the early 1980s (Parkin 1989: 154). By 1983 there were 16 local lists, and in 1984 and 1985 delegates from local groups met in national conventions and decided to co-ordinate the participation of Greens in the local administrative elections of May 1985 (Diani 1989a: 113). Around 150 Green lists contested 57 out of 75 constituencies in 1985, gaining 2.1 per cent of the overall vote and 141 provincial, communal and regional councillors. Given that Green political activity was still heterogeneous and dispersed, this result was viewed as a success.

A higher vote in the April 1987 elections was expected. The creation of the Federation of Green Lists in October 1986 had given the Greens a higher national profile – their decision to compete in the elections received more media attention than any previous political action by ecology groups (Diani 1989a: 122). This had subsequently been boosted by their participation in the anti-nuclear campaign. In the event, the Greens received 2.5 per cent of the vote and, with 13 deputies and two senators, entered national politics for the first time. Two years later, at the 1989 European elections, the Green Lists attracted 3.8 per cent of the vote and a separate group – the Verdi Arcobaleno (the Rainbow Greens, composed of New Left, émigré ecologists from the Radical Party and Proletarian Democracy) – won 2.4 per cent. The combined total

(6.2 per cent) for the Green camp was higher than that received by any of the minor parties of the governing coalition. Given that the Green Lists and Verdi Arcobaleno were still conducting separate campaigns, the Greens also performed extremely well in the regional elections of 1990 (see Table 9.1).

The early electoral experiences of the Greens were successful but constrained. They were successful in the sense that not only had they gained a foothold in both local and national politics relatively quickly – due in large part to the ease with which small parties can gain seats under the *imperiali* proportional system – but they had also begun to carve out a niche for themselves among other, better established parties on the libertarian left. In both the 1985 and 1987 elections, the protest vote had been more important than ecologism *per se* in delivering support to the Greens, but it was a vote for which the Radicals and Proletarian Democrats, not to mention the large Communist Party, were also competing. In May 1985, protest votes accounted for 71 per cent of Green support, 83 per cent of the Proletarian Democrat vote and 66 per cent of the Communist vote. But between May 1985 and December 1986 the percentage of Green voters for whom ecology was among the three most important issues facing the country increased from 4.8 to 27.5 per cent. At the same time, the percentage of Proletarian Democrat voters in the same category fell from 16.7 to 7.1 per cent, while the proportion of Radical voters for whom ecology was highly salient remained at a constant 9 per cent (Biorcio 1988b: 182). This reflected the fact that both the Radicals and Proletarian Democracy campaigned on much broader platforms, while the Greens focused exclusively on ecological issues. Proletarian Democracy – with its extensive network of local branches and new-found commitment to ecology – might have presented a greater threat but for its neo-Marxist concern with more traditional left-wing issues.

Nevertheless, the space provided for left–libertarian and eco-logical parties by the decline of Italy's traditional political sub-cultures was still restricted and this has limited the Greens' potential, especially at the national level. Two parallel develop-ments in Italian politics had created greater electoral opportunities for parties like the Radicals, Proletarian Democrats and Greens. On the one hand, the old model of 'polarised pluralism' with its centrifugal logic (Sartori 1966) – in which small centre parties could exploit the centre ground of Italian politics vacated by the Christian Democrats and Communists – had begun to break down

Table 9.1 Election results, 1985–1992 (percentages)

	Regional		Provincial		Communal		National[a]	Euro	National[a]
	1985	1990	1985	1990	1985	1990	1987	1989	1992
Christian Democrats (DC)	34.7	33.4	33.5	31.6	33.8	33.9	34.3	32.9	29.7
Communists (PCI)	30.8	24.0	29.8	23.8	28.7	22.9	26.6	27.6	–
Democratic Left (PDS)[b]	–	–	–	–	–	–	–	–	16.1
Communist Refoundation[b]	–	–	–	–	–	–	–	–	5.6
Socialists (PSI)	13.1	15.3	13.7	15.7	15.4	17.8	14.3	14.8	13.6
Northern Leagues	–	5.4	0.4	4.4	0.2	2.5	0.6	1.8	8.7
Neo-Fascists (MSI)	6.3	3.9	7.3	4.7	4.8	3.1	5.9	5.5	5.4
Republicans (PRI)	4.1	3.6	4.4	4.1	4.8	4.2	3.7	4.4[c]	4.4
Social Democrats (PSDI)	3.4	2.8	4.1	3.4	4.3	3.4	3.0	2.7	2.7
Liberals (PLI)	2.2	2.0	2.6	2.4	2.4	2.2	2.1	–	2.8
Green Lists	**1.8**	**2.4**	**1.0**	**2.4**	**0.9**	**1.3**	**2.5**	**3.8** }	
Rainbow Greens	–	**1.4**	–	**1.1**	–	**0.5**	–	**2.4** }	**2.8**
Green Alliance[d]	–	**1.2**	–	**1.7**	–	**1.9**	–	–	–
Radicals	–	–	–	–	–	–	2.6	–	1.2[e]
Proletarian Democrats	1.6	1.0	1.6	0.9	1.1	0.6	1.7	1.3	–[f]
Anti-Prohibitionists	1.1	1.0	–	0.9	–	0.3	–	1.2	–
La Rete	–	–	–	–	–	–	–	–	1.9

Notes: a Chamber of Deputies.
  b The Italian Communist Party (PCI) split into the Democratic Left Party (PDS) (the social democratic majority) and Rifondazione Comunista (Communist Refoundation) (the left-wing rump) in 1990.
  c Republicans and Liberals.
  d In many areas the Green Lists and Rainbow Greens campaigned together.
  e In 1992, the Radical Party's founder, Marco Pannella, led a personal list (the Lista Pannella) including the Anti-Prohibitionists.
  f Proletarian Democracy joined Rifondazione Comunista prior to the 1992 elections.

from the 1960s onwards, to be replaced by a 'centripetal pluralist' model (Farneti 1985: 182–189), in which new alliances in the centre (bringing the Socialists and lay centre parties closer to the Christian Democrats) encouraged new parties to emerge outside the mainstream, especially on the left. On the other, socio-economic change had begun to undermine the bases of traditional support for both Christian Democracy and Italian Communism by eroding their respective subcultural bases (Mannheimer and Sani 1987). In sum, electoral mobility had increased markedly by the late 1980s: the 'exchange vote' and 'attachment vote' which had underpinned the electoral stability of both the Christian Democrats and Communists through a 'logic of voter utility' or 'identification' was steadily giving way to an 'opinion vote', at least part of which was motivated by a 'logic of protest' against the traditional party system (Biorcio and Natale 1989). However, this new mobility did not necessarily liberate either opinion voters or those sympathetic with the new social movements completely from the grasp of the old parties. Nor did it deliver them directly to new parties such as the Greens.

This was partly because the old parties had played an important role as 'offstage but creative prompters in the origins, the dynamics, and the ultimate institutionalization of the new movements', producing a complex and interpenetrating set of relations between the 'wild, spontaneous, and anti-partisan new movements of the 1960s and 1970s' and the 'staid, tired, conservative institutions of the party system' (Tarrow 1990: 254). In effect, this meant that while some sectors of the new social movements were spawned by the old parties (as in the case of the joint Socialist/Communist Lega per l'Ambiente), they also retained substantial support across the spectrum of new social movement sympathizers. In 1986 only 3 per cent of Italian ecology movement supporters backed the Radical Party and 4 per cent the Proletarian Democrats, while the traditional parties still attracted the bulk of their support, ranging from 17 per cent for the Socialists to 27 and 35 per cent respectively for the Communists and Christian Democrats (Müller-Rommel 1990: 226–227). In the case of the latter two parties, this revealed the persistence of voting behaviour based on 'utility' or 'identification'. In the case of the Socialists it revealed the extent to which a rejuvenated party under the dynamic (and authoritarian) leadership of Bettino Craxi appealed to many in the new generation of voters (Giovannini 1988: 507). The strength of traditional voter identification is also revealed by the nature of electoral flows during the middle to late 1980s. During the period between 1983 and 1987, some two-thirds of the Green vote was transferred from the radical–socialist area and from certain lay centre parties, rather than from the Christian Democrats and Communists (Biorcio 1988b: 185). In 1987, both the Radical Party and the centrist Republican Party (the most fervent supporter of nuclear power) lost 0.5 per cent of their respective votes to the Green Lists; the Communist Party ceded only 0.2 per cent of its vote to the Greens and 0.4 per cent to Proletarian Democracy (Biorcio and Natale 1987; Draghi 1987). Thus, while the potential Green vote was much larger – some 12.4 per cent of left-wing voters and 8.9 per cent of centre-right voters were potential converts in the late 1980s – the actual Green vote was limited both by traditional voter ties and by competition from other left–libertarian parties (Biorcio 1988b: 194–195). In terms of geographical distribution, the Green vote in the 1987 elections was also restricted to certain areas. Most Green voters lived in towns with more than 100,000 inhabitants and were concentrated in the centre–north of the country, were secular rather than Catholic, aged between 18 and 24 and with a university education. This altered slightly in the 1989 European elections when 60 per cent of new Green voters came from the Mezzogiorno, boosting southern support from a quarter to a third of the Green total. Southern support also increased in the 1990 administrative elections in which the Greens made major advances in all areas, especially in the northern constituencies (see Table 9.2). Nevertheless, the Greens remained the party with the closest relationship between income and support: the poorer the area, the poorer their electoral performance (Magna 1989).

The persistence of divisions within the Green camp may also have limited the electoral appeal of the Greens. Although these divisions have been much less acute than those which have riven other European Green parties, either along 'red–green' or '*fundi–realo*' dimensions, they have none the less played an important role in shaping the movement. The creation of the Federation of Green Lists in 1986 was not universally welcomed: some local lists and influential figures opposed the December 1987 decision to make the Federation the only legal representative of the Liste Verdi, while others attacked the Federation's co-ordinating committee of 11 (which organized the 1987 election campaign) for acting as a de facto leadership group (Biorcio 1988a). There were also tussles

Table 9.2 Green List votes in the regional elections (1985 and 1990) and Chamber of Deputies (1987 and 1992) by constituency (percentage)

Constituency	Regional 1985	Regional 1990	Variation 1985–1990	National 1987	National 1992	Variation 1987–1992
Torino Novara Vercelli	3.5	7.3	+3.8	3.5	3.0	−0.5
Cuneo Alessandria Asti	3.1	5.2	+2.1	3.4	2.9	−0.5
Genova Imperia La Spezia Savona	2.8	5.7	+2.9	4.0	3.7	−0.3
Milano Pavia	2.6	5.8	+3.2	3.7	3.7	−
Como Sondrio Varese	2.2	5.4	+3.2	3.1	3.1	−
Brescia Bergamo	2.2	4.1	+1.9	2.8	2.4	−0.4
Mantova Cremona	2.5	4.7	+2.2	3.4	2.8	−0.6
Trento Bolzano	−	7.1	−	4.6	5.5	+0.9
Verona Padova Vicenza Rovigo	2.5	6.8	+4.3	3.4	3.0	−0.4
Venezia Treviso	3.0	8.0	+5.0	4.3	3.5	−0.8
Udine Belluno Gorizia Pordenone	−	3.8[b]	−	3.5	3.1	−0.4
Trieste	−	4.5[a]	−	3.3	3.6	+0.3
Bologna Ferrara Ravella Forlì	2.4	5.1	+2.7	2.3	2.8	+0.5
Parma Modena Piacenza Reggio E.	2.1	4.7	+2.6	2.8	2.6	−0.2
Northern Italy	**2.4**	**5.6**	**+3.2**	**3.4**	**3.3**	**−0.1**
Firenze Pistoia	2.2	3.8	+1.6	2.7	2.6	−0.1
Pisa Livorno Massa Carrara	1.5	4.3	+2.8	3.0	3.3	+0.3
Siena Arezzo Grosseto	0.6	2.9	+2.3	2.1	2.0	−0.1
Ancona Pesaro Macerata Ascoli	2.2	4.9	+2.7	2.6	3.2	+0.6
Perugia Terni Rieti	−	3.6	−	1.8	2.2	+0.4
Roma Viterbo Latina Frosinone	2.4	6.4	+4.0	3.0	3.3	−0.3
Central Italy	**1.9**	**4.3**	**+2.4**	**2.7**	**2.8**	**+0.1**
A'Aquila Pescara Chieti Teramo	1.2	3.0	+1.8	1.9	2.8	+0.9
Campobasso Isernia	−	1.4	−	1.1	1.6	+0.5
Napoli Caserta	−	4.6	−	0.7	2.6	+1.9
Benevento Avellino Salerno	−	3.0	−	1.2	2.0	+0.8
Bari Foggia	1.2	3.6	+2.4	1.6	2.3	+0.7
Lecce Brindisi Taranto	0.9	3.1	+2.2	1.7	1.9	+0.2
Potenza Matera	−	1.4	−	1.0	2.0	+1.0
Catanzaro Cosenza Reggio C.	−	2.0	−	0.8	1.7	+0.9
Catania Messina Siracusa Ragusa Enna	0.6[a]	1.0[c]	+0.4	1.2	1.5	+0.3
Palermo Trapani Agrigento Caltanissetta	0.6[a]	0.9[c]	+0.4	1.2	1.1	−0.1
Cagliari Sassari Nuoro Aristano	−	1.8[b]	−	−	2.3	−
South and Islands	**0.4**	**2.3**	**+1.9**	**1.2**	**2.0**	**+0.8**

Notes: a 1988
       b 1989
       c 1991

Source: Adapted from Biorcio (1988b: 184) and *La Repubblica*, 8 April 1992.

over the choice of candidates in 1987: women's groups wanted 50 per cent of list places (they eventually received 30) and others wanted list leaders to be grass-roots activists rather than the more entrepreneurial Greens whose rise to prominence was being assisted by a personality-obsessed Italian media. Electoral participation also made tensions more acute between libertarians (many of whom were still close to the Radical Party) and those with links through the Lega per l'Ambiente to the traditional left, who feared that a Green political force would pose a threat to the Communist Party. Nevertheless, although there were still many differences among the wide range of ecological groups and associations in the Green 'archipelago', all of them – except Italia Nostra (which decided to prioritize its pure ecology lobbying role) – supported participation in the 1987 polls and the Greens entered their first national electoral contest as a united force.

Damaging factionalism has been successfully avoided by the looseness of an organization which allowed the coexistence of different sectors of the movement in different lists. This has been helped by the absence of formal links between the Federation and Green MPs: MPs are not allowed to act as official representatives of the Green Lists and are accountable only to voters and the wider ecological movement (Diani 1989a: 120–121). However, the presentation of two separate Green formations in the 1989 European and 1990 administrative elections revealed the persistence of a potentially damaging division between two diverse groups of activists with different philosophies: the first focusing exclusively on ecological issues, and the second seeking to link them with the more general themes of left–alternative politics such as social justice, peace, Third World aid and minority rights (Biorcio 1992: 41–43). After the 1987 elections, a number of deputies elected from Radical and Proletarian Democrat lists proposed the creation of a united Verdi Arcobaleno group, which the Liste Verdi resisted, and they presented separate lists in 1987 and 1990. However, the unification of the two groups was sanctioned by the Liste Verdi at their December 1990 national assembly. Given the excellent results registered in the 1990 regional elections (see Table 9.2), those promoting the merger believed that it was possible to create a fourth force in Italian politics to contest the domination of the three traditional camps: Christian Democracy, Communism and the lay centre (embracing the Socialists, Social Democrats, Liberals and Republicans). They also sought to bring on board the Anti-

Prohibitionists whose success as a single-issue (drug liberalization) party had further fragmented the anti-establishment youth vote (Rhodes 1992: 437–438).

The first test of this strategy came in 1992 when the Greens competed in their second general election. It was not just the new unity which suggested the Greens might make a major electoral breakthrough. Elsewhere in Europe, other Green movements which had previously enjoyed only limited success had made major advances: in France, the Greens had won a combined 13.9 per cent in the regional polls, despite having campaigned as two separate parties. In Italy, the crisis facing the governing parties suggested that the Christian Democrats and Socialists might both lose support on a large scale, and given the potential support for the Greens which had always existed in the socialist–radical area, some of these discontented voters were expected to defect to the united Liste Verdi. Furthermore, although traditional Communist voters had not proven to be a source of Green support in the past, the divisive transition of the PCI from Euro-Communism to social democracy, and the creation of two new parties from within its ranks – the moderate Democratic Party of the Left (PDS) and left-wing Rifondazione Comunista – might also have been expected to liberate some voters for the Greens. In the event, the Green Lists' performance at the polls was mediocre. Their lower house vote rose marginally from 2.5 in 1987 to 2.8 per cent (boosting the number of Green deputies from 13 to 16), while their upper house vote increased from 2.0 to 3.1 per cent and their number of senators from two to four. Most significantly, the Greens lost support in major parts of the centre and north where, in theory, they should have performed best given the economic prosperity and strong secular–left tradition of these regions. At best, the outcome simply consolidated the Greens' position as a marginal lobby/parliamentary group at the national level, while remaining a much more significant force in communal, provincial and regional politics.

How can this indifferent result be explained? One contributing factor must be the absence of major mobilizing issues in the early 1990s. In retrospect, the Green movement's finest hour may have been in 1986 and 1987 when the anti-nuclear campaign, the referendums and their initial electoral success gave them national prominence for the first time. The success of the Greens and their partners in the anti-nuclear struggle effectively deprived them of one of their most important mobilizing issues. On issues such as hunting, the protection of wildlife and pollution, the Greens have far greater difficulty generating interest and support. Three national referendums against hunting and the use of pesticides held in 1990 failed because of the low turnout (43 per cent – a majority is required), and five regional referendums on the environment promoted by the Greens in Friuli Venezia Giulia in November 1991 were defeated. In January 1992, the power of Italy's 1,480,000 hunters was deployed to emasculate a new hunting law which failed both to restrict their access to much national parkland or fully to implement EC directives on protected species.

Similarly, while the creation of a new Environment Ministry in 1986 has only marginally improved environmental policy-making in Italy – it is underfunded and understaffed, and its implementation record poor (Lewanski 1990, 1993) – it has given a higher status to the environment and a consultative role to some of the larger environmental associations, depriving the Greens of yet another *cause célèbre*. There are still many mobilizing issues at the local level, but these can be dealt with most effectively by local action and the use of local referendums, dispersing both Green activity and Green identity at a time when there has also been a widespread loss of faith in national politics and government. Meanwhile, the salience of environmental issues has not increased greatly since the mid-1980s. According to the 1989 Eurobarometer, only 11.5 per cent of Italians consider the environment a high priority, placing Italy sixth in the EC in terms of environmental consciousness, after Belgium, Britain, Germany, Denmark and The Netherlands (Biorcio 1992: 16–18). There have even been signs that the entry of the Greens into national politics has polarized public opinion on environmental issues. Between 1985 and 1989 both the 'potential for mobilization' and the 'potential for counter-mobilization' on Green issues have increased – the first from 12 to 29 per cent of the electorate and the latter from 7 to 18 per cent (Biorcio 1992: 45–47). The most visible sign of this polarization is the clash between the Green groups and the powerful hunting lobby over access to land and the protection of species.

A second set of factors derive from the changing political context. A major part of the Green electorate is a protest vote, but since 1990 the nature of political protest in Italy has changed enormously, spreading from small parties on the margins of the political spectrum into the heart of the electorate, as a succession of scandals exposed the rotten core of a corrupt governmental system. But this did not assist the Greens to any great extent in 1992, partly because the issues at stake outstripped the capacity of the Greens to respond to them. Thus, when one prominent Green, Gianni Mattioli, accused the Italian media of boycotting their campaign, the director of *Telegiornale Uno* pointed out with some justification that the Greens had been completely absent from the key election debates. At a time when the major challenges facing Italy were far-reaching institutional reform, an uncontrollable public sector deficit and a flagging struggle against organized crime, it is hardly surprising that the Green message was marginalized. While some leading Greens attempted to respond to these issues, the Greens' only concrete reference to Italy's institutional problems during the election campaign was an unoriginal and underdeveloped proposal for electoral reform (Rhodes 1992: 438).

The nature of party competition has also changed over the last few years. Some features remain the same: as in the late 1980s, both the traditional left and New Left parties have continued to contest the left–libertarian/ecological terrain. Thus, in a major coup, the Italian Socialists managed to recruit Rosa Filippini – a high profile Green deputy – for its own list in 1992. Her view that the Greens amount to little more than the '*ennesimo partitino della sinistra*' (the umpteenth left-wing micro-party) is probably shared by a large number of those otherwise sympathetic to the movement. The Radical Party was similarly predatory: their leader, Marco Pannella, transformed the Radicals (in a typically dramatic gesture) into the Pannella List for the election, absorbing the Anti-Prohibitionists led by Marco Taradash in the process, something many leading Greens had hoped to achieve themselves. Pannella's offer to bring the Greens on to his list as well – creating a broad 'pro-democracy coalition' on the libertarian left – was rejected by the Green national congress as a thinly veiled threat to their autonomy.

But in 1992 there were also new competitors to contend with who have been particularly adept at exploiting the expansion of the protest vote. First, there were the new reformists who, while remaining members of the traditional parties, campaigned on cross-party lists demanding radical transformation of both the party system (via new electoral rules) and the institutions of government. By 1993, many of these – with their origins in the Christian Democrat, Republican, Socialist, Social Democrat and Liberal Parties – were creating the foundations of a new, large centre party in the Alleanza Democratica (Democratic Alliance) led by Christian

Democrat dissident Mario Segni. Second, the existence of other cross-party lists campaigning on issues adjacent to Green concerns only added to the confusing proliferation of ad hoc and semi-institutionalized groups competing for votes on the radical/libertarian left: a transversal alliance called Democrazia e partecipazione was supported by 17 pacifist organizations (as well as the Lega per l'Ambiente) and backed 750 candidates, including 157 Greens. Third, there were the new radicals, including Leoluca Orlando's anti-Mafia party, La Rete ('The Network'), and the left-wing rump of the former Communist Party, Rifondazione Comunista, which absorbed the remnants of Italy's New Left, including Proletarian Democracy, between 1990 and 1992, along with a small but significant section of the protest vote, as revealed by its unexpected electoral success (see Table 9.1, p. 177). Finally, the most successful protest party, the Lega Nord (Northern League) – which campaigns on a platform of radical institutional reform and quasi-federal devolution – may also have hindered the Greens in precisely that part of the country where their electoral potential has been the greatest – the prosperous, industrial north. The success of the Lega Nord (gaining 8.7 per cent of the national vote and 15.6 per cent in the north) may account for the fact that Green support fell in all but three northern constituencies in the vote for the Chamber of Deputies while rising in three central constituencies and improving everywhere in the south (see Table 9.2, p. 180). The pattern was repeated on a smaller scale in the limited number of communal elections which took place in June 1993: Rifondazione Comunista, the Lombard League (the largest component of the Northern League) and La Rete all benefited from a further erosion of the traditional parties' vote, while the various Green Lists received just over 2 per cent of the total votes cast, leaving them in roughly the same position as in the more general communal polls held in 1990 (see Table 9.1, p. 177). Their inability to capitalize on the collapse of the Socialist Party (following the incrimination of Craxi, its leader, on corruption charges) augurs especially ill for their future, given that much of their potential electorate lies precisely in the radical/socialist areas of the centre and north.

THE GREENS AND THE FUTURE OF ITALIAN DEMOCRACY

The future of the Verdi is uncertain. As elsewhere, they face a major crisis of image, organization and strategy, linked in part to the conventional split between Green fundamentalism and realism. In Italy, this crisis has three further dimensions. A national Green political force must carve itself a niche among the myriad parties and environmental associations which are simultaneously its allies and competitors for public recognition and support. At the same time, it must avoid contamination by the internecine and sectarian nature of Italian politics. Over the next few years it will also have to adjust to a reformed political system – including new electoral rules unlikely to favour small parties.

The '*fundi–realo*' division in Italy has been less important than elsewhere in Europe because the loose organization of the party – and the absence of any controlling link between the Federation of Green Lists and Green MPs – has prevented a major dispute over issues such as the rotation of MPs or the arrangement of party lists on an alphabetical basis. The imperatives of electoral competition in Italy have meant that those Greens with the highest public profile have always been *capoliste* (list leaders). Conflict over organization and strategy could yet split the Verdi as participation in national politics becomes more difficult and potentially compromising. The main challenge comes from the need to forge alliances with other parties. In 1992, the former Radical and member of the Green co-ordinating committee, Franceso Rutelli, was virtually alone among leading Greens in wanting to forge an alliance with La Rete, arguing that they shared a common cause in '*la politica pulita*' (clean politics). Limited alliances with La Rete and other like-minded parties were permitted in a number of senate constituencies where the Greens' prospects were least promising (as in the single list with the Party of the Democratic Left and the Republicans for the senatorial college in Calabria). Firmer alliances – if not mergers – of this kind are inevitable after the implementation of Italy's electoral reforms. They will present a difficult challenge to the 70 per cent of Green supporters who back political participation only if the activities of other parties are not emulated and a separate Green identity is maintained (Biorcio 1992: 49).

The 1992 elections also revealed the persistence of the internal division between the 'pure Greens' (or '*verdi doc*') and those with a New Left commitment to wider social issues, in particular pacifism, anti-racism and the north–south divide. This split tends to mirror that between the supporters of demonstrations and grass-roots activism (the *piazza*) and the advocates of national lobbying and parliamentary politics (the *palazzo*). Divisions between the two camps have widened as a result of the Greens' recent electoral stagnation and the selection of candidates prior to the 1992 polls. The selection process in 1992 did not provoke the often bitter debates which preceded the 1987 campaign, but it did create much discontent among the 'pure Greens' who fared worst in an allocation of list positions which confirmed the hegemony of former New Left activists in the parliamentary sphere. Previous Proletarian Democrat activists (such as Edo Ronchi) took the lion's share of prominent list positions, while among former Radicals, only Rutelli (perhaps the most well-known Green due to extensive media exposure) was ensured re-election, as *capolista* in Cagliari and second behind Massimo Scalia (then leader of the Green parliamentary group) in Rome. Prominent *verdi doc* figures – such as Sergio Andreis and Anna Donati – did worst: Andreis resigned from his position on the Pisa list due to the remote chances of election and Donati was demoted from Bologna to Parma. The only prominent figure from the 'pure' side of the movement to gain election was Fulco Pratesi, the former leader of the Italian World Wildlife Fund.

The changing composition of the Green parliamentary group seems to confirm a tendency noted by Biorcio (1992: 41), which, if taken to its logical conclusion, could lead to the dissolution or transformation of the Green 'Party': the reabsorption of the Greens into a wider project linked to a recomposition of the Italian left. For Greens like Rutelli and Scalia and former Proletarian Democrats such as Ronchi and Franco Russo – who now appear to have the upper hand at the national level – the Greens must make a bid for power and work for change across a wide range of policy areas. This view is epitomized by the *Terra nostra, vita, ambiente, solidarietà* campaign which seeks to counteract intolerance and racism in Italy by linking concern with the environment (broadly defined) with a call to assist immigrants in Italy as well as their countries of origin. They have been opposed by other major figures in the movement, including Alex Langer (Euro-MP and leader of the Greens in Trentino–Alto Adige), Alfonso Pecoraro Scanio (a regional councillor in Campania) and Annamaria Procacci (a representative of the *animalisti* – animal rights activists), as well as former '*verdi doc*' deputies like Donati and Andreis who would prefer a greater focus on specifically environmental issues and a return to street-level protest politics (Rhodes 1992: 438–439). The division was illustrated by two quite different responses to the outcome of the 1992 elections: while Russo stated that 'we now need to say clearly that we are no longer just an environmental lobby and must act like a fully fledged political force, taking initiatives on institutional reform', Pratesi maintained that 'we don't need to make more political demands but must prioritize environmental issues: we need less politics and more ecology' (*La Repubblica*, 7 April 1992).

Unfortunately for the Greens, this division is likely to be made more acute by the radical transformation of Italian politics. The overhaul of the 'political opportunity structure' is making the maintenance of a distinct Green identity in national politics much more difficult. As one commentator put it, 'the Greens must prepare to join with the new alignment – the reformist alliance or the "party of the honest" – without which Italy will be unable to save either democracy or the environment' (Valentini 1991). Recognition of this appears to lie behind the election of the former Socialist Environment Minister, Carlo Ripa di Meana, as the 'spokesman' (effectively leader) of the movement by 209 out of 350 delegates at the national congress of the movement in Montegrotto Terme in March 1993. A well-respected politician with a high public profile (he was EC Environment Commissioner until 1992), Ripa di Meana replaces the eleven-member co-ordinating committee as the national voice of the Greens and will attempt to widen their electoral appeal by addressing a wide range of issues, including unemployment and social justice (*La Repubblica*, 23 March 1993).

A second problem derives from the new electoral rules introduced in August 1993. The new electoral system is a complex mix of proportional and majoritarian elements, but the overall effect will be to reduce the number and influence of micro-parties in parliament and to force a major realignment of forces across the political spectrum. Mergers have already occurred on the libertarian left in anticipation of this development, most significantly the absorption of Proletarian Democracy by Rifondazione Comunista and the Anti-Prohibitionists by the Pannella List. The new electoral rules will present the Greens with unpalatable choices, for three-quarters of both lower house and upper house seats will be elected by a first-past-the-post vote in single-member constituencies and the remaining 25 per cent – designed to protect smaller parties – will be elected through a proportional system bolstered by a 4 per cent threshold. Given that the Greens are, on recent performance, unlikely to pass this threshold in the next general elections, they effectively have three options at the national level: alliance, merger or oblivion.

CONCLUSION

The early Green experience in Italy saw some notable successes, in the mobilization of widespread support for the anti-nuclear movement, in the forging of a close and productive alliance between moderate, protectionist, old middle-class activists and their more politicized, New Left counterparts, and in the launching of a national political force which quickly made its presence felt on the national political stage. But the political success of the movement has been restricted by electoral competition on the libertarian left and by the persistence of traditional voter identification among new social movement supporters. Changes in the 'political opportunity structure' – especially the impact of new electoral rules – may bring this brief episode of national political participation to an early close. What, then, does the future hold for the Italian Greens?

It is almost certain that they cannot now survive as a distinct political force in national politics. But the options of merger or alliance raise a number of questions about the destiny of activists from different sections of the movement. If, as now seems likely, the left-wing rump of the old Communist Party, Rifondazione Comunista, becomes an irresistible pole of attraction on the far left, those Greens with a past in the Radical Party or Proletarian Democracy may well join this new alliance of old left and new, libertarian, left forces. But given the nature of local alliances in joint lists for the 1992 general (and subsequent local) elections, others are likely to find a home alongside the moderate former Communists in the Democratic Party of the Left or in the new centrist formation emerging in the Alleanza Democratica. Individuals with a high public profile – such as Rutelli – will be able to champion the Green cause, even if they are using a larger political group as a means of achieving influence: Rutelli's recent candidacy for the mayoralty of Rome, sponsored by the Democratic Party of the Left, is an example which others will follow at the local level.

This suggests that even if the Greens are forced to vacate the national stage, they will still have a role elsewhere, either in local politics (especially in regional government where it is easier to mobilize local ecological concern and where, increasingly, environmental policy will be made) or, alternatively, at the European level. It has been clear from the experience of environmental policy-making in recent years that European Community directives have been the major impetus for progress within Italy, as in other

Mediterranean member states (Lewanski 1993; Pridham 1993: 24). The emergence of the EC as a major environmental decision-maker means that it is fast becoming a locus of both environmental lobbying and Green party politics. In sum, one can envisage a new division of labour within the Italian Green movement. Prominent Greens will continue to play a role in national politics, either within broader party alliances or via the lobbying or consultative influence of the traditional protectionist groups over environmental policy-making. At the local level, other Verdi will be active as communal, provincial or regional councillors and some may even be able to exercise a leadership role, as in the case of Rutelli. Meanwhile, Italian Green Euro-MPs will have an important function in helping shape European environmental legislation. Thus, while the future of the Italian Greens as a distinct, national political force is in doubt, the movement will continue to have a role, albeit one fragmented and dispersed throughout the Italian – and European – political systems.

POSTSCRIPT

The Verdi contested the March 1994 national elections as part of the broad Progressive Alliance that was led by the former communist Democratic Party of the Left (PDS) and included Rifondazione Comunista, the centrist Democratic Alliance, the anti-mafia Rete, the Socialists, Socialist Christians and the Independent Left. As expected, the Verdi won no seats on their own account, but their candidates on the Progressive lists managed to secure seven seats in the Senate (up by three on 1992) and eleven in the Chamber of Deputies (a reduction of five). This success reflected their influence within the alliance and the personal standing of leading Green politicians. However, their 2.7 per cent of the proportional vote suggests that their overall support remains largely unaltered: the tumultuous changes occurring in the Italian political system have therefore neither damaged nor benefited the Verdi to date. As for their identity in the new system, in April 1994 the Verdi joined the new Progressive federation alongside the PDS, Rete and Social Christians. Its loose structure should allow a distinctive Green identity to be preserved, although much will depend on the leadership of Carlo Ripa di Meana and the suppression of division in the Green camp.

REFERENCES

Accornero, A. (1992) *La Parabola del sindacato: ascesa e declino di una cultura*, Bologna: Il Mulino.

Alexander, D. (1991) 'Pollution, Policies and Politics: The Italian Environment', in F. Sabetti and R. Catanzaro (eds), *Italian Politics: A Review*, vol. 5, London: Pinter Publishers for Istituto Cattaneo, pp. 90–111.

Biorcio, R. (1988a) 'Ecologia politica e Liste Verdi', in R. Biorcio and G. Lodi (eds), *La sfida verde: il movimento ecologista in Italia*, Padova: Liviana Editrice, pp. 113–146.

—— (1988b), 'L'elettorato verde', in R. Biorcio and G. Lodi (eds), *La sfida verde: il movimento ecologista in Italia*, Padova: Liviana Editrice, pp. 181–208.

—— (1988c) 'Opinione pubblica, questione ambientale e movimento ecologista', in R. Biorcio and G. Lodi (eds), *La sfida verde: il movimento ecologista in Italia*, Padova: Liviana Editrice, pp. 27–47.

—— (1992) 'Il movimento verde in Italia', working paper no. 46, Barcelona: Institut de Ciències Politiques i Socials.

Biorcio, R. and Natale, P. (1987) 'Elezioni: la geografia dell'infedeltà', *Politica ed Economia* 12: 33–41.

—— (1989) 'La mobilità elettorale degli anni ottanta', *Rivista Italiana di Scienza Politica* 19: 385–430.

Ceri, P. (1988) 'The Nuclear Power Issue: A New Political Cleavage Within Italian Society?', in R. Nannetti, R. Leonardi and P. Corbetta (eds), *Italian Politics: A Review*, vol. 2, London: Pinter Publishers for Istituto Cattaneo, pp. 71–89.

—— (1990) 'Ecologismo radicale e autolimitato', *Politica ed Economia* 6: 57–60.

Diani, M. (1988) *Isole nell'arcipelago. Il movimento ecologista in Italia*, Bologna: Il Mulino.

—— (1989a) 'Italy: The "Liste Verdi"', in F. Müller-Rommel (ed.), *New Politics in Western Europe: The Rise and Success of Green Parties and Alternative Lists*, Boulder, Colo., San Francisco, Calif. and London: Westview Press, pp. 113–122.

—— (1989b) 'The "New" and "Old" Middle Class Within the Italian Ecology Movement, 1955–1988', paper for the workshop 'The New Politics and the New Middle Class', ECPR Joint Sessions, Paris, 10–15 April.

Doherty, B. (1992) 'The Fundi–Realo Controversy: An Analysis of Four European Green Parties', *Environmental Politics* 1: 95–120.

Draghi, S. (1987) 'Il modello dei flussi per capire il voto', *Politica ed Economia* 9: 23–24.

Farneti, P. (1985) *The Italian Party System*, London: Pinter.

Farro, A. (1991) 'Gli ingranaggi dell'ambientalismo', *Politica ed Economia* 6: 26–27.

Giovannini, P. (1988) 'Generazione e mutamento politico in Italia', *Rivista Italiana di Scienza Politica* 18: 487–510.

Hine, D. (1993) *Governing Italy: The Politics of Bargained Pluralism*, Oxford: Clarendon Press.

Inglehart, R. (1988) 'La nuova partecipazione nelle società post-industriali', *Rivista Italiana di Scienza Politica* 18: 403–445.

Kitschelt, H. (1986) 'Political Opportunity Structures and Political Protest: Anti-Nuclear Movements in Four Democracies', *British Journal of Political Science* 16: 57–85.

—— (1990) 'New Social Movements and the Decline of Party Organisation', in R.J. Dalton and M. Kuechler (eds), *Challenging the Political Order: New Social and Political Movements in Western Democracies*, Cambridge: Polity Press, pp. 179–208.

Lewanski, R. (1990) 'La politica ambientale', in B. Dente (ed.), *Le politiche pubbliche in Italia*, Bologna: Il Mulino, pp. 281–314.

—— (1993) 'Environmental Policy in Italy: From Regions to the EEC, A Multiple Tier Policy Game', paper for the workshop 'Environmental Policy and the Peripheral Regions', ECPR Joint Sessions, University of Leiden, The Netherlands, 2–8 April.

Lodi, G. (1988) 'L'azione ecologista in Italia: dal protezionismo storico alle Liste Verdi', in R. Biorcio and G. Lodi (eds), *La sfida verde: il movimento ecologista in Italia*, Padova: Liviana Editrice, pp. 17–26.

Magna, N. (1989) 'Le quattro Italie del voto europeo', *Politica ed Economia* 10: 33–43.

Mannheimer, R. and Sani, G. (1987) *Il mercato elettorale: identikit dell'elettore italiano*, Bologna: Il Mulino.

Müller-Rommel, F. (1990) 'New Political Movements and "New Politics" Parties in Western Europe', in R.J. Dalton and M. Kuechler (eds), *Challenging the Political Order: New Social and Political Movements in Western Democracies*, Cambridge: Polity Press, pp. 209–231.

Panebianco, A. (1988) 'The Italian Radicals: New Wine in an Old Bottle', in K. Lawson and P.H. Merkl (eds), *When Parties Fail: Emerging Alternative Organisations*, Princeton, NJ: Princeton University Press, pp. 110–136.

Parkin, S. (1989) *Green Parties: An International Guide*, London: Heretic.

Pridham, G. (1991) 'Italian Small Parties in Comparative Perspective', in F. Müller-Rommel and G. Pridham (eds), *Small Parties in Western Europe: Comparative and National Perspectives*, London: Sage, pp. 71–94.

—— (1993) 'National Environmental Policy-Making in the European Framework: Spain, Greece and Italy in Comparison', paper for the workshop 'Environmental Policy and the Peripheral Regions', ECPR Joint Sessions, University of Leiden, The Netherlands, 2–8 April.

Rhodes, M. (1992) '*Piazza* or *Palazzo*? The Italian Greens and the 1992 Elections', *Environmental Politics* 1: 437–442.

Sartori, G. (1966) 'European Political Parties: The Case of Polarised Pluralism', in J. LaPalombara and M. Weiner (eds), *Political Parties and Political Development*, Princeton, NJ: Princeton University Press, pp. 137–176.

Tarrow, S. (1990) 'The Phantom at the Opera: Political Parties and Social Movements of the 1960s and 1970s in Italy', in R.J. Dalton and M. Kuechler (eds), *Challenging the Political Order: New Social and Political Movements in Western Democracies*, Cambridge: Polity, pp. 251–273.

Valentini, G. (1991) 'Se ride quel Sole . . . ', *La Repubblica*, 11 December.

Chapter 10

Greece

Greens at the periphery

Nicolas Demertzis

Seen from the outside, there are many reasons why there should be a potent environmental movement in Greece. Yet there is no such movement. Of course, Greece is much less industrialized than most other European countries and has not so far experienced the severe environmental damage caused by extensive or heavy industry. Nor does Greece have any nuclear power plants. Low levels of industrialization and absence of nuclear installations do not, however, mean that there are no serious environmental disturbances which could serve as the basis for the formation of a substantial green movement. The small size of Greece's industrial establishments has not prevented them from littering and polluting the environment, not least because most are equipped with old-fashioned and fuel-inefficient machinery. Moreover, during the last 20 years there has been tremendous destruction of forests, extensive pollution of the sea, disorganized town planning, rapid extermination of the native fauna, dirty cities and, on top of everything, the Athenian smog caused mainly by the concentration of motor vehicles in an already hyper-concentrated capital where almost half the country's population lives.

This is a short extract from a much longer list of environmental problems which might be thought sufficient to provoke collective adversarial reaction. Of the above-mentioned problems, just two – the destruction of forests by yearly repeated fires and air pollution which, especially in summer in the Athens area, is the cause of many deaths and diseases (Gillman 1990) – could logically become the levers for a strong environmental or ecological movement. The fact that there is no such movement does not mean that people are unaware of the problems. On the contrary, the flow of information about them through various media is considerable. The absence of a systematic and collective response bears witness to the low ranking of environmental problems in people's need hierarchies. For almost 20 years the development of a large and dynamic Green movement has been hindered by a widespread lack of deep-rooted environmental consciousness among the Greek public. The fact that the environment plays a noteworthy role in agenda-setting procedures is due far more to its having been covered by commercially distributed news and spectacle than to fundamental collective public concern.

This, however, by no means implies that all through this period citizens' environmental initiatives, protectionist associations and ecological organizations were totally absent at both national and local level. On the contrary, it has been calculated that since 1974 more than 200 environmental and ecological clubs, associations, groups and organizations have been formed. Nevertheless, they have not constituted a movement in the proper sense of the word. That is, they have not influenced major parts of the population, they have worked sporadically and in isolation and with limited range and objectives. Where environmental initiatives have taken place, they tend to have been undertaken by largely isolated but frequently enlightened minorities rather than by active collectivities. By comparison with other western European countries, Greece has a quasi-movement rather than a well-established and deep-rooted Green movement.

HISTORICAL DEVELOPMENT OF THE GREEN MOVEMENT

If, however, one wants to do justice to what I have just called a 'quasi-movement', one should take a closer look at its course through time (Louloudis 1987: 8–21). Its history can be divided into two periods: from 1973 to 1981, and after 1981. In the first period, there were at least eight significant mobilizations regarding environmental problems, among them the cases of Megara (1973), Volos (1975), Pylos (1975) and Karystos (1977–1979). Aiming to prevent the building of new industrial installations, all of them occurred in places away from the capital. They had, therefore, a regional character. These mobilizations included demonstrations, strikes, public debates, propagation of demands and ideas through local media and so on. A common feature was that, since Greece has an overconcentrated administrative structure, these mobilizations could not succeed unless they were, in one way or another, extended to the central decision-making headquarters of Athens. The transference of appeals to the national level proved in all cases to be decisive and all eight mobilizations ultimately achieved most of their objectives. However, their accomplishments were usually not so much the outcome of their own efforts and dynamics as they were due to the incidental incorporation of regional and local environmental uprisings into the competition between political parties at the central level. In this respect, it should be mentioned that political parties, especially leftist ones, have been reluctant to take part in this sort of mobilization, whose rationale was sometimes entirely different from the parties' own. The leftist parties only came to terms with them either to attempt to absorb the mobilization out of long-term strategic considerations or for immediate political advantages.

Another common trait of this period was the protectionist character of mobilizations; the prevailing element was environmentalism rather than deep ecology. The simple environmentalist nature of those mobilizations could be partially explained by the role of intellectuals who were involved during that period. They mostly came from the natural sciences and usually advocated scientific and technical solutions to the various problems. This was not accidental since it was they who, during the 1970s, first taught and brought into Greek universities and other institutions the environmental problematic in a scientific and systematic manner. It is of importance here that those mobilizations were frequently stimulated by sheer economic motivations by vested material interests, glossed up ideologically by appeals to tradition and homeland. The environment was not consistently recognized as a societal value in itself.

Despite apparent similarities, the situation during the second period (1981 to date) is different. Again, there have been mobilizations, among them one in 1988 in northern Greece (Kalamas) which really shook public opinion. Though mobilizations did occur more frequently in Athens (the most prominent of them initiated by Chernobyl in 1986), most took place at regional and local level once again. But, beyond these superficial similarities, one can ascertain new traits: a proliferation of environmental and ecological associations and groups, reinforcement of an autonomous feminist problematic, an increase in humanist intellectuals' involvement in environmental debates and activities and a remarkable growth of environmental and ecological literature. It should also be mentioned that 'alternativeness' as a vague but adversarial socio-economic project was more apparent than in the previous period. We could, therefore, say that since 1981 there has been a sort of transition from environmentalism to political ecology or from shallow to deep ecology.

This does not imply a clear-cut distinction nor a well-defined collective identity for all those who participate in major mobilizations. Again, what frequently underlies mobilizations at the local level are private and non-organized economic interests which cannot in the first place be mediated by existing political networks. Such was the case with the Kalamas River affair (August–September 1988), the most publicized environmental mobilization ever in Greece. Successive mobilizations have not, however, given rise to a substantial Green movement. Green thinking remains isolated in minority circles, unable to permeate the mentality and everyday life activities of wider social strata (Karimalis 1987: 234–235; Plassara 1987: 284–286; Spanopoulos 1987: 292–293).

By international standards, we still cannot speak of a Green movement in Greece. It is not simply a question of the ambivalences in the identity of many groups which participate in various kinds of mobilizations, nor their deficiencies in defining their foes and alternative projects for societal reconstruction that Touraine (1977: 77–101) identified as the prerequisites for a movement. Something more fundamental is missing, the *sine qua non* for a social movement to develop as such: mass involvement as well as durable support and attractiveness. As it is, the cause of environment or ecology is restricted to small devoted groups whose influence is, and probably will continue to be, quite fragmented and limited. The non-development of environmental social consciousness might be advanced as an explanation of the weakness of the Green movement, but this in turn requires explanation. What makes for this lack of environmental consciousness? A number of factors deserve mention.

The first is the postwar economic development which lasted until the early 1970s (Mouzelis 1978). It was modernization based extensively on small manufacturing, middle range industry, fragmentation of capital and property, as well as on tourism and the massive remittances of emigrants. Non-agricultural production has been concentrated mainly in construction, consumption and the tertiary sector. At the same time, a great deal of economic activity is parasitic and 'grey', recent estimates putting the black economy at more than 35 per cent of GNP. All these factors have led to an unforeseeably rapid vertical as well as horizontal social mobility which has put into question traditional lifestyles and identities. Moreover, social mobility has been accompanied by geographical mobility, the result being rapid and unplanned urbanization buttressed principally by small private property.

Second, this modernization has given rise to very crowded middle social layers whose mentality is highly atomistic and state-oriented. Contemporary orientation towards the state is related to traditional Greek statism (Mouzelis 1986; Lyrintzis 1984: 99–118). For reasons both historical (legacies of the Byzantine and Ottoman empires, the absence of a potent and productively inclined bourgeoisie) and political (the weak civil and human rights tradition, political modernization from above, clientelistic political representation), the state intervenes decisively in societal relations as a powerful distributor of incomes, resources and advantages of all sorts. The western tradition of the state as 'night-watchman' has never appeared in Greece. Nor has state intervention led to a welfare state. From the beginning, the state has been a power and administrative centre for the absorption of potential unemployment as well as for balancing opposed societal interests through non-productive financial, protective and distributive policies. It is precisely these policies which reproduce almost the whole society's dependence on the state. This is essentially the reason for administrative overconcentration and the unusually large and unproductive public sector.

Consequently, the mode of domination has been deeply embedded in clientelism and populism rather than in contractual and institutionally guaranteed parliamentary and democratic procedures. This is related to the weakness of civil society in Greece, both as a relatively independent public sphere and as a setting in which various social movements can emerge. Together with other dimensions of the social and political system, the weakness of civil society leaves room for a ubiquitous individualism, fostered by small private property that often makes difficult the articulation of collective consciousness. Given this individualism, rapid upward social mobility has brought about a raising of expectations, a reorientation of reference groups and an intense sense of relative deprivation (Demertzis 1990: 70–96). These have been expressed through an ever-moving stream of consumerism and greedy material prosperity which make it difficult for the environment to be protected and accorded a central place in public interests. Under such circumstances, the natural environment is not conceived as a public good or as something endowed with its own inherent value but as a field and means for maximum economic exploitation.

Another important factor that has contributed to limited environmental consciousness among the Greek public is the priority given to the democratic cause over other political and social concerns, especially during the years immediately after the abolition of the military dictatorship (1967–1974). Whereas for most European countries the 1970s was the decade of Green movement formation, intellectuals and other radical groups in Greece were primarily concerned with the restoration of democratic institutions rather than with the critique of an environmentally calamitous model of socio-economic modernization.

Since 1974, political parties have been the primary agents for the mediation and articulation of societal demands, including those concerning the environment. The 'partyness' of Greek society conducts interest aggregation from above (Papadopoulos 1989: 66–67). Thus, even if there have been environmental demands, they have been for the most part addressed to the traditional parties and, consequently, were deprived of their ecological as well as radical potential.

All in all, disorganized economic development, speedy urbanization and upward social mobility, statism and poorly articulated civil society, have co-ordinated historically to make a well-rooted environmental consciousness unlikely in Greece. Underdevelopment of societal environmental consciousness has not, however, prevented Green parties from emerging out of the various environmental groups and associations.

THE DEVELOPMENT OF THE GREEN PARTY

Ecological and environmental groups started thinking about forming a unified political body as early as 1984. This, however, proved to be more difficult than it might have seemed, partly because other parties could absorb relatively easily environmental demands into their programmes and policies, and because the numerous groups and associations were dispersed over the country, making co-operation and communication difficult. Moreover, the quite deep differences and divisions among these groups made unified action almost impossible, as did their adherence to 'anti-systemic' activism and their scepticism of electoral politics.

A number of meetings did take place where possibilities for constructing a unified Green party were explored, but it was not until autumn 1989 that a federation of more than 100 groups and associations was set up. Meanwhile, some of them had participated in the 1986 local elections. Results were rather disappointing in terms of votes and seats, but it was at least a first step. Two years later a loose eco-political scheme was founded under the title Enosi Politon (Citizens' Union). This proved short-lived both because only a small number of groups and intellectuals was involved and because of its self-declared preliminary organizational character; for the majority of the participants, the Citizens' Union was meant to be the forerunner of a much wider political–ecological organization.

In February 1989, through close co-operation with German Greens and the contribution of some extra-parliamentary leftist groups, members of the Citizens' Union decided to participate in the June 1989 election for the European Parliament, and to postpone setting up the Green federation until the end of that year. In the meantime, other political agents took part in elections under 'environmental' or 'ecological' banners. These were ephemeral, did not constitute parties in any proper sense of the term and had minimal significance in terms of votes, organization and programme.

Although the conditions for a substantial environmental movement were lacking, Greek ecologists did participate in three successive elections under the title Ecologists–Alternatives.

Though the European election coincided with the general election of June 1989, Ecologists–Alternatives decided to take part only in the former, mainly because it was reckoned that, given the intensity of national party competition, their chances in the national parliamentary election were extremely limited, whereas the European election was relatively neglected by the major parties. In the event, they narrowly failed to reach the threshold of 1.36 per cent necessary to win a seat.

The Greens were ambivalent about the 1.1 per cent they actually got. It was interpreted either as a negative sign that environmental ideas and political ecology needed to be further cultivated at ground level before being tested in the political arena, or, alternatively, it was seen as a first doubtful but primarily positive and encouraging message for further political involvement. The second interpretation prevailed in the meetings and debates that followed that election. Thus when the Federation of Ecological Organizations was formed in October 1989, it was decided to participate under that banner in the national election of November 1989.

Expectations and predictions that the Greens would double their vote in the general election proved unfounded, but the 0.58 per cent they did get was sufficient to win them a seat in the national parliament. As a result, they started to get more publicity because this was the first time in more than half a century that a non-traditional leftist party had entered the Greek parliament. That single parliamentary seat was reckoned by Ecologists–Alternatives to justify their taking part in the next national election a few months later. Again, expectations triumphed over reality; in April 1990 they managed to increase their votes only marginally but retained their single seat.

In local elections the Greens have fared rather better. In October 1990 they managed to multiply their votes in many regions and cities and secured a number of seats on municipal councils. The relatively small-scale problems of local communities and the highly personalized character of local political communication made it feasible for Green candidates to exercise personal influence more easily. Yet with few exceptions, the numbers and percentages concerned were still very small.

Since their official introduction to the political scene, Ecologists–Alternatives have not penetrated the boundaries of the Greek party system but remain on its thresholds. Potential influence has not yet been converted into positive voting. It is characteristic that although a few months before the 1990 election 8 per cent of the population ranked the environment first in their issue preferences, Ecologists–Alternatives received only 0.77 per cent of the votes. This means not only that the existing party system is capable of appropriating the ecological problematic, but also that the low development of environmental consciousness affects Green Party performance. The formation of a Greek Green party, late though it was by comparison with most European countries, does not appear to have met or represented any widespread new post-materialist needs, values or demands.

Although there are no systematic calculations, all the indications are that Ecologists–Alternatives were, like Green parties in western Europe, mostly preferred by the young and the new middle class as well as by the more highly educated. It has to be noted that although most groups participating in the Ecologists–Alternatives came from various regions and constituencies, in the 1989 European election the Green vote in urban areas was double that in semi-urban ones, and more than double that in rural areas; 41.4 per cent of Green votes were concentrated in Athens. The same held true for the next two national elections: Athens accounted for 47.2 and 44.4 per cent of Green votes in the November 1989 and April 1990 elections respectively.

A closer inspection of the results of those polls shows that the Green vote in the wealthier, well-preserved new middle-class areas is much greater than in low income and environmentally damaged areas and districts. It seems that there is a disconnection between the areas and constituencies confronted with serious environmental problems and the electorate's preference for the Greens. It is characteristic that in the constituency of Thesprotia, where the great mobilization over the Kalamas River took place, the Green candidate got only 0.36 per cent in the 1989 poll and 0.49 per cent in the 1990 election. Results were similarly meagre in all the other places where environmental mobilization had occurred, as well as in other constituencies with extensive environmental problems. Although the Greens polled more strongly in local elections, the disconnection between environmentally burdened areas and the Green vote still remained. For example, in Elefsis, reckoned to be the most ecologically damaged city in Europe, the Greens polled only 2.9 per cent.

The Federation of Ecological Organizations formed in October 1989 accommodates nearly 100 groups and associations which range from pure conservationists to extra-parliamentary far leftists. Since October 1989 something like a dozen of the founding constituent groups have withdrawn. Most of the constituent groups come from various regions and provincial cities and towns. The decentralized character of the federation continues to contrast with the concentration of Green votes in Athens.

The Federation has a loose organizational structure consisting of a 45-member co-ordinating secretariat, a nine-member presidency and committees on specific issues such as the parliamentary support of their delegate and the ethnic minorities. According to the rotation principle, members of both the secretariat and the presidency are supposed to change every three months, but this has not happened because of acute organizational problems, the unwillingness of ordinary members to undertake official tasks and the personal squabbles between some prominent members. Like their counterparts elsewhere, the Greek Greens espouse acknowledged 'new politics' means and goals, yet, as far as their organizational structure is concerned, neither the members of the secretariat nor the members of the presidency have ever been elected. Instead, they are appointed by the major constituent groups.

The founding Congress was postponed four times. First scheduled for December 1990, then for April 1991, June 1991 and autumn 1991, it eventually took place in January–February 1992. The main reasons for these postponements lie in the inner discords of the Federation. Apart from the 'deep versus shallow ecology' and the '*fundi–realo*' disputes, a devastating debate took place in the Federation concerning its organization. On the one hand, it was argued that there should be a balance between the centre and the periphery, namely, between the Federation as a co-ordinating centre and the local constituent groups; on the other hand, an argument was raised against the very co-ordinating character of the Federation and in favour of the autonomy of the constituent groups. This disagreement was amplified not only by the above-mentioned discords and divisions, but also by the lack of preparation of the Greek Greens to enter the political arena.

All these antitheses were intensified during the founding Congress in February 1992. That Congress ended in total failure since a considerable number of far left activists withdrew both from the Congress and the Federation. One of the immediate consequences was that their single parliamentary representative declared herself independent from the Ecologists–Alternatives, thus depriving the Federation of an important means of political action.

THE POLITICAL OPPORTUNITY STRUCTURE

The weak electoral profile of the Greek Greens cannot be explained entirely by the atrophy of environmental consciousness and the consequent enfeeblement of a Green movement. The inertia of the Greek political party system also plays a major role. In analysing the structure of the party system in Greece and the position of the Greek Green Party in it, one can rather better understand its relatively late formation and its limited electoral base as well as its future prospects.

Despite various extra-constitutional interruptions, the Greek party system has been characterized by remarkable continuity and stability. It has deep historical roots inherited from two periods which determined the political cleavages of the country: the National Schism of 1915–1922, and the Civil War of 1945–1949. The first gave rise to right and anti-right coalitions, the second to a communist left and anti-communist division. In the years after the Second World War the two cleavages overlapped so as to allow the non-right-wing camp to overtake the right.

Alongside these cleavages, a tri-polar political system has been constructed which corresponds to three clear-cut political camps with their respective identifications and loyalties: the left, the centre and the right (Mavrogordatos 1983a, 1983b: 70–94; Diamandouros 1983: 43–69; Papadopoulos 1989: 58–61; Nikolakopoulos 1985: 65–85). Before 1981 none of the poles corresponded to a particular single party. Thus, although there was usually a multi-party system, it was actually run according to a tri-polar logic. With the restoration of constitutional democracy in 1974 this system gradually started to fade. The outcome of the 1981 election marked its end. Three distinct major parties now represent the three political families; in recent elections they have between them won almost the sum total of votes cast in national as well as European elections.

Most students of the Greek party system agree that it is 'frozen' (Mavrogordatos 1984; Nikolakopoulos 1989: 100–108; Papadopoulos 1989: 62–64; Paschos 1984: 192–211). Party loyalties and identifications based on traditional cleavages remain intact and voting volatility is extremely low (Verney 1990: 131).

Party systems and electoral systems feed on each other. Changes to the electoral law to suit the governing party are typical of the Greek political system. At various times since the early 1950s, electoral laws have been designed so as to exclude the left from participation in government. Most national elections have been run by a system of 'reinforced' proportional representation (Featherstone 1990: 105–106; Verney 1990: 131–133) which always provides a working parliamentary majority to the major party by depriving lesser ones of several seats they would have gained under a strictly proportional system.

In order to secure its future position, shortly before the general election of June 1989, PASOK introduced a hybrid system intermingling reinforced proportionality and 'pure' PR (Pridham and Verney 1991: 50). In the new system, 288 of the 300 seats are filled from 56 constituencies. The remaining 12 go to 'Deputies of State' elected on a nationwide PR basis. The 288 seats are allocated by means of two distributions. In the first, allocation in each constituency is calculated by dividing the number of valid votes cast by the number of seats plus one. Any remaining seats are allocated on the second distribution in which the country is divided into 13 constituencies, this time without the 'plus one' clause (Pridham and Verney 1991: 55–56). Single parties or coalitions which field candidates in at least three-quarters of all constituencies and get at least 2 per cent of the total vote are granted at least three seats from the second distribution provided that they have not won any on the first. Parties with 1 per cent of the total vote are entitled to one parliamentary seat. This electoral system is much more open and permissive than any since 1974. Yet, though it has operated through three successive polls, the party system has exhibited remarkable inertia. Contrary to predictions and positive opinion polls, Ecologists–Alternatives have barely managed to win a single seat.

Given that in 1988–1989 the political scene was torn by scandals and obvious political corruption (Featherstone 1990: 103–105; Pridham and Verney 1991: 49, 54), observers and students of Greek politics predicted a decisive rupture in party loyalties. It was precisely this assumption that persuaded the Greens to enter electoral politics. But the assumption was proved wrong; the party system stood still. More particularly, though there were shifts in voters' allegiances, they took place within the three camps rather than disengaging voters towards new options. The right achieved its best result but PASOK's populism averted severe losses even though it was PASOK's leadership which had been accused of much economic and political corruption. Recent upheavals in eastern Europe had thrown the traditional left into crisis and many of its voters moved towards either PASOK or New Democracy. The proportion of the left vote which transferred to the Greens lagged far behind predictions. Given the low ranking of the environment in the public's need hierarchies, as well as the stormy political arena of the time, it may well be that a considerable part of the Ecologists–Alternatives' votes were not actually Green but protest votes.

CONCLUSION

The formation of the Green Party in Greece can be attributed to: a voluntaristic compensation for the green movement's low profile; activists' incomplete understanding of the Greek party system;

contingent circumstances such as the uneasiness of the political scene; the exceptionally permissive electoral law of 1989. This appears to contrast sharply with the experience of western Europe where, in most cases, Green parties have been the outcome of a deep-rooted set of social needs expressed through potent movements and ruptures of political cleavages.

What, then, are the prospects for the Greens in Greek politics? To answer this question one has to take into account some nascent dimensions of the political and party system which, for the first time, have faintly appeared during the last few years in Greece. It is increasingly recognized that the mode of domination in Greek society, based principally on clientelistic politics and populist practices, is an impediment to economic success and modernization in general. Various voices have been raised against this mode of domination and in favour of a reorganization of representation structures. This does not imply that such a restructuring is immediately at hand – the party system is still well buttressed by traditional political practices which lead modernization processes into blind alleys – but it is an important tendency which may be realized in the long or even medium term. Arguments against the continuation of the current mode of domination are supported by a slight dislocation of traditional political cleavages.

This dislocation does not come principally from a transmutation of values in a post-materialist direction (Inglehart 1977, 1981). It is stimulated by the inability of the existing party system to meet the requirements of administrative and economic rationalization. The Greek public is generally unaffected by post-materialist priorities, although one can trace such trends among the young and the educated upper middle class. Hence, whereas in the mid-1980s the distance in Greece between right and left on the respective axis was the largest in Europe (Papadopoulos 1989: 63), by the end of the decade it had diminished. The opposition between the two extremes has thus been reduced and one can observe a certain convergence towards the centre. It was precisely this leaning to the centre that made possible the six-month coalition between right and left in 1989.

It is premature to assume that this convergence is going to last. On the contrary, some indications in recent government policies point to its contingent character. The alteration of the electoral law is one instance. Once again, the party in government has altered the terms of political competition in its own favour: the October

1993 general election was conducted by the familiar reinforced proportional representation system, but this time with a 3 per cent threshold. This, and the renewed fragmentation of the Greens – the Federation having disintegrated almost a year before the election and many Greens having subsequently attached themselves to other parties, notably the Left Alliance – robbed the Greens of any chance of parliamentary representation.

For the time being the issue is open, but the modernizing imperatives of European integration may determine future developments. With the restructuring of traditional political cleavages, Greens, either alone or in coalition with other parties, might yet win a better place on the left of the Greek party system. This presupposes their reforming into a 'systemic' political force (Katsoulis 1990: 40–42) and their resolving their internal inconsistencies. The Federation lacked specific rules for its organization and decision-making. It also lacked an articulated alternative programme founded on political ecological principles. To overcome their difficulties, Greek Greens would, among other things, have to bridge the gulf between *Fundis* and *Realos*. So far they show no signs of doing so.

REFERENCES

Demertzis, N. (1990) 'The Greek Political Culture in the 80s', in Hellenic Political Science Association (ed.), *Elections and Parties in the 80s: Evolution and Prospects of the Political System*, Athens: Themelio (in Greek).

Diamandouros, N. (1983) 'Greek Political Culture in Transition', in R. Clogg (ed.), *Greece in the 1980s*, London: Macmillan.

Featherstone, K. (1990) 'The "Party-State" in Greece and the Fall of Papandreou', *West European Politics* 13(1): 101–115.

Gillman, P. (1990) 'A Touch of the Vapours', *Sunday Times Magazine*, 14 October: 44–54.

Inglehart, R. (1977) *The Silent Revolution*, Princeton, NJ: Princeton University Press.

—— (1981) 'Post-Materialism in an Environment of Insecurity', *American Political Science Review* 75(4): 880–900.

Karimalis, G. (1987) 'The Ecological Movement has a Future', in Ch. Orphanidis (ed.), *The Ecological Movement in Greece*, Athens: Meta te Vroche (in Greek).

Katsoulis, E. (1990) 'The Frozen Party System in a Transitory Society: Evolutions, Perspectives', in Hellenic Political Science Association (ed.), *Elections and Parties in the 80s: Evolution and Prospects of the Political System*, Athens: Themelio (in Greek).

Louloudis, L. (1987) 'Societal Demands: From Environmental Protection to Political Ecology', in Ch. Orphanidis (ed.), *The Ecological Movement in Greece*, Athens: Meta te Vroche (in Greek).

Lyrintzis, Ch. (1984) 'Political Parties in Post-Junta Greece: A Case of Bureaucratic Clientilism?', in G. Pridham (ed.), *The New Mediterranean Democracies: Regime Transition in Spain, Greece and Portugal*, London: Frank Cass.

Mavrogordatos, G. (1983a) 'The Emerging Party System', in R. Clogg (ed.), *Greece in the 1980s*, London: Macmillan.

—— (1983b) *Stillborn Republic: Social Coalitions and Party Strategies in Greece, 1922–1936*, Berkeley, Calif.: University of California Press.

—— (1984) 'The Greek Party System: A Case of Limited but Polarized Pluralism?', *West European Politics* 4(2): 156–169.

Mouzelis, N. (1978) *Modern Greece: Facets of Underdevelopment*, London: Macmillan.

—— (1986) *Politics in the Semi-Periphery: Early Parliamentarism and Late Industrialism in the Balkans and Latin America*, London: Macmillan.

Nikolakopoulos, E. (1985) *Parties and Parliamentary Elections in Greece. 1946–1964*, Athens: National Centre of Social Research (in Greek).

—— (1989) *Introduction to the Theory and Practice of Electoral Systems*, Athens: Satoulas (in Greek).

Orphanidis, Ch. (ed.) (1987) *The Ecological Movement in Greece*, Athens: Meta te Vroche (in Greek).

Papadopoulos, Y. (1989) 'Parties, the State and Society in Greece: Continuity Within Change', *West European Politics* 12(2): 55–71.

Paschos, G. (1984) 'Bipartism and the Functioning of the Polity', in Hellenic Political Science Association (ed.), *The 1981 Election*, Athens: Estia (in Greek).

Plassara, K. (1987) 'The Present and the Future of Greece's Ecological Movement', in Ch. Orphanidis (ed.), *The Ecological Movement in Greece*, Athens: Meta te Vroche (in Greek).

Pridham, G. and Verney, S. (1991) 'The Coalitions of 1989–90 in Greece: Inter-Party Relations and Democratic Consolidation', *West European Politics* 14(4): 42–69.

Spanopoulos, K. (1987) 'Ecology is Eros for Life', in Ch. Orphanidis (ed.), *The Ecological Movement in Greece*, Athens: Meta te Vroche (in Greek).

Touraine, A. (1977) *The Voice and the Eye*, Cambridge: Cambridge University Press.

Verney, S. (1990) 'Between Coalition and One-Party Government: The Greek Elections of November 1989 and April 1990', *West European Politics* 13(4): 131–138.

Chapter 11

Czechoslovakia

Greens in a post-Communist society

Petr Jehlicka and Tomas Kostelecky

In the months following the November 1989 upheaval, the growing Green Party seemed to be one of the decisive political forces in Czechoslovakia.[1] The environment ranked as a top priority issue in opinion polls and the Green Party was perceived by the general public as the leading exponent of environmental reform. However, as the results of the June 1990 general election revealed, the Greens failed to capitalize on this advantage and, after joining an obscure coalition before the 1992 election, the Czech Green Party lost both its identity and a majority of its members. Now, despite having three deputies in parliament, the Greens have fallen into near oblivion. In Slovakia the party split into 'pro-Czechoslovak' and 'real Slovak' Greens before the 1992 election; neither has deputies in the new Slovak parliament. Why and how the brave hopes of 1989 should have been so thoroughly disappointed is the subject of this chapter.

THE EMERGENCE OF THE GREEN PARTY

In the 1980s Czechoslovakia had arguably the most devastated environment in Europe. Some of its regions were undoubtedly ecological disaster areas (see Figure 11.1, p. 217), and far-reaching environmental degradation affected the health of a population which has one of the shortest life expectancies in Europe. As everybody could see the deepening ecological degradation, even the Communist regime could not maintain that environmental groups and their claims and objections were illegitimate. Some environmental organizations, for example, the Czech Union of Nature Protectionists (CUNP), Brontosaurus, Tree of Life and the Slovak Union of Protectionists of Nature and the Countryside (SUPNC), functioned legally albeit under the strict control of the

Communist regime. Other groups, for example, the Ecological Society or Children of the Earth, were completely illegal. Although the official organizations were relatively numerous (the CUNP had about 25,000 members in 1989), they were not very effective. In general, all legal ecological movements and unions were intentionally kept atomized and in isolation by the Communist authorities, but, in practice, the core activists of such groups often cooperated closely with activists from illegal groups. Both sides benefited from this collaboration: unofficial groups could achieve some of their aims through the medium of legal organizations, while the latter's activities became more effective by utilizing the often highly qualified experts associated with the illegal groups.

As a result, the environment became more or less the main legal basis for opposition to the Communist regime, especially in the Czech lands. Environmentalists' arguments could not, as the protests of human rights dissidents usually were, be easily swept aside by the authorities and, since environmental activities were not completely illegal, more people could safely participate in them. In consequence, many activists were primarily opponents of communism and only secondarily supporters of the environmental cause. This is not to say that human rights defenders and environmentalists were entirely separate; in 1983, for example, the Ecological Section of the Biological Society prepared for Charter 77 the *Report on the Ecological Situation in Czechoslovakia* which described the extent of the ecological catastrophe in Czechoslovakia.

Civic resistance was much weaker in Slovakia than in the Czech lands, and the role of environmentalists during the events of November 1989 and afterwards in the Slovak capital, Bratislava, was crucial. Almost all leading figures of Public Against Violence (PAV), the movement which carried out the November revolution in Slovakia and won the first free election in that republic seven months later, were members of the Bratislava branch of the SUPNC. While the opposition to the regime in the Czech lands could be labelled 'civic–environmental', in Slovakia it was rather 'environmental–Christian'.

The great demonstration in Teplice against the passivity of local Communist authorities in dealing with environmental problems preceded by a week the beginning of the 'velvet revolution' in Prague (17 November 1989) and can be seen as further evidence of the prominent role of the environmental cause in bringing down the regime.

The Green Party was established on 21 November 1989, the first political party founded after the 'velvet revolution'. The announcement of its foundation suggested that the party already had 5,200 members and 11,000 signatures supporting its legalization. On 26 November, the new party published the main items of its programme. The most important were the call for reform of the political system, abolition of the leading role of the Communist Party and free elections. Curiously, the environment was not mentioned. In an interview for the People Party's daily on 28 November, the founders of the Prague Committee admitted that they had in their ranks neither experts on the environment nor well-known activists. Parallel to the establishment of the Prague party, local Green groups mushroomed all over the Czech Republic, mainly in larger cities. Another green grouping, the Green Alternative, was founded in Prague on 1 December and tried to attract humanistically oriented academics and young people. Although a few well-known public figures were involved, this group also failed to attract well-known ecologists.

At the beginning of December, I. Dejmal, previously known as an editor of the samizdat *Ecological Bulletin*, published a pamphlet (Dejmal 1989) stating that, while the Green Party was developing spontaneously in many parts of the country, the Prague Committee consisted of people who did not enjoy the confidence of the environmental movement and had even taken part in the persecution of ecological activists. Nevertheless, it was the Prague Committee which used television to call a national meeting of all Green preparatory committees for 9 December.

The 9 December meeting was not properly organized: the representativeness of delegates was doubtful and there were none from Slovakia. Almost no interest was expressed in co-operation with environmental NGOs. A crucial meeting followed a month later, by which time there existed Moravian–Silesian and Slovak committees of the Green Party. The Green Alternative fused with the Green Party and negotiations were held with representatives from the regions. A separate Bohemian meeting took place on the same day. The overall results were a preliminary proposal for a party programme, approval of its logo and the name 'Green Party', the establishment of a Bohemian regional committee and the acceptance of the regional structure of the future federal party.

The preparatory committee of the Green Party in Slovakia was founded at the same time. However, the emergence of the Green Party in Slovakia was different. Mesik (1990) explains:

> The interest of the secret police in the infiltration and prospective dominance of the developing Green Party was fairly logical, and could have been foreseen, and was exactly the same in Slovakia as in Bohemia and Moravia. However, the reaction of the environmental protection movement in both republics was different. Key figures in the Slovak environmental movement, who originally did not intend to abandon their super-political position within the framework of the movement and did not plan to join the Greens, responded to an attempt by the secret police to control the Green Party's nuclei by joining the new party. The present situation is that the core of the management and activists in the Green Party in Slovakia consists of former members of the environmental protection movement.

In mid-February 1990 the first national congress of the Green Party was convened in Brno. Among more than 300 delegates, Prague was again represented by members of its now discredited committee but, despite considerable effort, they did not succeed in penetrating the party leadership (Makasek 1990). The congress approved an organizational structure of basic groups at the municipal level and, above them, district associations. Co-ordination committees were formed for the Czech regions, Bohemia and Moravia–Silesia, and for Slovakia.[2] These committees were only very loosely roofed over by a national council composed of nine members, three each from the Czech regional committees and three from Slovakia. Their period in office was set at eight months in deference to the (later abandoned) principle of rotation. After the Brno congress, the party began to prepare for the first free elections for more than 40 years.

THE CZECHOSLOVAK POLITICAL SYSTEM 1990–1992

The Federal Assembly was composed of two chambers with equal rights and responsibilities: the Chamber of People elected in the whole of Czechoslovakia in proportion to population (and so with twice as many Czech deputies as Slovak), and the Chamber of Nations, consisting of Czech and Slovak sections each of 75 members. There were also separate Czech and Slovak National Councils.

The electoral system – proportional representation with multi-member constituencies – was qualified by thresholds: 5 per cent of the vote in the territory of one republic was necessary for a party to enter the Federal Assembly and the Czech National Council, whereas only 3 per cent was sufficient to elect deputies to the Slovak National Council.

Besides the Green Party, many new parties and movements emerged after 1989 and complemented several parties legally recognized during the Communist period. Civic Forum, originally a broad alliance of most of the anti-communist political forces in the Czech Republic, split after the 1990 election to leave three main successors: the Civic Movement, the Civic Democratic Alliance and the Civic Democratic Party. Civic Forum's Slovak counterpart, Public Against Violence, also split: the popular leftist and nationalist Movement for Democratic Slovakia formed in April 1991, and the remainder of the PAV became the liberal and pro-Czechoslovak Civic Democratic Union.

On the right, the dominant part of the Christian Democratic Union was the Czechoslovak People Party, a predominantly Catholic party established at the turn of the century which had collaborated with communists throughout their rule. Its Slovak counterpart was the Christian Democratic Movement. Most other important parties in 1990 were on the left. The Slovak National Party had a single policy – independence for Slovakia – whereas the Movement for Self-Governing Democracy/Society for Moravia and Silesia claimed autonomy for Moravia and Silesia within Czechoslovakia. The most important part of the Alliance of Agrarians and Countryside, the Agrarian Party, represented co-operative farmers. Czechoslovak Social Democracy aspired to be a western-style party, but was too much anchored in prewar memories and too much under the influence of reform communists. Both the Communist Party of Bohemia and Moravia and the Party of Democratic Left (former Slovak communists) remained trapped in the past, although the leadership of the Slovak party tended to be more 'social democratic'.

THE GREENS IN THE 1990 PARLIAMENTARY ELECTIONS

The election law guaranteed 4 hours of TV and radio broadcasts for each participating party, but the Green Party's media performance was fairly unattractive and obscure. Before the election, a fortnightly publication, *The Greens*, began to appear, at first only in Bohemia but, due to lack of funds, publication ceased after the eleventh issue. In Slovakia, the Greens had a weekly two-page supplement in the trades unionist daily.

During the campaign, the Greens avoided attacking other parties; only from the Communists did they keep their distance. It was decided as early as the Brno congress that former members of the Communist Party would not be allowed to stand as candidates of the Green Party. Later, it was also decided that Green candidates would be checked to make sure they were not on lists of secret police agents. The fact that Prague candidates refused to submit to such checks was one reason why their opponents called the Greens 'melons' (green outside, red inside).

The slogan most often used in the Green Party's campaign was: 'Vote for the Greens, you are voting for life.' The Greens declined to locate themselves on a left–right spectrum, declared themselves a party 'standing neither left nor right, but ahead' and tried to appeal to ecological sentiment and the responsibility of people for the environment. At the local level, their campaign concentrated on organizing such events as 'green marches' and cleaning parks, Greens often organizing pre-electoral meetings in small communities with social democrats (Vajdova 1990). Greens were frequently attacked by other parties: in spite of their constant effort to keep their distance from the Communists, they were accused of 'cryptocommunism' and, in Slovakia, were sometimes blamed for idealism and naivety, even by former nature protectionists in the leadership of Public Against Violence.

According to newspaper opinion polls, the Greens maintained a stable 11 per cent support from the end of February until the beginning of May; in mid-May 8 per cent intended to vote for the Greens, while a few days before the poll this had dropped to the 4 per cent they actually received. The Greens had not foreseen their vote falling below the thresholds but, on the contrary, had anticipated post-election collaboration with the presumed winners – the Civic Forum and Public Against Violence. Their self-confidence was encouraged by the numbers joining the party: at the end of January 1990 the Greens were estimated to have 15,000 members in the Czech Republic[3] and, at the Brno congress in February, 80,000 in the whole country.[4]

The Greens ran successfully only for the Slovak National Council, where the threshold was lower than in other legislative bodies,

Table 11.1 Parliamentary election, June 1990 (percentage of votes)

Political party	FA–CR[1]	FA–SR[2]	CNC[3]	SNC[4]
Civic Forum	51.6		49.5	
Public Against Violence		34.9		29.3
Communist Party	13.6	13.6	13.2	13.3
Christian and Democratic Union	8.7		8.4	
Christian Democratic Movement		17.8		19.2
Society for Moravia and Silesia	8.5		10.0	
Slovak National Party		11.2		14.0
Alliance of Agrarians	3.9	2.3	4.1	2.5
Social Democracy	4.0	1.7	4.1	1.8
Green Party	3.3	2.9	4.1	3.5
Coalition of Minorities	0.0	8.5		8.7
Democratic Party		4.0		4.4

Notes: 1 FA–CR Average votes for both chambers of the Federal Assembly in Czech Republic.
2 FA–SR Average votes for both chambers of the Federal Assembly in Slovak Republic.
3 CNC Votes for Czech National Council.
4 SNC Votes for Slovak National Council.
Turnout: 95 per cent.

winning six of the 150 seats (see Table 11.1). Key figures of the Czech Greens and representatives of NGOs took part in a discussion of that failure in the ecological monthly, *Nika* (Cekalova *et al.* 1990). Very significantly, the Greens were a party of second choice; for most voters the most important thing was consolidation of political change – many followed the slogan 'Ecology will wait for democracy.' Others considered the economy as the primary problem in spite of the catastrophic state of the environment and feared that success for the Greens might slow down the pace of economic reform. The media campaign by Civic Forum and Public Against Violence against smaller parties probably hit the Green Party too.[5] Lack of money, unpersuasive TV broadcasts and too narrow a programme all contributed to the unexpectedly poor electoral performance. The Green Party also paid the price for its lack of interest in contacts with environmental NGOs, whose members do not seem to have voted for the Greens. In addition, the leaders of the Greens in the Czech Republic were almost completely unknown to the general public and even to environmentalists. The fact that all parties included ecology in their programmes and rhetoric also played a significant role. Detailed analysis by Rehak and Rehakova (1991) revealed a close similarity between the programmes of the Green Party and those of parties presenting themselves as centrist (Civic Forum, Public Against Violence, Democratic Party) or centre-leftist (Socialists, Social Democrats).

The Green vote was relatively evenly distributed spatially (co-efficient of variation 34.5 per cent – only those of Civic Forum and the Communists were more uniform). Nevertheless, the vote mirrored territorial differences in the state of the environment (see Figures 11.1, 11.2 and 11.3): north-western Bohemia emerged as a Green stronghold, while southern Moravia and the Hungarian minority districts of southern Slovakia produced their worst results (see Figure 11.2).

If we assume that most people who voted Green did so because they were concerned about the environment, the territorial distri-bution of the Green vote should depend on: the degree of environmental degradation, the extent to which people are aware of that devastation, mortality and morbidity rates which are attri-buted to the quality of the environment and the influence of regionally specific demographic patterns. We attempted to quantify these potential explanatory factors using accessible statistics and subjected the data to stepwise multiple regression analysis (avail-ability of data limited analysis to the Czech Republic). Explanatory factors and independent variables used for this analysis are shown in Table 11.2.

Table 11.3 presents the variables that entered the regression equation. Their standard coefficients express the approximate significance of individual variables in the regression model. As the combination of these four variables explains 76 per cent of the variation, the model can be considered successful. The indepen-dent variables entering the regression equation point to the positive relationship between damage to the environment and the share of votes for the Green Party. Further, the negative relation between the share of votes for the predominantly Catholic Christian Democratic Union and that for the Greens appears to confirm the general antagonism between Catholicism and support for Green parties (Jehlicka 1994). Relatively smaller gains for the Green Party in urban districts compared with the highly polluted rural districts of north-western Bohemia explain the negative association between the percentage of built-up area in a district and the share of votes for the Greens.

Table 11.2 Potential explanatory factors and independent variables used in regression model

Explanatory variable	Independent variable
Quality of the environment	Aggregate index of environmental crisis Emissions of SO_2 Emissions of fly-ash
Mortality	Mortality between 40 and 60 years (male) Mortality between 40 and 60 years (female) Life expectancy at age 60 (male) Life expectancy at age 60 (female)
Morbidity	Proportion of children with congenital physical defects
Influence of other political parties	Proportion of votes for Christian Democratic Union
Migration attraction	Net migration Net migration on health grounds
Age of population	Proportion of children under 15 Proportion of retired persons
Education	Proportion of people with university degree
Structure of land use	Proportion of built-up area
Standard of living	Average monthly income
Commercial attraction	Retail turnover per capita

Table 11.3 Basic characteristics of the regression equation

Independent variable	Standard regression coefficient
Proportion of built-up area	−0.598
Proportion of votes for Christian Democrats	−0.519
Aggregate index of environmental crisis	0.550
Proportion of children with congenital physical defects	0.131

Note: Variation explained: 76 per cent.

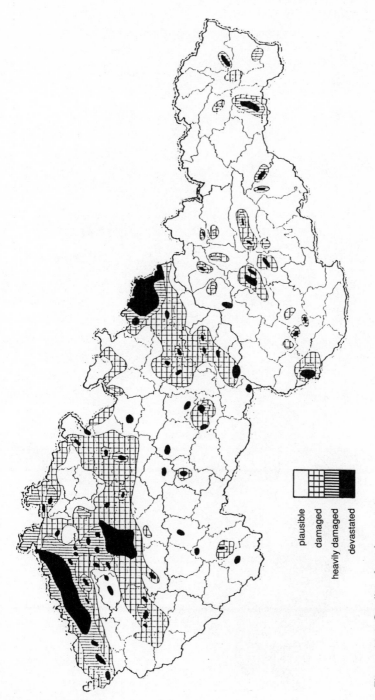

Figure 11.1 Quality of environment

plausible
damaged
heavily damaged
devastated

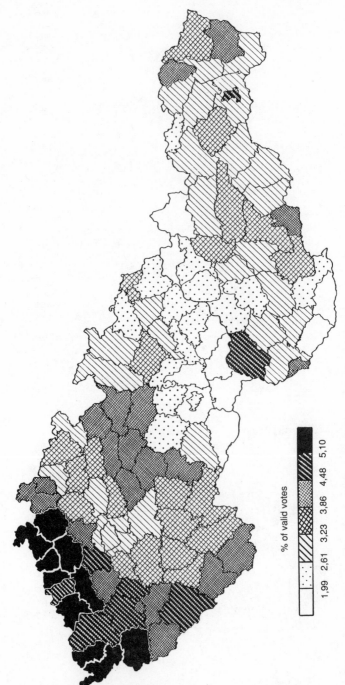

% of valid votes

| 1,99 | 2,61 | 3,23 | 3,86 | 4,48 | 5,10 |

Figure 11.2 Votes for the Green Party in parliamentary elections, 1990

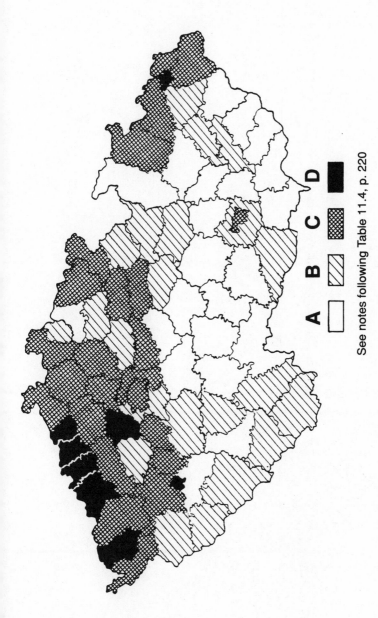

A B C D

See notes following Table 11.4, p. 220

Figure 11.3 Districts by the quality of environment (Czech Republic)

Table 11.4 Votes for the Green Party according to population size of municipality and quality of environment in districts (Czech Republic)

Environmental quality	Population size of municipality							
	–199	200–499	500–999	1,000–1,999	2,000–4,999	5,000–9,999	10,000–19,999	20,000+
A[1]	2.18	2.25	2.20	2.25	2.53	3.14	3.20	3.34
B[2]	2.41	2.93	3.03	3.17	3.33	3.93	4.22	3.69
C[3]	3.28	3.46	3.60	3.76	4.00	4.00	4.37	4.17
D[4]	6.07	5.17	5.75	5.42	7.11	6.24	6.99	5.54
National average	2.65	2.97	2.99	3.08	3.43	3.84	4.22	4.01

Notes: 1 A Districts with a high standard of environment, relatively favourable indexes of social environment, favourable mortality indexes.
2 B Districts with above average standard of environment, average indexes of social environment, unfavourable mortality indexes.
3 C Districts with below average standard of environment, different indexes of social environment and mortality.
4 D Districts with extremely damaged environment, very low indexes of social environment and increased mortality.

Also of interest is the connection between the vote for the Greens and the size of the municipality. To analyse this, we divided municipalities into eight categories and calculated the average percentage of votes for the Greens in each. Then, using the classification of districts according to the degree of environmental degradation (Moldan 1990; see also Figure 11.3), we divided municipalities into four categories. Results are shown in Table 11.4.

The results for the Czech Republic confirmed the general trend: the bigger the municipality the higher the vote for the Greens. When individual municipalities were evaluated district by district, the influence of the degree of environmental devastation was apparent. Further, the generally positive relation between the Green vote and size of municipality does not apply to districts with an extremely damaged environment; there the Greens received more votes in the smallest villages than in cities of over 20,000.

THE GREENS IN THE 1990 LOCAL ELECTIONS

Before the local elections of November 1990, the Greens decided, depending on local conditions, to enter coalitions with all parties except for Communists and Republicans in the Czech Republic and Communists and Nationalists in Slovakia. As Slovak data are not available, we have only analysed results in the Czech Republic. Here Greens concluded electoral alliances with 29 of the 53 parties, the most frequent partners being Socialists (16.2 per cent), Social Democrats (15.8 per cent) and Christian Democrats (15.4 per cent). The overall winner, Civic Forum, took only fourth place (13.9 per cent), while the Agrarian Party was the fifth most frequent partner (7 per cent). However, these figures have to be interpreted very cautiously as they reflect the density of local parties' networks as much as (if not more than) the political preferences of local Green groups. The Prague Greens, who generally created coalitions with small, usually opposition parties of various orientations, again differed from the rest of the party, entering few coalitions with Civic Forum or the Socialists (Jehlicka and Kostelecky 1992).

Figure 11.4 gives a survey of the Green Party's electoral results in each district. The territorial distribution apparent in the parliamentary election was basically preserved, but with districts in northwest Bohemia differing even more sharply from the rest of Bohemia. Greens won an extraordinarily high share of votes in heavily polluted districts. In Decin, a city of over 50,000, the Greens

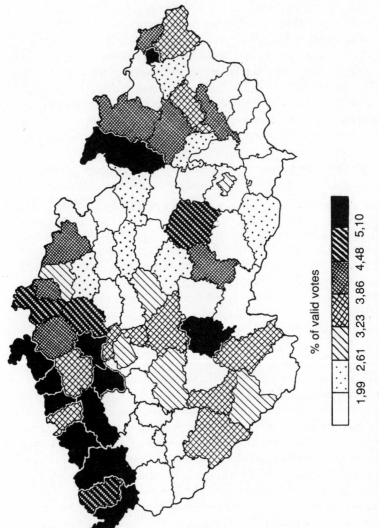

% of valid votes

1,99   2,61   3,23   3,86   4,48   5,10

Figure 11.4 Votes for the Green Party in local elections, 1990

captured a quarter of the vote. These results reflected not only the 'natural potential' for Green votes in areas where the environment was most seriously damaged but also the ability of local groups of the party to make full use of this potential. A high share of votes for Greens in northern Moravia and Silesia can to a large extent be attributed to locally good co-operation between the party and non-political environmental organizations whose members stood for election on Green lists.

The 1990 local elections concluded the first year of the party's existence, a period of organizational activity, of creating the party and preparing for elections. By contrast, the following period, up to the parliamentary election of June 1992, may be characterized as a period of intense internal conflicts leading to marginality. During these two years, the Green Party withdrew its original support for the government and became part of the opposition in both the Czech Republic and Slovakia.

THE GREENS BETWEEN THE ELECTIONS OF 1990 AND 1992

At the beginning of this period, tensions emerged between the Prague Greens and the rest of the Bohemian party. The top positions in the Bohemian regional organization were occupied by representatives of the countryside where the Greens found strongest electoral support. But, because. of the dominant position of Prague as the centre of political life and the high absolute number of Green votes in Prague, the regional organization had to take the Prague organization seriously. Already during 1990 the Prague organization had, contrary to the party's rules, declared itself an independent regional organization (Jehlicka and Kostelecky 1992).

A second serious problem confronted the Green Party in the shape of relations with the Extra-Parliamentary Assembly, an obscure assembly of small Czech parties (Republicans, the Friends of Beer Party, Free Thinkers' Party and others) which had not surmounted the threshold for representation in the various parliaments, established after the 1990 parliamentary election. The Bohemian regional Green Party organization, unlike the Moravian and Slovak branches, joined the Assembly but cancelled its membership after two months when it realized that membership discredited the party. The more radical and less environmentalist Prague organization, however, continued to take part. This not only lowered the prestige of the Greens in the eyes of the general public, but also led to the alienation of the Moravian and Slovak branches of the party. The result was a de facto split into four very loosely connected organizations: Bohemian, Moravian, Slovak and Prague.

The behaviour of the Prague Greens was primarily motivated by the general election due to take place in June 1992. Greens not only in Prague but in the Czech Republic as a whole wanted to reverse the 1990 electoral failure. Given the vanishing environmental concern of the public[6] and the relatively high threshold for a single party, the only possibility to achieve a national presence for the Greens seemed to be that of joining a coalition composed of several small parties. As participation in the Extra-Parliamentary Assembly did not prove fruitful, other parties were approached. In December 1991, after long negotiations, and by a process of elimination, the Green Party succeeded in joining the Liberal Social Union (LSU) already composed of the Czechoslovak Socialist Party and the Agrarian Party.

The establishment of the LSU coalition was purely instrumental. First, all member parties feared they would not overcome the threshold separately. Second, whereas the Socialists, as former satellites of the Communists, had a relatively well-developed network of district offices and sources of income (publishing house and buildings in Prague) but very poor electoral support, the Agrarians, as a 'new' (post-1989) party, had minimal material resources but a more numerous potential electorate. While the Socialist Party, a traditional part of the Czech political spectrum before the Second World War, concentrated exclusively on urban voters, the Agrarian Party was a purely rural party defending the interests of co-operative farmers. It was difficult to find common ground between these parties except in their opposition to the government and their desire to enter parliament. In view of the devastation of the countryside caused by co-operative agriculture, whose continuation the Agrarian Party promoted, the coalition of the Green Party with the Agrarians looked very strange. From the very beginning there was strong opposition to the Greens' membership of the LSU: only 60 per cent of delegates at the Bohemian Greens' conference voted in favour of entry into the coalition, whereas 40 per cent voted against; between half and two-thirds of members left the party in protest at the outcome.

The Slovak Greens' membership of the LSU was even more complicated. On the one hand, the Green Party still claimed to be a united federal party and, accordingly, the whole party was supposed to enter the coalition but, as the other members of the LSU did not have branches in Slovakia, they did not intend the LSU to run in Slovakia. Moreover, by this time the Greens in Slovakia were already divided into 'pro-federal' and nationalist factions. Despite proclamations that the Green Party was something inherently different from conventional political parties, the Slovak Greens fell into the same trap as many others. During the debate about the Language Act in the Slovak National Council in 1991, all Green Party deputies but one joined the nationalist parliamentary bloc in the effort to restrict the rights of the large Hungarian minority. The division among Slovak Greens clearly followed the overall pattern of political orientation in Slovak society: Greens from eastern Slovakia advocated preservation of the federal status of the party, whereas representatives from western Slovakia and its capital Bratislava favoured an independent Slovak Green Party and an independent Slovakia.

Although polls suggested that the Green Party was generally considered 'acceptable' (only 1 per cent said they would never vote for it (Boguszak 1991)), a January 1992 survey (Sasek 1992) showed the extreme volatility of the party's support: only 31 per cent of those who voted Green in 1990 intended to do so in 1992, a lower rate of repeat voting than for any other party. Two opinion polls conducted a few days before the 1992 election confirmed the result of previous surveys: the LSU found its voters in the countryside and, thanks to the Green Party, among young people, a below average proportion of university graduates among them (Boguszak 1992; Hartl 1992).

THE GREENS AND THE JUNE 1992 ELECTION

As a result of the fragmentation of parties from 1990, twice as many contested the 1992 election. The parties split along two lines: originally united parties such as the Communists and Social Democrats split along the national line into Czech and Slovak parties; the broad movements, Civic Forum and Public Against Violence, split into three and two main successors respectively, motivated by political differentiation. The Greens were divided into three in 1992, although two officially maintained the status of a common party: Czech and Moravian Greens were hidden in the LSU, whereas their Slovak counterparts stood under the name of the Green Party. Green 'nationalists' in Slovakia ran separately as the 'Green Party in Slovakia'. The LSU was the only important party composed of parties which ran separately in the 1990 election.

In 1992 electoral thresholds were increased depending on the number of parties in coalitions: the 5 per cent limit for a single party remained, both for the federal and republic parliaments, whereas a coalition of two or three parties needed 7 per cent and a coalition of four or more parties 10 per cent of the vote on the territory of one republic to get into the federal parliament. The limits for the Czech National Council were set differently: a coalition of two parties needed 7 per cent, a three-party coalition 9 per cent and a four-party coalition 11 per cent. Given that combined support for Socialists, Agrarians and Greens in 1990 amounted to 10 per cent, the prospects for their coalition were uncertain. The LSU's reaction was decisive: in order to qualify for the 5 per cent threshold, they declared the coalition a single movement with a collective membership.

The LSU's leaders justified their satisfaction with the electoral results by their successful entry into both the Czech and federal parliaments. Yet the LSU in 1992 gained little more than half the combined support of the three separate parties in 1990 (compare Tables 11.1, p. 214 and 11.5); in every district the coalition gained fewer votes in 1992 than the three parties together in 1990. The dominance of the Agrarian Party among LSU voters was clear: the coalition gained most votes in typical rural districts with high proportions of inhabitants living in small villages, and LSU voting in 1992 coincided with that for the Alliance of Agrarians and the Countryside in 1990.

Although it is impossible to 'unwrap' the package of LSU votes to distinguish how people voted for its constituent parties, there is indirect evidence that the Greens gained fewer votes than in 1990. First, no Green candidate on the LSU list in northern Bohemia gained sufficient preferences to secure election although six Green Party members were elected elsewhere, three to the Federal Assembly and three to the Czech National Council. Second, if the results of Agrarians, Socialists and Greens in the 1990 election are put together and compared with the result of the LSU in the 1992 election, significant losses are seen, mainly in the erstwhile 'Green stronghold' of northern Bohemia where only the Green Party had been significant in 1990. Green losses there were paralleled by an upsurge of the racist (anti-Gypsy), extreme right-wing Republican Party.

Table 11.5 Parliamentary election, June 1992 (percentage of votes)

Political party	FA–CR[1]	FA–SR[2]	CNC[3]	SNC[4]
Civic Democratic and Christian Democratic Party*	33.7		29.7	
Movement for Democratic Slovakia		33.7		37.3
Party of Democratic Left		14.2		14.7
Left Bloc	14.4		14.0	
Slovak National Party		9.4		7.9
Christian Democratic Movement		8.9		8.9
Czechoslovak Social Democratic Party	7.2		6.5	
Coalition of Hungarian Parties	0.1	7.4		7.4
Republicans	6.4	0.4	6.0	0.3
Christian Democratic Union	6.0		6.3	
Liberal Social Union	6.0		6.5	
Civic Democratic Alliance	4.5		5.9	
Slovak Social Democratic Party		6.5		4.0
Society for Moravia and Silesia	4.6	0.2	5.9	0.1
Civic Movement	4.6		4.6	
Civic Democratic Union		4.0		4.0
Democratic Party and Civic Democratic Party*		3.8		3.3
Slovak Christian Democratic Movement		3.3		3.1
Green Party in Slovakia		2.5		2.1
Green Party**				1.1

Notes: 1 FA–CR The average of votes for both chambers of the Federal Assembly in the Czech Republic.
2 FA–SR The average of votes for both chambers of the Federal Assembly in the Slovak Republic.
3 CNC Votes for the Czech National Council.
4 SNC Votes for the Slovak National Council.
* Coalitions.
** Green Party ran only in Slovakia under its own name, the Czech Greens were part of the Liberal Social Union.
Turnout: 85 per cent.

If in 1990 the Green Party could be seen as a protest party, in 1992 that role was taken over by the Republicans. Surveys carried out in 1992 described a typical Republican voter as a man under 30 with a middle level of education (Sasek 1992), a profile similar to that of potential Green voters. If in 1990 the most distinctive political feature of the north Bohemian region was its 'greenness', two years later it was its brown 'Republicanism'. This reflects the overall trend: in 1990 opinion polls showed degradation of the environment to be the leading problem; in 1992 crime was most important, followed by hardship and unemployment. North Bohemia was precisely the region where the effects of these problems were concentrated.

While the nationalist Green Party in Slovakia (1,000 members) put up candidates both for the Federal Assembly and the Slovak National Council, the pro-federal Green Party (200 members) ran only for the Slovak National Council, its candidates at federal level standing on lists of a minor pro-federal party, Democrats '92. Neither won any seats. Overall, the combined support for both Slovak Green parties was slightly lower than that for the Green Party in 1990 (see Tables 11.1 and 11.5). The biggest decline occurred in the Hungarian-populated districts of southern Slovakia, an area of already low support in 1990 and, paradoxically, that most affected by the construction of the infamous Gabcikovo Dam on the Danube.

A survey,[7] conducted a year after the Greens' entry into the LSU provoked an exodus of members to right-wing parties in protest against the leftist orientation of the Agrarians, found that 51 per cent of Greens placed themselves on the right of the left–right continuum. Other evidence of the centre-right orientation of Greens can be seen in their choice of newspaper and their views on the party's membership of the LSU: 15 per cent considered the latter a betrayal of Green principles; 40 per cent believed the Greens should not have entered the LSU because their party had nothing in common with its coalition partners; 30 per cent believed entry into the LSU was justified because it enabled Greens to get into parliament; only 8 per cent saw the LSU as a logical result of the previous convergence of the parties.[8]

CONCLUSION

During its three-year existence, the Czechoslovak Green Party proved unable to compete successfully with other parties. The causes of its failure were both endogenous and externally imposed. The first problem emerged even before the Green Party's official foundation: even the party's present representatives do not deny that the Communist secret police participated in the formative process, at least in Prague. The accusation of co-operation with the secret police appeared truly devastating in elections construed as a plebiscite on the Communist regime. Second, the Greens never succeeded in attracting any well-known environmental experts into their ranks, and this might explain why the media gradually lost interest in the party. Third, the Greens in the Czech Republic never managed to bridge the gap between the party and environmental NGOs. Conversely, in Slovakia a kind of personal union existed between the Green Party and the old environmental protection movement.

In general, unpredictability and inscrutability became part of the Green Party's image. It flirted with several obscure parties in the Extra-Parliamentary Assembly and, given the centre-right orientation of most party members, its eventual entry into the Liberal Social Union, in alliance with a party representing the co-operative farmers responsible for devastating the Czech countryside, brought no benefit either, the price of gaining three deputies in the Czech parliament being the loss of two-thirds of the membership. The very loose party structure, often resulting in uncertainty as to who had the right to speak on behalf of the party and serious differences among pronouncements by different party representatives, added to the public's confusion about what the party stood for. Continual conflicts within the party did not improve its credibility.

The party failed in the 1990 election primarily because of factors beyond its control. Soon after the political upheaval of 1989, despite the severe environmental degradation inherited from the previous regime, environmental issues lost their appeal. Greens had assumed that 'greenness' itself would bring them success, but new hot topics emerged from the deep social and economic changes accompanying the transition from the old system to the new. The practical application of originally only verbal slogans about market economy, liberalization of prices and privatization from the beginning of 1991 led to profound changes in the values and attitudes of large groups of the population. New opportunities were accompanied by growing uncertainty and anxiety as people were exposed to problems they were not accustomed to dealing with. This development gradually resulted in people's concentration on personal and concrete everyday life problems at the expense of 'more abstract' issues such as the environment. A majority of Czechs concentrated on catching up with western Europe in material terms; environmental considerations were perceived as a potential impediment. Rising Czech–Slovak tensions, which switched the attention of politicians, media and the public to the real possibility of the country's disintegration (Jehlicka and

Kara 1993), were another distraction. The Green Party had no answers to these questions.

It is clear now that the vision of Green Party success which seemed well within reach in the autumn of 1989 belonged to the realm of dreams. The Green Party was unable to come up with a consistent set of policies and ideas. Other, more important (and less abstract) issues always overshadowed ecological considerations. While in 1990 a majority of society might have thought that 'the environment will wait for democracy', at present it looks as if 'the environment will wait for prosperity'. If so, the Green parties in both the Czech lands and Slovakia may have a long wait for success.

NOTES

1 Czechoslovakia, established in 1918 after the dismemberment of Austria–Hungary, existed for 74 years (with a six-year break 1939–1945) until 31 December 1992, when it was divided into independent countries, the Czech and Slovak Republics.

2 From 1968, Czechoslovakia was a federative country composed of two republics, Czech and Slovak. Each had its parliament (national council) and government. The top federal bodies were a federal government and a two-chamber parliament. However, the decision of the Green Party to establish a party composed of two regional organizations (Bohemian and Moravian–Silesian) and a Slovak Republic organization, reflected an historical division of the Czech lands into three regions: Bohemia, Moravia and Silesia.

3 'Zelene svitani' (Green dawn), Mlada fronta, 25 January 1990.

4 'Zelena aby' (Green misgivings), Mlada fronta, 19 February 1990.

5 Voters were warned that a 'lost' vote (for a party which would not overcome the threshold) would be partly an indirect vote for Communists, because these lost votes would be divided among parliamentary parties in proportion to their actual gains.

6 Since the middle of 1991, various opinion polls provided clear evidence that environmental issues were no longer of primary concern, but had fallen in relative importance to a position ranging from third to eighth depending on the poll and formulation of questions.

7 In 1992–1993, Jehlicka, supported by the Global Security Programme, University of Cambridge, and with the assistance of the party, surveyed all 700 Green Party members in Bohemia. Three hundred questionnaires (45 per cent) were returned.

8 Fifty-three per cent of Green Party members had never been members of an environmental NGO, while 33 per cent were members and 9 per cent had belonged to some group in the past. If 62 per cent were aware of the poor relationship between the party and NGOs, only 6 per cent believed that the party and these groups had nothing in common and 23 per cent believed the relationship was very close.

REFERENCES

Boguszak, M. (1991) 'Rok po volbach a rok pred volbami, Strana zelenych' ('A Year After and a Year Before the Election, the Green Party'), *Lidove noviny* 177.

—— (1992) 'Liberalne Socialni Unie' ('Liberal Social Union'), *Mlada fronta Dnes* 130.

Cekalova, J., Kamaryt, R. and Makasek, I. (1990) 'Uspech ci neuspech Strany zelenych' ('Success or Failure of the Green Party'), *Nika* 4.

Dejmal, I. (1989) 'Socialni ekologicke hnuti versus politicke zelene strany' ('Social Ecological Movement Versus Green Political Parties'), *Depese Niky* 11/12.

Hartl, J. (1992) 'Socialni profily stran' ('Social Profiles of Political Parties'), *Lidove noviny* 125.

Jehlicka, P. (1994) 'Environmentalism in Europe: An East–West Comparison', in C. Rootes and H. Davis (eds), *A New Europe? Social Change and Political Transformation*, London: UCL Press.

Jehlicka, P. and Kara, J. (1993) 'Ups and Downs of Czech Environmental (Awareness and) Policy', paper presented at ECPR Joint Sessions, Leiden, 2–8 April.

Jehlicka, P. and Kostelecky, T. (1992) 'The Development of the Czechoslovakian Green Party since the 1990 Election', *Environmental Politics* 1(1).

Makasek, I. (1990) 'Zeleni maji federalni stranu' ('The Greens have a Federal Party'), *Depese Niky* 2.

Mesik, J. (1990) 'Co este chyba zelenym' ('What is Still Wrong with the Greens'), *Kruh* 23: 8–10.

Moldan, B. (eds) (1990) *Zivotni prostredi Ceske republiky* (*The Environment in the Czech Republic*), Praha: Academia.

Rehak, J. and Rehakova, B. (1991) 'Predvolebni programy 1990' ('Pre-Election Programmes in 1990'), *Sociologicky casopis* 2.

Sasek, M. (1992) 'Volebni preference v Usti nad Labem' ('Electoral Preferences in Usti nad Labem'), Usti nad Labem: Faculty of Social Sciences and Economics, North Bohemian University (unpublished).

Vajdova, Z. (1990) 'Parlamentni volby na lokalni urovni mensich mest a obci' ('Parliamentary Election on the Level of Small Towns and Villages'), Praha: Institute of Sociology of the Czechoslovak Academy of Sciences (unpublished).

Chapter 12

Environmental consciousness, institutional structures and political competition in the formation and development of Green parties

Chris Rootes

The rise of Green parties in Europe has been variously attributed to the development of environmental consciousness, the pattern of opportunities and constraints imposed by institutional arrangements and the shifting balance of political competition.[1] It is time to assess the balance of the evidence.

ENVIRONMENTAL CONSCIOUSNESS

There can be no doubt that the development of the electorate for Green parties has been built upon unprecedented awareness of environmental problems. However much Green party theorists and activists insist on the distinction between environmentalism and ecologism, between anthropocentrism and biocentrism, most people in even the most environmentally aware European societies identify Green parties primarily with concern for the environment in the loose sense of opposition to pollution and environmental degradation. But, if consciousness of environmental deterioration is a necessary condition of support for Green parties, it is by no means a sufficient one; there is no simple correspondence between the state of environmental consciousness in a country and the level of development or electoral fortunes of its Green party.

Two of the countries where environmental consciousness has been most consistently high and where the environment has regularly ranked highly as a salient political issue – Denmark and The Netherlands – have produced only tiny and poorly supported Green parties, while in others where environmental awareness is less highly developed – such as Belgium and France – Green parties have been relatively successful. In Italy, where levels of both general concern about the national and global environment and 'personal complaint' about the state of the citizen's own environment were higher even than in Germany (Hofrichter and Reif 1990: 134), the Greens have made only very modest electoral progress.

In the newly democratic countries of southern and eastern Europe, the political saliency of environmental issues has been less than in northern and western Europe, and Green parties, where they exist, have made only very modest progress. In these states, the consolidation of democracy and the pursuit of economic modernization have displaced the environment as an issue affecting electoral choice. It is not that there is no public recognition of environmental degradation in these countries. On the contrary, large majorities profess concern about the environment, but their environmental consciousness is more likely than in northern Europe to take the form of 'personal complaint' than 'global concern' (Hofrichter and Reif 1990). Clearly, awareness of environmental problems is one thing; preparedness to put the environment ahead of other considerations and to make it the basis of political choice is quite another.

The environmental protests of the late days of Communist regimes excited expectations of success for eastern European Green parties but, as Jehlicka and Kostelecky observe (Chapter 11), with the benefit of hindsight it is clear that environmental movements attracted so much support less because they reflected the burgeoning of ecological awareness than because they served as relatively safe vehicles for more general anti-regime protest. In any event, they could not be translated into green politics, much less into electoral success for Green parties.[2]

Another factor which contributed to the failure of the Greens in Czechoslovakia and elsewhere in central and eastern Europe was the re-emergence of nationalism. Yet, if the Czech and Slovak Greens succumbed to the appeals of nation over those of ecology, the Belgian experience shows that ecological consciousness is not doomed always to be subordinated to the appeals of ethnicity and nationalism. Clearly, Greens can effectively transcend such divisions, and their failure to do so in post-Communist states reflects the depth of the economic and political crises those states face, as much as the general level of social, economic and political development of societies which until recently were relatively isolated from many of the forces which conditioned the development of ecologism in western Europe.

Switzerland (Chapter 8) offers an example of a country in which nationalism underwrites ecological awareness and the politics of a Green party. The nationalism which the Swiss Greens exhibit in their reservations about Swiss membership of the European Union derives in part from a perfectly Green desire to defend Switzerland's decentralized political structures and long traditions of local autonomy as well as the high levels of environmental protection already achieved. Nevertheless, Greens have not been immune to the straightforwardly nationalist pride which motivates the majority of the Swiss to wish to continue to keep European co-operation at arm's length.

Much – too much – of the discussion of the prospects of Green parties stresses the obstacles presented by the underdeveloped state of environmental (let alone ecological) consciousness among mass publics. There is a considerable body of evidence that most people do not have, and probably do not have the means to develop, systematic world-views such as ecologism (Converse 1964; Klingemann 1979). Rohrschneider (1993), however, suggests that where the issue domain is clear and where active environmental movements maintain the visibility of the issues, mass publics are quite capable of developing consistent ecological attitudes.[3]

If Rohrschneider's findings cast doubt on the assumption that ecologism, as a systematic world-view, is beyond the capacities of all but élites and the highly educated, there is nevertheless evidence that it is among the highly educated that an ecological world-view is most likely to be developed. British data analysed by Witherspoon and Martin (1993) suggest that it is the simpler and less sophisticated forms of environmental concern which are most likely to be found among the less well educated, and that those attitudes that approximate most closely to an ecological world-view are more likely to be found among the higher educated (cf. Jehlicka 1994).[4] This may help to explain why the correlation between postmaterialism and support for Green parties is generally only modest: among the people who vote for Green parties and support environmental movements, as well as highly educated 'post-materialist' ecologists who are not so much fearful for their own security as concerned about global environmental problems whose effects are more remote, there are people, usually less well educated, who are motivated principally by fear of the threats that pollution and nuclear waste pose to their own material security.

The Green vote is often portrayed as a 'protest' vote but, as several of our contributors attest, those who vote for Green parties usually insist that they are motivated by concern for the environment rather than by generalized political discontent. If the instability of the Green vote over time has in many cases encouraged the view that it is an inherently unstable protest vote, particular ingenuity has been deployed to make the case that even the relatively stable core of support for the Greens among the highly educated members of the new middle classes is a protest vote. Alber (1989), for example, argues that the Green movement represents not so much the politics of a new middle class as the protest of students, the unemployed and the economically inactive, a protest arising from the structural blockage of their chances for upward mobility in countries where the production of graduates has outpaced the growth of opportunities for suitable employment.

A similar argument is developed by Bürklin (1987). Bürklin shows from an analysis of West German survey data that support for the Greens is disproportionately concentrated among voters aged under 35 and educated at least to university entrance level; such people, although they comprised just 7.7 per cent of the electorate, accounted for 28 per cent of Green voters in 1984. Bürklin interprets the Green vote as essentially a reflection of the frustrations of people who are highly educated but who, largely because of the condition of the labour market, are relatively poorly socially integrated. They are not attracted to the SPD because, as the party of government from 1969 to 1982, it appeared to them to be a party of the 'established'. But, Bürklin argues, the lack of social integration of the highly educated young is an essentially transitory condition; as they become better socially integrated, so they will become reconciled to more conventional party politics.

The problem with this analysis is that it treats higher education and lack of social integration as essentially independent phenomena. However, if being socially integrated is defined as being married, being employed, having children in the household, owning a house or apartment, attending church regularly and not living in a big city (Bürklin 1987: 115), then being relatively poorly socially integrated is likely to be highly correlated with being young and highly educated, especially where, as in Germany, the process of higher education is often protracted. Bürklin also neglects to consider the extent to which non-integration into society may be a product of deliberate choice by people who feel estranged from conventional society on grounds of political principle. If such considerations are taken into account, electoral support for the

Greens might then be seen, not as the product of a malfunction in the labour market, but as an expression of political principles not otherwise accommodated within the political system (cf. Rootes 1994). In any case, Green supporters are not principally youthful idealists whose idealism is likely to be tempered by realism as they age and assume the responsibilities of work and family. The Green electorate, like the membership of many Green parties, is, on average, getting older, and it is no longer the youngest who are disproportionately supporters of the Greens but those who are in early middle age and securely established in the teaching and caring professions.

Everywhere it is the highly educated members of the new middle classes who comprise most of the memberships of Green parties and who are disproportionately represented among Green voters. The proportion such people comprise of the citizenry is everywhere increasing and, although they may not (yet) be sufficiently numerous to sustain electoral majorities, it is they who provide most of the political activists and opinion leaders of advanced societies. The fact that the stratum which constitutes the Greens' social base is increasing in strategic importance may portend better medium-term prospects for Green politics than a mere headcount might suggest. Nevertheless, if the rise of a higher educated new middle class provides the social base for the Green wave, the direction in which that wave washes, the force it develops and how well it endures, is to a great extent influenced by the channelling effects of institutionalized political structures.

THE IMPACT OF INSTITUTIONAL STRUCTURES

It might be thought that Green parties are a natural development out of environmental movements, but there is no clear correlation between the popularity of environmental protection organizations and the strength of Green parties. It has been estimated that, in terms of the proportion of population who are members of environmental organizations, The Netherlands and Denmark lead the way (17 and 10.9 per cent respectively) from West Germany (7.5 per cent), Britain (4.7 per cent) and Belgium (3.4 per cent), with the other western European countries some way behind (van der Heijden *et al.* 1992: 18).[5]

Green parties have not usually begun simply as party-political translations of less directly political environmental social movements. One reason is that, as Richardson insists (Chapter 1), political ecology, which is the political philosophy which guides Green parties, is a more radical and inclusive world-view than environmentalism. Where Green parties have grown directly out of social movements, it is more often out of specifically anti-nuclear movements than more inclusive environmental movements. One reason for this is that environmental movements often have long histories, are well institutionalized and well embedded in relation-ships with official conservation agencies, and may involve a wide range of constructive and reformist practical activities that only rarely spill over into direct political confrontation and mass mobil-ization. Anti-nuclear movements, on the other hand, are more novel and their concerns more urgent. Because they are usually organized around attempts to prevent the construction of new nuclear installations, the time-scale for possible success is relatively short, and so intense but relatively short-lived mass mobilization seems more appropriate. Moreover, because anti-nuclear move-ments are usually conceived as single-issue campaigns, they are typically organized as broad coalitions of pre-existing groups, very often including small left-wing parties whose members are attracted not merely by the opportunity to proselytize, but by the fact that the anti-nuclear issue involves considerations of international relations and critique of the forms of the state.

Thus the way the anti-nuclear issue combines environmental concern with issues of concern to other political groupings builds in the likelihood that anti-nuclear movements will be broad coalitions of environmentalists, ecologists, political radicals gener-ally and the radical left in particular. Under the right conditions, the contacts forged in such movements may, as they did in West Germany, evolve into Green parties. Both the Austrian (Haerpfer 1989: 23) and Swedish Green parties had their origins in referen-dum campaigns against nuclear power, and anti-nuclear move-ments made important contributions to the early development of Green parties in Finland (Paastela 1989: 81) and Luxembourg (Koelbe 1989: 131) as well as in Germany and France.

In many countries, Green parties exist alongside and in uneasy alliance with more organizationally diffuse green movements. In Belgium, Agalev more or less drifted into the status of a political party and coexists with a movement of the same name. In France, where political ecology emerged as early as anywhere, Greens resisted the lures of party status more determinedly than elsewhere and even now neither Les Verts nor Génération écologie is a conventional party *comme les autres*, in the case of Les Verts because of the principled inhibitions of ecologists who reject the prevailing political order and the forms of organization normal to it.

Similar reservations were, of course, famously prominent in the early development of the German Greens, and continued throughout the first decade of their formal existence as a party. Ambivalence about the party as an appropriate form of political organization is implicit in the omission of the word 'party' from Die Grünen's title. In fact, the very formation of the party was essentially an opportunistic response to the possibilities for publicity presented by the European elections of 1979 and to the prospect of gaining from the funding provided by the Federal Republic to registered political parties. In an unusually clear-cut way, the existence in Germany of laws and procedures governing the registration of political parties was both a constraint upon the political organization of the Greens and a spur to their reconstitution as a political party.

The British experience was quite different. A handful of individuals, concerned about environmental issues, interested in ecology, but isolated from any social movement, mused about forming a political party and discovered that there was no regulation of parties in Britain: there were no restrictions upon the formation of parties and, beyond the then very nominal deposits required of parliamentary candidates, no restrictions upon individuals offering themselves for election. Equally, however, the incentives to party formation were meagre: in national parliamentary and European elections each candidate is entitled to free distribution of a campaign address and parties are given radio and television broadcast time on the basis of the number of constituencies they are contesting and the strength of their representation in the outgoing parliament, but otherwise there is no public funding of campaigns or party activity. But if starting a Green party was easy in Britain, attracting support or even interest from the already well-developed environmental movement was not. Given the peculiarly unfavourable conditions of the British electoral system, environmental activists found it difficult to imagine how a Green party might be electorally successful. Moreover, a well-institutionalized environmental movement feared that it might jeopardize its access to bureaucrats and traditional politicians by the adoption of an overtly political stance. In Britain, then, the institutional structure of politics not only militates against electoral success for the Greens but encourages the maintenance of a discreet distance between the environmental movement and the Green Party.

Institutional structures have enabled French ecologists to make some electoral impact despite the weakness of the French environmental movement. Save for the 1986 election, elections for the National Assembly have, like parliamentary elections in Britain, been conducted on the basis of single-member constituencies. Unlike the British system, however, a two-ballot arrangement means that French voters are, in the first round, offered a relatively riskless opportunity to cast a symbolic vote. Moreover, the personalized contests of presidential elections offer unusually favourable conditions for a movement better known for its personalities than its organization. Nevertheless, it is especially at local level and, since the decentralizing reforms of the last decade, at regional level, that the Greens have enjoyed most electoral success. Their great leap forward came when the Socialist government's introduction of a measure of proportional representation for the 1983 local elections enabled ecologists to gain over 750 council seats despite attracting rather fewer votes than in 1977, when they had captured just 30 seats. The translation of those successes and their good results in the 1989 European elections (also achieved under conditions of proportional representation) into votes and seats in national elections is thwarted by the majoritarian system by which the National Assembly is elected, and the quite different conditions of political competition which that system dictates. Indeed, the absence of realistic prospects of national political representation has been one of several factors discouraging stable party formation among French ecologists.

The Belgian case offers an instructive contrast. There the institutional structure was relatively favourable for the Greens. Even before the recent adoption of a federal constitution, Belgium was a quasi-federal state in which elections were conducted by the unusually permissive d'Hondt system of proportional representation. For electoral purposes, the country is divided into separate electorates for Flanders, Wallonia and Brussels. The linguistic divisions of the country are reflected in the coexistence of separate Green parties based in the Flemish and French-speaking populations but, because those linguistic differences are substantially institutionalized in the structure of regional government, the size of the separate political arenas is small and it was relatively easy for

Ecolo and Agalev to move from modest local and regional successes to representation in the national parliament.

The importance of political institutions in opening or fore-closing opportunities for the development of Green parties can be emphasized by contrasting the cases of two countries with reputations as pioneers in environmental awareness and reform – Sweden and Switzerland. In Sweden, a relatively centralized unitary state, elections are conducted by proportional representation with the whole country voting as a single electorate, and a 4 per cent threshold discourages voters from experimenting with small new parties. As a result, despite some success at local level, the Swedish Green Party struggled for nearly a decade to translate its opinion poll rating into votes sufficient to enable it to surmount the 4 per cent threshold in national parliamentary elections.

If even moderately successful Green parties have difficulty in surmounting thresholds of visibility and credibility to gain seats in national parliaments in centralized states, it is not surprising that Greens should have done relatively well in that most decentralized of European states, Switzerland. In Switzerland a predominantly ecological 'dark' Green party enjoys a measure of electoral success in a confederal system in which the national parliament is unusually marginalized both by regional autonomy and by frequent recourse to referendum. But moderate electoral success in a radically decentralized system has its frustrations too. As Church indicates (Chapter 8), a Green party still too small to have broken into the 'cartel of power' of national governments formed from the 'magic circle' of more established parties finds it difficult to influence decisions, to agree to the compromises required by a peculiarly consensual political culture, and to garner the resources necessary successfully to initiate referendum campaigns.

The fact that Green parties have usually done better at local, regional and European levels can, in part, be explained simply in terms of the relatively relaxed attitudes of voters to 'second order' elections in which lower turnouts tend to amplify the voices of agitated minorities. But it may also be the case that Greens are more comfortable and more persuasive with the issues and styles of politics at local and supranational levels than they are with the 'old politics' of national parliaments; community and internationalism are, after all, more consonant with Green politics than are national considerations.

The advent of direct elections to the European Parliament has been an important factor in stimulating the formation and development of Green parties in several countries. For Green parties which have already succeeded in establishing local or regional bastions, the European elections have provided a stimulus to national-level organization, and have the advantage of being, in effect, *national* second-order elections conducted (except in Britain) by proportional representation. Several parties (notably the French who remain unrepresented in their national parliament) have benefited considerably from the visibility and resources that come with the election of members to the European Parliament. The existence of a Green group in the European Parliament and the way its members have used the resources of the parliament has assisted the wider diffusion of the Green message in a more systematic way than did the earlier 'diffusion by example' of the German model.

Nevertheless, even the impact of European Union institutions and the examples of successful Green parties elsewhere are mediated by national political structures. In general, in countries with federal constitutions and proportional representation electoral systems, the institutional matrix is much more favourable for the development and success of Green parties, and for the development of mutually beneficial relationships between Green parties and the environmental movement, than it is in centralized unitary states with majoritarian electoral systems. But such relatively temporally invariant factors as institutional structures scarcely suffice to explain why Green parties *sometimes* do surprisingly well even in the least hospitable systems; nor are they sufficient to explain why Green parties are more successful in some countries with facilitative political systems than in others with not dissimilar political structures.

POLITICAL COMPETITION

Just as highly developed and widespread awareness of environmental issues, national or global, is no guarantee of the development of a successful Green party, neither is a decentralized political system operating under conditions of proportional representation. In European surveys, the citizens of Denmark and The Netherlands have usually manifested higher levels of environmental consciousness than most of their fellow Europeans, and both countries have electoral systems which are unusually hospitable to small parties; yet neither has been a pace-setter in the development of Green parties. The Danish Green Party, De Grønne, was not established until 1983 and, despite modest early success in local elections, it has failed to win representation in a national legislature with only a 2 per cent threshold (Schüttemeyer 1989). In The Netherlands, as Voerman (Chapter 6) makes clear, the situation is more complicated, but the recent formation and modest electoral success of Groen Links (Green Left) should not obscure the failure of the longer established and more purely ecological De Groenen.

In both Denmark and The Netherlands, despite high levels of environmental consciousness, well-developed environmental movements and low threshold electoral systems, Green parties have failed to flourish. The explanation lies in the state of political competition. In both countries, the relative weakness of governments, itself a reflection of the fragmented party systems produced by highly proportional electoral systems, has made mainstream parties, especially those of the left, relatively accessible to the environmental movement and so defused some of the momentum which Green parties might otherwise have channelled.

More directly, in both countries, the New Left parties which emerged out of or were transformed by the political upheavals of the 1960s survived to occupy some of the political space which in other countries has come to be occupied by the Greens. In Denmark, the Socialist People's Party has proved both responsive to new issues and electorally successful, leaving little room for a Green party to develop (Jamison et al. 1990: 115). The strict proportionality of the Dutch electoral system presents even fewer barriers to political innovation than does the Danish one but, because it imposes fewer constraints towards the aggregation of interests, it has produced an even more fragmented and intensely competitive party system in which minor parties find it difficult to attract or retain the attention of the electorate. The Greens emerged belatedly on a political stage already crowded with bit players hungry for larger roles. The relative success of the German Greens in due course encouraged the electorally marginal 'small left' parties of The Netherlands to co-operate and opportunistically to try to corner the environmentalist vote by establishing a 'Green Platform' for the 1984 European elections. The previously established regional Green parties quickly distanced themselves from the Green Platform and formed a separate Green party, but failed to make a significant impression. Meanwhile, the dismal electoral fortunes of the several 'small left' parties, once they returned to competing with one another, produced increasing pressure towards collaboration and, after campaigning together under a 'Green Left' banner in the 1989 election and producing a modest gain over the combined total of their separate results in the 1986 election, Groen Links was formalized as a unified party in 1990.[6]

In Italy, as in Denmark and The Netherlands, high levels of environmental concern and a permissive electoral system have so far produced only modest gains for the Greens. The relative weakness of the Italian environmental movement, despite Italians' professed support for it (Fuchs and Rucht 1994; Ashford and Halman 1994), suggest that in Italy it may be especially difficult to convert diffuse goodwill into mobilized allegiance. In any case, until recently, the domination of the political landscape by the parties of the Catholic and Communist subcultures and the extreme fragmentation of the centre and radical left confined the Greens to a minor supporting role. The fact that the Greens were able to make any impact at all, despite their own fragmentation, owes much to the decentralized character of the Italian political system and the fact that, although national elections were conducted by an exceptionally permissive form of proportional representation, the country was divided for the purpose into regional constituencies. It has thus been possible for Greens to organize on a purely local and regional level and yet still secure the election of deputies to the national parliament.

The Italian Greens may, as Rhodes suggests (Chapter 9), have a particularly uncertain future in the more majoritarian political system which has operated since March 1994, but for the moment they seem to be among the beneficiaries of the collapse of the old political subcultures and the disarray of the old centre parties contaminated by past proximity to power. One such benefit is the defection to the Greens of nationally prominent 'clean' politicians disgusted by the corruption of their former colleagues. The election of an ex-Radical turned Green, on a ticket backed by former Communists, as mayor of Rome in 1993 is only a straw in the wind, but it is an indication of the way in which the Greens, once they can establish a presence on the political stage, may benefit from other players' need of allies as the rules of political competition are redrawn. The danger for the Greens is that the political crisis will overwhelm them, that their voice will be lost in the tumult and that nervous voters will flee to the apparently safer if less clean hands of the more politically experienced.

If the collapse of traditional political subcultures appears to be beneficial for the Italian Greens, it is, paradoxically, the *persistence* of traditional political subcultures which Rihoux (Chapter 5) suggests has created opportunities for the Greens in Belgium. Because the traditional Belgian parties are so tightly bound to their 'pillars', it has been difficult for them to respond to new issues that have no relation to those pillars. Nevertheless, the Belgian Green parties have made more progress in periods in which the Socialists have been in government and when there has, accordingly, been a vacuum of opposition on the left. Despite the dissimilarity of their origins, Agalev having grown out of the Catholic revival movement in Flanders whereas Ecolo grew out of dissatisfactions with the limitations of ethno-linguistic politics on the part of some activists of the francophone Rassemblement Wallon, the changing balance of political competition in Belgian national politics has encouraged increasingly close co-operation between Agalev and Ecolo and has rewarded them with an increased share of the vote.

The conditions of political competition in West Germany were uniquely propitious for the development of a Green party. The socialist and Marxist left had been marginalized by the deliberate centrism of the SPD with the result that there was, especially in the wake of the extra-parliamentary opposition of the late 1960s, a relatively large minority of leftists unattached to any of the parties represented in the Bundestag. Largely independently, the Citizens' Initiatives of the 1970s developed a substantial pool of environmentalist activists. The conjunction of these two forces was encouraged by an electoral system which financially rewards parties roughly in proportion to the votes cast for them, but which restricts parliamentary representation to parties which attract at least 5 per cent of the vote. Such a system in effect offers financial inducements to party formation and electoral participation, but also presents an unusual incentive to co-operation among interest groups and parties which separately could not hope to surmount the 5 per cent threshold. Furthermore, the federal constitution of the West German state meant that modest success in the smallest state was sufficient to propel the Greens into parliamentary politics.

Thus it was that the Greens, despite being a loose and fractious coalition of environmentalists, ecologists, Marxists and anarchists, took the form of a political party and in 1979 entered the parliamentary arena by the least defended gate, the city-state of Bremen, and went on to secure representation in the federal parliament and the parliaments of most of the states. Their subsequent progress has not been monotonic, but both their greatest setback (their failure to surmount the 5 per cent threshold in the 1990 'unification' election) and their triumphs in the 1992 state elections, can to a great extent be explained by the then prevailing conditions of political competition (Chapter 2).

The French case (Chapter 3) presents a quite different picture. Although political ecology emerged as a national political phenomenon in France even earlier than it did in West Germany (an ecology candidate won 1.3 per cent of the vote in the 1974 presidential election), a less favourable electoral system and quite different conditions of political competition have prevented ecologists from translating diffuse local support into national parliamentary representation.

The successes of Les Verts in the European elections of 1989, and of both Les Verts and Génération écologie in the 1992 regional elections, owed something to the systems of proportional representation employed for these elections. But they owed at least as much to a state of political competition in which both the left and the traditional right appeared equally discredited at a time when a resurgent Front National demonstrated that there were prospects of success beyond the confines of mainstream politics. Local and regional successes combined with the unpopularity of the Socialists to encourage Les Verts and Génération écologie to join forces in an attempt to overcome the effects of the majoritarian electoral system in the campaign for the 1993 National Assembly elections. In the event, the renovation of the traditional right under Balladur and the deepened unpopularity of the Socialists so changed the balance of political competition that the Greens' results were disappointing.

Britain (Chapter 4) is an even clearer case where a high level of diffuse support for environmentalism has, because of an almost uniquely inhospitable electoral system, failed to translate into votes for a Green party. Yet, in the 1989 European elections, the UK Green Party, by winning almost 15 per cent of the vote, scored a success unprecedented in the annals of European Green politics. The most adequate explanation of this result is in terms of the extraordinary conditions of political competition which operated in 1989 in a low turnout election for a parliament few voters credited with much importance. The failure of that success to be repeated in subsequent local elections and, even more strikingly, in the 1992 general election, serves only to confirm the conclusion that, under the conditions of political competition normal in Britain, the Green Party's prospects are distinctly unpromising.

Nor was the balance of party political competition favourable for the development of a Green party in Sweden. In the 1970s, the one environmental issue of great contention, the opposition to nuclear power, found advocates within the established party system in the shape of the Centre Party and a Communist Party which had so successfully transformed itself into a New Left party (VPK – Left Communist Party) that its electorate was more solidly anchored among the higher educated than among the working class.

The Swedish Green party, Miljöpartiet de gröna, was formed in 1981, against the wishes of most leading environmental activists, in reaction to the disappointing outcome of the 1980 nuclear energy referendum and out of disillusionment with the performance of the Centre Party while in office (1976–1978). In an intensely competitive system, the anxiety of other, better established parties to recruit environmental activists and to proclaim their environmentalist credentials left little room for the Greens to develop. In particular, the receptivity of the Social Democrats to both New Left and environmental issues presented obstacles to Swedish Greens with which their German counterparts, for example, have not had to contend (Jamison et al. 1990: 59–60). Nevertheless, in 1988 the party succeeded in surmounting the 4 per cent threshold to secure parliamentary representation. It did so because the impact of Chernobyl and a summer of media bombardment about pollution problems and incidents combined to raise the profile of environmental issues upon which the Greens, in light of the discrediting of the Centre Party, were uniquely well placed to capitalize. In contrast, in 1991 the Greens succumbed to a situation of political competition transformed by the intervention of a new centre-right party, fell just short of the 4 per cent level, and so lost their place in parliament.

Greece (Chapter 10) is in some respects representative of a class of less-industrialized but rapidly urbanizing countries where widespread popular recognition of environmental problems has failed to translate into large-scale support for an ecology party. As Demertzis observes, a Greek Green party was formed not in response to any deep-rooted shift in social conditions or ecological consciousness, but because the opportunity for a new party appeared to have been created by political conditions and electoral reforms dictated by considerations of political competition between the major parties. It has failed, partly because of a national preoccupation with the fruits of economic development, but also because the political battleground is dominated by the still-unresolved struggle between right and left in a democratic system which has yet to prove that it is fully consolidated.

This latter factor is even more important in the newly democratic states of central and eastern Europe. Despite popular awareness of all too evident environmental degradation, economic anxieties loom larger and the status of democracy and even of national integrity is still too fragile for there yet to have been any 'normal' elections in these states, the first post-Communist elections in particular having been treated by many as plebiscites on the Communist regimes. The very fact that environmentalist activism was one of the few forms of independent political expression permitted under those regimes inevitably excited suspicions that environmental organizations and, by extension, embryonic Green parties, had been infiltrated by agents of the state security services. If the Czechoslovak case (Chapter 11) is anything to go by, in the post-Communist states of eastern Europe concern with the stabilization of democracy and the continuation of institutional reform, on the one hand, and the resurgence of nationalism, on the other, have combined with the political ineptitude of Green politicians to all but extinguish the Green vote.

CONCLUSION

If the Greens have, as newcomers to competitive political systems, to face the problem of building a loyal electoral base, they are confronted by a special combination of constraints and opportunities. As parties of principle, they are severely constrained in the extent to which they can trim their sails in response to the capricious breezes of popular sentiment or even, as the ubiquitous debates between 'fundamentalists' and 'realists' testify, in the interests of organizational efficiency and effectiveness (Doherty 1992).

The question of where the Greens might most appropriately be placed on the left–right continuum is a vexed one. Even if it appears that the left–right axis is of declining importance, it is difficult to sustain the proposition that it is simply cross-cut by a new green–grey one. In most cases, Green party members and voters alike incline, in varying degree, towards the left of the conventional political spectrum and they have often made greatest progress in circumstances in which the established left parties have been in government or have been otherwise disabled from performing effectively as an opposition. Yet the existence of a vacuum of effective opposition on the left has not always worked to the advantage of the Greens; the French Greens, for example, failed in 1993 to reap the expected benefits from the discomfiture of the Socialists. Clearly, the Greens are not inevitable beneficiaries of the decay of traditional party alignments. The nationalist right may appeal to a different and less well educated constituency, but other new parties might, by appealing especially to the young, divert votes from the Greens as Rossem has from Agalev in Belgium.

The volatility which characterizes the Green vote is a persistent theme. For the most part, the problems of the Greens are in this respect simply the familiar problems of any new party which must attempt to recruit support either from those who have already established voting habits or from those who have none. Old habits are hard to break, and especially hard to replace with new ones, while people who have no habits of political allegiance are disproportionately people who are less interested in politics and less likely to vote at all. The young, who have at least the excuse that they have had no opportunity to develop voting habits, are especially likely to be uninterested in politics, to abstain from voting and to be volatile in their choices when they do vote. It is the special misfortune of Green parties that, both because of their (admittedly fading) novelty and the content of their programmes, they appeal, more than most parties, to the young. But if that is their misfortune, it is also grounds for cautious optimism. It does, after all, augur better to appeal disproportionately to the swollen ranks of the inconstant young than to the shrinking generations of the steadfast elderly. The greying of the Green vote suggests that the association of Green voting with youth may, in any case, be spurious, and that the more meaningful correlation may be with higher education. If so, the prospects of the durability of support for Green parties may be better. In any case, as the increasing rate of repeat voting for longer established Green parties such as Die Grünen indicates, if Green parties can maintain visibility and credibility, the habituation of political allegiance may begin to work to their advantage.

The diversity of experiences of Green parties in Europe is such as to defy easy generalization. A fairly advanced level of economic development appears to be a condition of the development of heightened environmental awareness, and particularly of global environmental consciousness, but the remarkable thing is that the levels of environmental consciousness as revealed by surveys are very high for *all* the European countries for which we have data. However, the salience of the environment as a political issue and the priority citizens are prepared to accord to it varies considerably. It is not merely the level of economic development and standard of living which influence citizens' political priorities, but also the perceived stability or otherwise of democratic institutions, and, among other considerations of political culture, questions of identity, cultural, regional and national.

Even where citizens do accord highest priority to ecological issues, whether that priority is translated into activism in social movements, support for one or another established political party or votes for a Green party, will be greatly influenced by the impact, actual and perceived, of the pattern of opportunities constituted by social and political institutional arrangements, and by the altogether more contingent balance of political competition – competition among parties for votes and for the allegiance of activists, and competition over issues, to capitalize upon ascendent issues, to turn issues of broad popular concern to partisan political advantage, to dominate a particular 'issue-space'.

It is this last factor – the contingent balance of political competition – which makes theorizing and prediction so difficult, because although one can point to the ways in which social, economic and political institutional considerations create the framework for political competition, how that competition is worked out in practice depends on any number of the caprices of humanity and nature. And, because Green politics is, after all, politics, the outcomes of the complex processes of political competition will depend in no small part on the actions and reactions of Greens themselves. Their philosophical, strategic and tactical disputes, their personality conflicts, their political inexperience, all have complicated their progress, but if none had been prepared, against improbable odds, to mount the Green challenge, there would be no Green parties to write about.

NOTES

1 I avoid using the term 'political opportunity structures' because it has too often been used to obscure the analytically important distinction between factors which are, on the one hand, genuinely structural in that they derive from more or less temporally durable and often formally institutionalized arrangements, and, on the other, conditions which are essentially contingent and usually more temporary (Rootes 1992).

2 Interestingly, Greens have fared better in states which were formerly part of the Soviet Union itself: in August 1993 Greens sat in the national parliaments of Armenia, Estonia, Georgia, Lithuania and Ukraine.

3 Rohrschneider interprets 1980s Eurobarometer data as showing that mass publics exhibit more consistent and internally coherent ecological beliefs and attitudes in Germany and The Netherlands than in Britain and France. The reason, he suggests, is that in Germany and The Netherlands active and visible movements and parties have kept environmental issues high on political agenda, whereas the more moderate British environmental movement and, especially, the smaller and less visible French movement have failed to exercise a comparable constraining effect upon public opinion. It should be noted that Rohrschneider appears to use the terms 'ecological' and 'environmental' interchangeably.

4 Witherspoon and Martin, analysing data from the 1991 British Social Attitudes Survey, distinguish three kinds of attitudes towards the environment: global green awareness, concern about pollution and concern about nuclear power and hazardous wastes. Concern about pollution is spread quite evenly through the population, whereas it is especially the less well educated and women who voice concern over nuclear power and hazardous wastes; in both cases, scientific, technical and medical professionals exhibit *less* concern than average. Global green awareness has a quite different social profile: scientific, technical and medical professionals are not underrepresented, while those most overrepresented are the middle-aged, the highly educated, women and people living in the south of England. Of the three attitude scales Witherspoon and Martin devised, it is 'global green awareness' which most closely approximates to an ecological world-view.

5 Given the variety of organizations involved and the varying meanings of 'membership' and the varying accuracy with which it is recorded, the precision of such percentages might be open to dispute, but the rank-ordering is probably right.

6 The Dutch case is the most significant instance of the transformation of an existing party or parties into a nominally Green party. It might be seen as representing a distinctive route: the pre-emptive formation of a Green party by the left, in this case a move ostensibly directed against the risk that the extreme right Centre Party might attempt to represent itself as a Green party. An altogether more extreme and cynical case is that of the formation of Os Verdes by the Portuguese Communist Party in an attempt to outflank the autonomous Greens and to compensate for its own lack of appeal to the young.

REFERENCES

Alber, J. (1989) 'Modernization, Cleavage Structures and the Rise of Green Parties and Lists in Europe', in F. Müller-Rommel (ed.), *New Politics in Western Europe: The Rise and Success of Green Parties and Alternative Lists*, Boulder, Colo., San Francisco, Calif. and London: Westview, pp. 197–210.

Ashford, S. and Halman, L. (1994) 'Changing Attitudes in the European Community', in C. Rootes and H. Davis (eds), *A New Europe? Social Change and Political Transformation*, London: UCL Press.

Bürklin, W. (1987) 'Governing Left Parties Frustrating the Radical Non-Established Left: The Rise and Inevitable Decline of the Greens', *European Sociological Review* 3(2): 109–126.

Converse, P.E. (1964) 'On the Nature of Belief Systems in Mass Publics', in D.E. Apter (ed.), *Ideology and Discontent*, New York: Free Press, pp. 206–261.

Doherty, B. (1992) 'The Fundi–Realo Controversy: An Analysis of Four European Green Parties', *Environmental Politics* 1: 95–120.

Fuchs, D. and Rucht, D. (1994) 'Support for New Social Movements in Five Western European Countries', in C. Rootes and H. Davis (eds), *A New Europe? Social Change and Political Transformation*, London: UCL Press.

Haerpfer, C. (1989) 'Austria', in F. Müller-Rommel (ed.), *New Politics in Western Europe: The Rise and Success of Green Parties and Alternative Lists*, Boulder, Colo., San Francisco, Calif. and London: Westview, pp. 23–37.

Hofrichter, J. and Reif, K. (1990) 'Evolution of Environmental Attitudes in the European Community', *Scandinavian Political Studies* 13: 119–146.

Jamison, A., Eyerman, R. and Cramer, J., with Laessoe, J. (1990) *The Making of the New Environmental Consciousness*, Edinburgh: Edinburgh University Press.

Jehlicka, P. (1994) 'Environmentalism in Europe: An East–West Comparison', in C. Rootes and H. Davis (eds), *A New Europe? Social Change and Political Transformation*, London: UCL Press.

Klingemann, H.-D. (1979) 'Measuring Ideological Conceptualization', in S. Barnes, M. Kaase *et al.*, *Political Action*, London: Sage, pp. 215–284.

Koelbe, T. (1989) 'Luxembourg', in F. Müller-Rommel (ed.), *New Politics in Western Europe: The Rise and Success of Green Parties and Alternative Lists*, Boulder, Colo., San Francisco, Calif. and London: Westview, pp. 131–137.

Paastela, J. (1989) 'Finland', in F. Müller-Rommel (ed.), *New Politics in Western Europe: The Rise and Success of Green Parties and Alternative Lists*, Boulder, Colo., San Francisco, Calif. and London: Westview, pp. 81–86.

Rohrschneider, R. (1993) 'Environmental Belief Systems in Western Europe', *Comparative Political Studies* 26(1): 3–29.

Rootes, C.A. (1992) 'Political Opportunity Structures, Political Competition, and the Development of Social Movements', paper presented at First European Conference on Social Movements, Berlin, October.

—— (1994) 'A New Class? The Higher Educated and the New Politics', in Louis Maheu (ed.), *New Actors and New Agendas: Social Movements and Social Classes Today*, Beverly Hills, Calif. and London: Sage.

Schüttemeyer, S.S. (1989) 'Denmark: "De Grønne"', in F. Müller-Rommel (ed.), *New Politics in Western Europe: The Rise and Success of Green Parties and Alternative Lists*, Boulder, Colo., San Francisco, Calif. and London: Westview, pp. 55–60.

van der Heijden, H.-A., Koopmans, R. and Giugni, M. (1992) 'The West European Environmental Movement', *Research in Social Movements, Conflicts and Change* supplement 2: 1–40.

Witherspoon, S. and Martin, J. (1993) 'Environmental Attitudes and Activism in Britain', JUSST working paper no. 20, SCPR and Nuffield College, Oxford.

Postscript

Greens in the June 1994 elections to the European Parliament[1]

Chris Rootes

The Greens enjoyed mixed fortunes in the June 1994 elections to the European Parliament. Provisional results suggest that the Green Group won 23 seats compared with the 27 they held in the outgoing Parliament.

The revival of the electoral fortunes of the German Greens, long signalled by the opinion polls, was confirmed when, on a 58 per cent turnout, Die Grünen took 10.1 per cent of the vote, their best ever result in a nation-wide election. That result gave them 12 seats in the European Parliament and, coupled with the failure of the French Greens, a majority in the European Parliament's Green Group.

The poor French result was not unexpected. Les Verts were in considerable disarray in the wake of the party's tumultuous Assembly in Lille in November 1993 when Waechter and his strict autonomist line were decisively defeated by a coalition put together by Voynet and ostensibly committed to closer cooperation with other progressive parties. Nevertheless, Les Verts and Lalonde's Génération écologie presented separate lists for the European election. The effects of their inability to reconstitute their electoral alliance of 1993 were compounded by the advent of two new players in the electoral competition, Bernard Tapie's Energie Radicale and Philippe de Villiers' L'Autre Europe, both of which scored 12 per cent of the vote. As a result, Les Verts and Génération écologie were reduced to 2.96 per cent and 2.02 per cent of the vote respectively. Their combined vote thus fell just short of the 5 per cent which, had they presented a joint list, would have entitled them to seats in the European Parliament.

In Britain, Green candidates, contested all 84 divisions and averaged 3.2 per cent. Although this was better than their showing in the 1992 General Election, it was, at first glance, worse than their results in the May 1994 local elections when Green candidates in contest with three or more other candidates averaged over 8 per cent in London and over 5 per cent in England outside London. The local election results were never likely to be a good guide to those of the European election both because Greens concentrated their local election candidacies in areas where they were strongest and because strictly local factors were less likely to be infuential in the nationwide contest for seats in the European parliament. In the event, the Greens achieved their best local election results in Oxford, the site of their breakthrough in the 1993 County Council elections: Mike Woodin won Oxford Central at his sixth attempt and another Green came second by only 11 votes in Oxford St Clements. If the local elections suggested the consolidation of a few geographical concentrations of support, there was little pattern in the results of the European election. The party Chair, Jean Lambert, achieved the Greens' best result (6.4 per cent) in London North East, but the next best results (5.6 per cent in Hereford and Shropshire and 5 per cent in Sussex South and Crawley) were in more rural areas based on seats in which the Greens had achieved two of their best three results in 1989. The European election in Britain was widely interpreted as a referendum on the standing of the British national government, and so was keenly fought by all three major parties, but especially by a resurgent Labour Party. Ecological issues were not prominent in the campaign, and intense electoral competition and the intervention of the newly formed UK Independence Party forced the Greens into fifth place in a number of places where they had polled well in 1989.

In Greece, the European election confirmed the fragmentation of the Greens. No fewer than six lists, two of them former members of the now defunct Federation of Ecologists-Alternatives, represented themselves as Green or ecological and together they accounted for 2.2 per cent of the vote, but since these 'quasi parties' were so diverse, their combined vote can scarcely be interpreted as the sum total of the Green vote in Greece. Ecological issues were little mentioned in the campaign except by the left-wing Synaspismos party.

Elsewhere, Greens, although they generally polled less well than in 1989, generally did at least as well as in recent national elections. Green Left won 3.7 per cent in the Netherlands in an unprecedentedly low poll (35.6 per cent turnout), and the Verdi managed 3.2 per cent in Italy. In Belgium, both Ecolo and Agalev lost ground (4.8 and 6.7 per cent of the national vote respectively), but Ecolo retained the support of 13 per cent of the francophone electorate. The surprise successes of the elections were those in Ireland where Greens won two of the 15 Irish seats, and in Luxembourg where an alliance of two Green parties won 10.9 per cent and one of the six Luxembourgeois seats; in both cases the result was attributed to local anxieties about environmental issues, including waste reprocessing. In Denmark, the Socialist People's Party, which sits with the Green Group in the European Parliament, won 8.6 per cent of the vote and retained its single seat.

Although the 1994 elections gave Greens less to celebrate than did those of 1989, they can scarcely be said to mark the demise of the Green challenge. But they do demonstrate the extent to which the electoral fortunes of the Greens are dependent upon the balance of party political competition in the several nation states and, as the contrasting fates of the German and French parties show, upon the ability of Green parties to present themselves as credible contenders for office.[2]

NOTES

1 These remarks are based principally upon the reports of the provisional results of the European elections published in the Financial Times (14.6.1994), The European (17.6.94) and The Economist (18.6.1994), supplemented by information supplied by Clive Church, Alistair Cole, Nicolas Demertzis, Mario Diani, Dick Richardson and Chris Rose. I am indebted to them for their help.
2 On the transformation of Die Grünen into a 'moderate and prag-matic party with an unambiguous aspiration toward government', see Poguntke and Schmitt-Beck (1994).

REFERENCE

Poguntke, T. and Schmitt-Beck, R. (1994) 'Still the Same with a New Name? Bündnis 90/Die Grünen after the Fusion', German Politics 3(1): 91–113.

Index

Accornero, A., on Italian political system 172
acid rain 7, 30, 103
Affigne, A., on Swedish Greens 129
Agalev (Belgium) 18, 91, 237, 239–40, 244; electoral base 105–6; financial stability 105; membership 105; and national power 106; on non-environmental issues 104–5
Agalev (Belgium) electoral success 96–103; formation of 94–9
Alber, J., on Green protest vote 235; on unemployment and Green Party membership 121
Alexander, D., on environmental legislation 175
Amis de la Terre, Les 46, 49, 51, 92–3, 95; *see also* Friends of the Earth
Andreis, Sergio (Italian Green) 187
Anger, Didier, and Les Verts (France) 52, 53, 54
anthropocentric politics 9–11
Ashford, S. and Halman, L., on environmentalism in Italy 243
Association for Transport and the Environment 152
Austria, Green Party in 237

Bassand, M., on Swiss environmentalism 152

Belgium Agalev party *see* Agalev (Belgium); Anders Gaan Leven ('Live Differently') group (AGL) 94; Democratie Nouvelle 92, 93, 95; Ecolo party *see* Ecolo (Belgium); electoral system 98; environmental/ecological awareness 232, 233; far-right parties 91; Flemish party system 91; French party system 91; Green parties in 18, 91–108; nationalism 233; nuclear power 101; 'pillarized' political system 103–4, 106, 239–40, 244; regionalist parties 91, 92; socialism and Green parties 101, 104; Wallonie-Ecologie (WE) group 92–3, 95
Bell, D., on post-industrial society 14
Bennahmias, J.L. and Roche, A., on French Greens 50, 59–60, 61
Bennulf, M., on Green voters 133, 137; on materialism/post-materialism scale 135, 139; on Swedish Greens 129
Bennulf, M. and Holmberg, S., on environmental awareness 128, 132; on post-materialism 135; on Swedish voters 139, 140
Bhopal disaster 30
Biffaud, O. and Jarreau, P., on Les Amis de la Terre 49
Bildt, Carl 140
biocentric philosophy 7–11